Fodor's

U.S. & BRITISH

V̶I̶R̶G̶I̶N̶

I̶S̶

Portions of this book appe

WELCOME TO
THE U.S. & BRITISH
VIRGIN ISLANDS

This chain of over 120 islands—some inhabited, most not—share beautiful scenery and beaches, excellent opportunities for water sports, and great places to stay. Divided between British and American rule, they're a popular draw for Americans as the U.S. dollar is used everywhere. The biggest resorts are in the U.S. Virgin Islands, but bring your passport and you can also escape to the British Virgin Islands for an even slower pace and an even more relaxed feel. Whichever one you choose, plan to recline with a Painkiller dark-rum cocktail in hand.

TOP REASONS TO GO

★ **Beaches:** Almost every island here has a great beach of white or golden sand.

★ **Sailing:** This archipelago is one of the world's top sailing destinations.

★ **Resorts:** You'll find everything from luxurious beachfront hideaways to simple inns.

★ **Shopping:** Bargains abound, especially in the U.S. Virgin Islands.

★ **Island Culture:** Each island has its own traditions and unique identity.

★ **Food:** From local favorites to gourmet dining rooms, you'll eat very well.

Fodor's U.S. & BRITISH VIRGIN ISLANDS

Publisher: Amanda D'Acierno, *Senior Vice President*

Editorial: Arabella Bowen, *Editor in Chief*; Linda Cabasin, *Editorial Director*

Design: Tina Malaney, *Associate Art Director*; Chie Ushio, *Senior Designer*; Randy Glance, *Production Designer*

Photography: Jennifer Arnow, *Senior Photo Editor*; Mary Robnett, *Photo Researcher*

Production: Linda Schmidt, *Managing Editor*; Evangelos Vasilakis, *Associate Managing Editor*; Angela L. McLean, *Senior Production Manager*

Maps: Rebecca Baer, *Senior Map Editor*; David Lindroth, *Cartographer*

Sales: Jacqueline Lebow, *Sales Director*

Marketing & Publicity: Heather Dalton, *Marketing Director*; Katherine Punia, *Publicity Director*

Business & Operations: Susan Livingston, *Vice President, Strategic Business Planning*; Sue Daulton, *Vice President, Operations*

Fodors.com: Megan Bell, *Executive Director, Revenue & Business Development*; Yasmin Marinaro, *Senior Director, Marketing & Partnerships*

Copyright © 2015 by Fodor's Travel, a division of Random House LLC

Writers: Carol M. Bareuther, Carol Buchanan, Lynda Lohr, Susan Zaluski

Editor: Eric Wechter

Production Editor: Carolyn Roth

25th Edition

ISBN 978-1-101-87825-5

ISSN 1070–6380

SPECIAL SALES

This book is available at special discounts for bulk purchases for sales promotions or premiums. For more information, e-mail specialmarkets@penguinrandomhouse.com

PRINTED IN THE UNITED STATES OF AMERICA

10 9 8 7 6 5 4 3 2 1

CONTENTS

CONTENTS

ABOUT
THIS GUIDE

Fodor's Recommendations

Everything in this guide is worth doing—we don't cover what isn't—but exceptional sights, hotels, and restaurants are recognized with additional accolades. **Fodor's**Choice★ indicates our top recommendations; and **Best Bets** call attention to notable hotels and restaurants in various categories. Care to nominate a new place? Visit Fodors.com/contact-us.

Trip Costs

We list prices wherever possible to help you budget well. Hotel and restaurant price categories from **$** to **$$$$** are noted alongside each recommendation. For hotels, we include the lowest cost of a standard double room in high season. For restaurants, we cite the average price of a main course at dinner or, if dinner isn't served, at lunch. For attractions, we always list adult admission fees; discounts are usually available for children, students, and senior citizens.

Hotels

Our local writers vet every hotel to recommend the best overnights in each price category, from budget to expensive. Unless otherwise specified, you can expect private bath, phone, and TV in your room. For expanded hotel reviews, facilities, and deals visit Fodors.com.

Top Picks	Hotels &
★ **Fodor's**Choice	**Restaurants**
	🏠 Hotel
Listings	🛏 Number of
✉ Address	rooms
✉ Branch address	⊙ Meal plans
☎ Telephone	✗ Restaurant
🖷 Fax	⬱ Reservations
⊕ Website	👔 Dress code
✉ E-mail	═ No credit cards
🎫 Admission fee	$ Price
⊙ Open/closed times	**Other**
Ⓜ Subway	⇨ See also
⊹ Directions or Map coordinates	☞ Take note
	🏌 Golf facilities

Restaurants

Unless we state otherwise, restaurants are open for lunch and dinner daily. We mention dress code only when there's a specific requirement and reservations only when they're essential or not accepted. To make restaurant reservations, visit Fodors.com.

Credit Cards

The hotels and restaurants in this guide typically accept credit cards. If not, we'll say so.

EUGENE FODOR

Hungarian-born Eugene Fodor (1905–91) began his travel career as an interpreter on a French cruise ship. The experience inspired him to write *On the Continent* (1936), the first guidebook to receive annual updates and discuss a country's way of life as well as its sights. Fodor later joined the U.S. Army and worked for the OSS in World War II. After the war, he kept up his intelligence work while expanding his guidebook series. During the Cold War, many guides were written by fellow agents who understood the value of insider information. Today's guides continue Fodor's legacy by providing travelers with timely coverage, insider tips, and cultural context.

EXPLORE THE U.S.
& BRITISH VIRGIN
ISLANDS

WHAT'S WHERE

1 St. Thomas. The familiar and foreign mingle perfectly here. Resorts run the gamut from plain and simple to luxurious, but tranquil it isn't. Go for the shopping, sights, and water sports.

2 St. John. The least developed of the USVI, two-thirds of the island is a U.S. national park. With its excellent snorkeling, good restaurants, and comfortable villas and resorts, many find this the perfect island.

3 St. Croix. The largest of the U.S. Virgin Islands is 40 miles (64 km) south of St. Thomas. Choose St. Croix if you like history, good restaurants, decent shopping, and good (but not great) beaches.

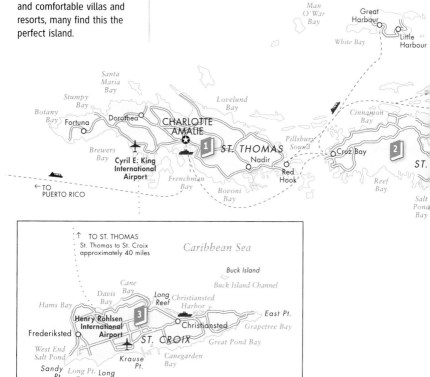

1

Bones Bight
Red Pond
Loblolly Bay
6
Table Bay
The Settlement
Flamingo Pond
Lower Bay
Budrock Pond
ANEGADA
White Bay

A T L A N T I C   O C E A N

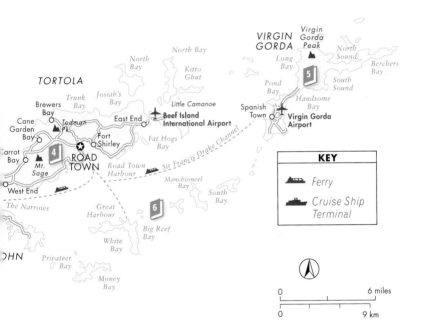

VIRGIN GORDA
Virgin Gorda Peak
North Sound
Long Bay
Berchers Bay
North Bay
Pond Bay
South Sound
5
TORTOLA
North Bay
Kitto Ghut
Handsome Bay
Trunk Bay
Josiah's Bay
Little Camanoe
Spanish Town
Virgin Gorda Airport
Brewers Bay
East End
Beef Island International Airport
Cane Garden Bay
Tadman Pk.
Fort Shirley
Fat Hogs Bay
Sir Francis Drake Channel
arrot Bay
Mt. Sage
ROAD TOWN
Road Town Harbour
Manchioneel Bay
South Bay
West End
The Narrows
Great Harbour
6
Big Reef Bay
White Bay
OHN
Privateer Bay
Money Bay

KEY

🛳 *Ferry*

🚢 *Cruise Ship Terminal*

0 ———— 6 miles
0 ———— 9 km

4 **Tortola.** A day might not be enough to tour this island because you're meant to relax while you're here. Go to Tortola if you want to do some shopping and enjoy a larger choice of good restaurants than you can find on the other British Virgins.

5 **Virgin Gorda.** Progressing from laid-back to more laid-back, mountainous and arid Virgin Gorda offers beautiful beaches but fewer restaurants and far fewer shopping opportunities than Tortola.

6 **Other British Virgin Islands.** There are actually about 50 islands in the British Virgin chain, many of them completely uninhabited, but most have a single hotel or at least a beach that is popular with sailors.

VIRGIN ISLANDS PLANNER

Ferries in the Virgin Islands

There is frequent and regular daily ferry service connecting St. Thomas, St. John, and Tortola. In most cases, you can leave your St. John or Tortola hotel early in the morning and still make a flight back home from St. Thomas if you are leaving in midmorning.

There's daily ferry service between Tortola and Virgin Gorda, but on most days you have to make a connection if you are coming over from St. Thomas or St. John, so it's important to take a ferry to Road Town and not West End if you need to make this change. While there is direct service several times a week between Virgin Gorda and St. Thomas via St. John, this is a fairly long trip, so you must sometimes spend a night in St. Thomas or Tortola before your return flight.

There is no ferry service between St. Thomas and St. Croix, but you can take a seaplane, which has frequent daily departures from a terminal in the heart of Charlotte Amalie, St. Thomas.

For more information on USVI ferry schedules, check out the website ⊕ www.vinow.com. For BVI ferry schedules, check out the website ⊕ www.bviwelcome.com.

Flying to the Virgin Islands

It's fairly easy to get to St. Thomas by air from the United States, with many nonstop flights as well as connecting flights from San Juan. There's no air service to St. John; you must take a ferry from St. Thomas. For St. Croix, you must usually connect in either Miami, San Juan, or St. Thomas. The only air service to the British Virgin Islands is through Tortola (always a connecting flight on a smaller plane). You can get a charter flight from Tortola or another nearby island to Virgin Gorda or Anegada, or take one of the ferries that connects Tortola to the rest of the Virgin Islands.

Getting Around

Once in the Virgin Islands, you can use ferries to hop from one island to another, though not all services are daily, and some ferries don't run frequently (or reliably). There are also small planes, but they aren't really cost-effective if you plan on visiting several islands (unless you have a large transportation budget).

Many visitors rent cars, especially in the USVI and on Tortola and Virgin Gorda, but taxis will suffice if you don't plan on doing a lot of independent exploring or eating too often outside your resort. You can also rent a jeep on Anegada, though some people opt for taxis there, too. Jost Van Dyke is small enough that most visitors walk or use an island-based taxi service. On the smaller private islands, there may be no cars at all.

The major chains are represented in the USVI and on Tortola, but only local companies operate in Virgin Gorda and the smaller islands. It's a good idea to reserve a car in advance since companies can run out, particularly during the high season.

Be aware that, while cars will be standard U.S. vehicles, you drive on the left in the Virgin Islands—even in the U.S. Virgin Islands. Roads are often not well marked regardless of which island you are on, so it's a good idea to pick up a detailed road map once you land.

For more travel info, see the Travel Smart chapter.

Restaurant Basics

Everything from fast food to fine cuisine in elegant settings is available in the Virgin Islands. Prices run about the same as you might expect to pay in New York City (so 20% more than you'd pay in most places in the U.S.). Don't be afraid to sample local fare at roadside stands throughout the islands. One popular island-style fast-food basic is the *pate,* a fried pastry filled with conch, salt fish, or hamburger, which islanders call, simply, "meat." Most restaurants, except the simplest roadside stands, take major credit cards. Dress is generally casual, though there are a few upscale places that still require men to wear a jacket, but never a tie. Virgin Islanders, however, would never wear swim attire in town, and most upscale restaurants will expect men to wear long pants at dinner. Mealtimes are similar to what you'll find at home.

Hotel Basics

There are many types of lodgings in the Virgin Islands, from luxury resorts to moderately priced hotels to small inns. Many visitors opt to rent a private villa, which might range from a sumptuous retreat on the beach to a simpler house in the hills. Many of these have private pools. The high season generally runs from mid-December through mid-April. After that, rates may drop by a third or more, with the lowest rates reserved for the period in the late fall, when hurricanes are most common. Rates during the Christmas holidays may be double those during the rest of the year.

Calling Home

If you have a GSM mobile phone, then regular phone calls in the USVI may be included in your wireless plan; however, you may have to pay extra to send or receive text messages or to use data features. Most companies charge hefty roaming fees for the BVI, but from some points on the west end of Tortola, you can pick up a signal from St. John.

Internet

Most hotels offer Internet service, often Wi-Fi. This service is not always free, so check with your resort regarding any charges. There are still Internet cafés on all the U.S. Virgin Islands and on Tortola. There are no Internet cafés elsewhere in the BVI.

Smoking

You can still smoke almost everywhere in the USVI, including bars and restaurants. However, smoking is not allowed in any public places in the BVI, including bars and restaurants.

FERRY ROUTES AND TRAVEL TIMES

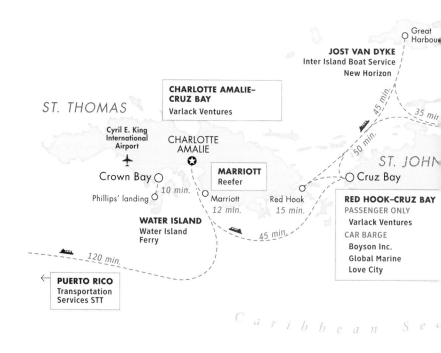

A T L A N T I C O C E A N

Great Harbour

JOST VAN DYKE
Inter Island Boat Service
New Horizon

ST. THOMAS

CHARLOTTE AMALIE–CRUZ BAY
Varlack Ventures

Cyril E. King
International
Airport

CHARLOTTE
AMALIE

45 min.

35 min.

50 min.

ST. JOHN

Crown Bay

10 min.

Phillips' landing

MARRIOTT
Reefer

Marriott
12 min.

Red Hook
15 min.

Cruz Bay

RED HOOK–CRUZ BAY
PASSENGER ONLY
Varlack Ventures
CAR BARGE
Boyson Inc.
Global Marine
Love City

WATER ISLAND
Water Island
Ferry

45 min.

120 min.

← **PUERTO RICO**
Transportation
Services STT

C a r i b b e a n S e a

0 ——— 6 miles
0 ——— 9 km

*St. Croix Island is made to fit for this diagram. It is not true to scale.

Christiansted

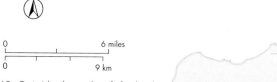

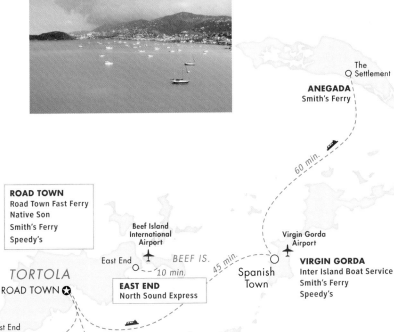

The
Q Settlement
ANEGADA
Smith's Ferry

60 min.

ROAD TOWN
Road Town Fast Ferry
Native Son
Smith's Ferry
Speedy's

Beef Island
International
Airport

Virgin Gorda
Airport

BEEF IS.

East End
O
10 min.

45 min.

Spanish
Town

VIRGIN GORDA
Inter Island Boat Service
Smith's Ferry
Speedy's

TORTOLA
ROAD TOWN ✪

EAST END
North Sound Express

West End
O
20 min.

30 min.

Great
Harbour
O

WEST END
Inter Island
Boat Service
Native Son
Smith's Ferry

PETER ISLAND
Peter Island Ferry

FERRY SCHEDULES:
U.S. Virgin Islands ⊕ www.vinow.
com/stjohn/getting_there

British Virgin Islands ⊕ www.
bviwelcome.com/ferries.php

Ferry Companies:

Boyson Inc. **General II** and
Mister B (St. John car barge)
☎ 340/776-6294

Global Marine's Tug Life aka
Roanoke (St. John car barge)
☎ 340/779-1739

Inter-Island Boat Service (St.
Thomas/St. John/Jost Van Dyke)
☎ 340/776-6597 in St. John,
284/495-4166 in Tortola

Love City Car Ferries' Captain
Vic (St. John car barge)
☎ 340/779-4000

Native Son ☎ 340/774-8685 in
St. Thomas, 284/495-4617 in
Tortola ⊕ www.nativesonferry.
com

New Horizon Ferry Service
☎ 284/495-9278 in Tortola

North Sound Express
☎ 284/495-2138 in Tortola

Peter Island Ferry (Peter Island
Resort) ☎ 284/495-2000 in
Tortola ⊕ www.peterisland.
com

Reefer (Marriott French-
man's Reef/Morningstar
Beach) ☎ 340/776-8500
in St. Thomas ⊕ www.
marriottfrenchmansreef.com

Road Town Fast Ferry
☎ 284/494-2323 in Tortola,
340/777-2800 in St. Thomas
⊕ www.roadtownfastferry.com

Smith's Ferry ☎ 340/775-7292
in St. Thomas, 284/494-
4454 in Tortola ⊕ www.
bviferryservices.com

Speedy's Ferries ☎ 284/494-
6154 in Tortola ⊕ www.
bviferries.com

Varlack Ventures (St. John)
☎ 340/776-6412 in St. John
⊕ www.varlack-ventures.com

Water Island Ferry (Water Island)
☎ 340/690-4159

U.S. & BRITISH VIRGIN ISLANDS TOP ATTRACTIONS

Visiting The Baths, Virgin Gorda

(A) The unusual boulder formations at The Baths create delightful tide pools and grottoes and make this beach one of the most unique in the Caribbean. The swimming and snorkeling here are absolutely amazing, despite the crowds that can gather, especially on cruise-ship days. However, similar, less crowded beaches are nearby.

Staying at Concordia Eco-Resort, St. John

(B) Now that Maho Bay Camps has, sadly, closed after almost 40 years, you can still get a similar eco-resort experience with a bit more comfort at Concordia, which is operated by the same management. Unlike Maho, it's not on the beach, but it does have a pool and great views.

Diving in Anegada

(C) Whether you are into reef or wreck diving, the clear, bright blue waters here make visibility tremendous, and the protected reef system is still alive and teeming with fish.

Tossing Back a Painkiller, Jost Van Dyke

(D) Whether you go for the original at the Soggy Dollar Bar or the unique rum punch at Foxy's Tamarind, no trip to the Virgin Islands would be complete without a stop for nightlife and a few swigs of something at Jost Van Dyke (as if the beautiful beach at White Bay weren't enough).

Snorkeling at Coki Beach, St. Thomas

(E) The best beach on St. Thomas for snorkeling is right next to the island's popular aquarium attraction, Coral World. You can buy food from the huts and have a thoroughly fun beach day. It's not a quiet beach, but the amenities make an extended stay a lot easier.

Hiking the Reef Bay Trail, St. John

(F) St. John's best hike is led by rangers from the National Park Service. Along the way, you'll see island flora and fauna,

the ruins of the Reef Bay plantation, and petroglyphs. Best of all, a safari bus will take you to the trailhead, and a boat will bring you back to Park Service headquarters for a reasonable price.

Taking in the View from Sage Mountain, Tortola

(G) The views from Tortola's highest peak are stunning. On a very clear day, you can see both St. Croix (some 40 miles [64 km] away) and Anegada (a mere 20 miles [32 km] away).

Sampling Cruzan Rum at its Factory, St. Croix

(H) After a tour of the distillery and processing facilities here, you can sit down in the pub and taste some samples of the many different kinds of rum that are still produced here. Connoisseurs can even buy bargain-priced vintages, though the fruity varieties will satisfy most rum-soaked palates.

Visiting the Caves, Norman Island

(I) It is believed that uninhabited Norman Island was the inspiration for Robert Louis Stevenson's *Treasure Island*. Boaters are drawn to three sea-level caves at Treasure Point, which are a popular sight for snorkelers since they are deep enough to resemble a night dive.

Chartering a Yacht, Tortola

(J) The charter-yacht capital of the Caribbean is one of the best places to go for either a bareboat or crewed yacht charter. Boaters can easily reach more than 50 different islands and dozens of anchorages and snorkeling spots, including many deserted beaches that are not reachable any other way.

WEDDINGS AND HONEYMOONS

There's no question that the Virgin Islands are a popular destination for a honeymoon. Romance is in the air here, and the white, sandy beaches, turquoise water, swaying palm trees, balmy tropical breezes, and perpetual summer sunshine put people in the mood for love. It's easy to understand why the Virgin Islands are fast becoming a popular wedding destination as well. They are easy to reach from the United States and offer a broad array of hotels and resorts. A destination wedding is no longer exclusive to celebrities and the superrich. You can plan a simple ceremony right on the beach or use your resort's chapel. Every large resort has a wedding planner, and there are independent wedding planners as well. Although the procedures in the British Virgin Islands are a little different, planning your wedding is relatively simple regardless of where you are.

Getting Married in the USVI

You must first apply for a marriage license at the Superior Court (in either St. Thomas or St. Croix; St. John has no court office). The fee is $50 for the application and $50 for the license. You have to wait eight days after the clerk receives the application to get married, and licenses must be picked up in person on a weekday, though you can apply by mail. To make the process easier, most couples hire a wedding planner. If you plan to get married at a large resort, most have planners on staff to help you with the paperwork and all the details, but if you're staying in a villa, at a small hotel or inn, or are arriving on a cruise ship, you'll have to hire your own.

The wedding planner will help you organize your marriage-license application as well as arrange for a location, flowers, music, refreshments, and whatever else you want to make your day special. The wedding planner will also hire a clergyman if you'd like a religious service or a nondenominational officiant if you prefer. Indeed, many wedding planners are licensed by the territory as nondenominational officiants and will preside at your wedding.

Superior Court Offices St. Croix Superior Court ☎ *340/778–9750*. **St. Thomas Superior Court** ☎ *340/774–6680*.

Wedding Planners Anne Marie Weddings ☎ *340/626–4658, 888/676–5701* ⊕ *www.stjohnweddings.com*. **Weddings the Island Way** ☎ *340/777–6505, 800/755–5004* ⊕ *www.weddingstheislandway.com*.

Getting Married in the BVI

Getting married in the BVI is a breeze, but you must make advance plans. To make things go more smoothly, hire a wedding planner to guide you through the ins and outs of the BVI system. Many hotels also have wedding planners on staff to help organize your event. Hotels often offer packages that include the ceremony; accommodations for you, your wedding party, and your guests; and extras like massages, sailboat trips, and champagne dinners.

You must apply in person for your license ($110) weekdays at the attorney general's office in Road Town, Tortola, and wait three days to pick it up at the registrar's office there. If you plan to be married in a church, announcements (called *banns* locally) must be published for three consecutive Sundays in the church bulletin. Only the registrar or clergy can perform ceremonies. The registrar charges $35 at the office and $100 at another location. No blood test is required.

Contacts BVI Wedding Planners and Consultants ☎ *284/494–5306*   ⊕ *www.bvi weddings.com*.

How to Dress

In the Virgin Islands, basically anything goes, from long, formal dresses with trains to white bikinis. Floral sundresses are fine, too. For the men, tuxedos are not the norm; a pair of solid-colored slacks with a nice shirt is. If you're planning a wedding on the beach, barefoot is the way to go.

If you decide to marry in a formal dress and tuxedo, you're better off making your selections at home and hand-carrying them aboard the plane. Yes, it can be a pain, but ask your wedding-gown retailer to provide a special carrying bag. After all, you don't want to chance losing your wedding dress in a wayward piece of luggage. And when it comes to fittings, again, that's something to take care of before you arrive in the Virgin Islands.

Your Honeymoon

Do you want champagne and strawberries delivered to your room each morning? A breathtaking swimming pool in which to float? A five-star restaurant in which to dine? Then a resort is the way to go. If you're on a tight budget or don't plan to spend much time in your room, there are also plenty of cheaper small inns and hotels throughout the USBVI to choose from. On the other hand, maybe you want your own private home in which to romp naked—or just laze around recovering from the wedding planning. Maybe you want your own kitchen in which to whip up a gourmet meal for your loved one. In that case, a private villa rental is the answer. That's another beautiful thing about the Virgin Islands: the lodging accommodations are almost as plentiful as the beaches, and there's bound to be one to match your tastes and your budget.

Popular Honeymoon Resorts

If you are looking for some serious time together with few distractions, you can always head to one of the private-island resorts in the BVI. **Guana Island** and **Peter Island** are luxurious, but **Cooper Island Beach Club** offers both privacy and moderate prices.

Many honeymooners choose the laid-back luxury of **Caneel Bay** on St. John or the **Rosewood Little Dix Bay** or **Biras Creek** on Virgin Gorda. Those looking for more creature comforts might consider the **Ritz-Carlton** on St. Thomas or the **Renaissance Carambola Beach Resort** on St. Croix (which has a good golf course). The **Sugar Mill Hotel** on Tortola is simple and small but still gracious, while the **Surfsong Villa Resort** on Beef Island, Tortola, offers the privacy advantages of a villa with some hotel amenities. St. Thomas's **Sugar Bay Resort and Spa,** though also popular with families, has an on-site wedding coordinator and is the island's only true all-inclusive resort.

IF YOU LIKE

The Beach

Even if you're not a connoisseur, a day or two on the sand is central to a complete vacation here. Your hotel may border a beach or provide transportation to one nearby, but don't limit yourself.

You could spend one day at a lively, touristy beach that has plenty of water-sports facilities and is backed by a bar, and another at an isolated cove that offers nothing but seclusion. Here are our favorites:

The Baths, Virgin Gorda, BVI. Swimming among the giant boulders here is a highlight of any trip, despite the crowds.

Buck Island, St. Croix, USVI. The softest sandy beach in St. Croix isn't exactly *on* St. Croix.

Cane Garden Bay, Tortola, BVI. This silky beach is often Tortola's busiest.

Coki Beach, St. Thomas, USVI. Come here for St. Thomas's best off-the-beach snorkeling.

Long Bay West, Tortola, BVI. Although the water is not calm, this is one of Tortola's finest beaches and is still quite swimmable.

Magens Bay, St. Thomas, USVI. St. Thomas's busiest beach is one of the most beautiful in the Caribbean, if not the world.

Trunk Bay, St. John, USVI. This national park beach is picture-perfect, and has an underwater snorkeling trail.

West End Beaches, St. Croix, USVI. Find a spot near Sunset Grill and relax.

White Bay, Jost Van Dyke, BVI. You won't have to travel far to find a bar on this long stretch of sand.

Diving and Snorkeling

Serious divers usually head to the BVI, but don't neglect St. Croix, which is also a good dive destination.

Anegada, BVI. The reefs surrounding this flat coral-and-limestone atoll are a sailor's nightmare but a snorkeler's dream.

The Baths, Virgin Gorda, BVI. Snorkelers in the BVI need not worry that they'll miss out because they can't reach the deeper reefs and wrecks. Virgin Gorda's most popular beach is dotted with giant boulders that create numerous tide pools, making it a great place to explore underwater. It's especially good for kids.

Buck Island, St. Croix, USVI. Buck Island Reef National Monument is St. Croix's best-known snorkeling spot, where there's a marked trail among the coral formations. Take a catamaran for a more relaxing trip.

The Reefs of St. Croix, USVI. Cane Bay Wall is the most popular dive site in St. Croix, and that's where you can find the highest concentration of dive operators.

Snorkeling Tours, St. John, USVI. If you want to do a day-sail-and-snorkeling trip, then St. John is a good place to leave from. You'll have easy access to a wide variety of islets and cays, so the boat can drop anchor in several places during a full-day sailing trip.

The Wreck of the *Rhone*, off Tortola, BVI. This exceptionally well-preserved royal mail steamer, which sank in 1867, is one of the most famous wreck dives in the Caribbean. But snorkelers won't feel left out in these clear waters.

History

Columbus, pirates, European colonizers, and plantation farmers and their slaves are among the people who have left their marks on these islands, all of which are benefiting the tourism industry, a relatively recent development.

The U.S. National Park Service maintains several sites in the U.S. Virgin Islands, so keep your annual America the Beautiful Pass handy for free or discounted admissions.

Annaberg Plantation, St. John, USVI. You can sometimes see living-history demonstrations at the most popular plantation ruins on St. John.

Christiansted, St. Croix, USVI. With several historic buildings, including Fort Christiansvaern, the island's main town is a place to do more than just shop and dine.

Copper Mine Point, Virgin Gorda, BVI. The remains of a 16th-century copper mine are a popular tourist site here.

Old Government House Museum, Tortola, BVI. The former seat of the island's government is now a museum. It can be found right in the heart of Road Town.

Seven Arches Museum, St. Thomas, USVI. A trip to this museum, in a restored 18th-century home, will give you a sense of how St. Thomas residents lived in the colonial heyday.

Whim Plantation Museum, St. Croix, USVI. A lovingly restored plantation house is St. Croix's best-preserved historical treasure. It's also an island cultural center.

Sleeping in Style

The Virgin Islands have some fine resorts, though not all the best places are necessarily the most luxurious. St. Croix in particular is known more for its small inns than for big, splashy resorts. In the British Virgin Islands (and even St. John), the best options are usually much more laid-back. You're paying for a sense of exclusivity and personal attention, not lavish luxury. You won't be disappointed by these choices.

Bitter End Yacht Club, Virgin Gorda, BVI. If you've ever wanted to sail—or if you simply want to relax on the quiet beach—this lively and comfortable retreat on the island's far eastern end is the ticket.

Caneel Bay, St. John, USVI. Caneel has been a standard-bearer since it opened in the 1950s, but the sense of luxury here is decidedly laid-back. Still, it's hard to resist those seven gorgeous beaches.

Carringtons, St. Croix, USVI. Claudia and Roger Carrington's small, friendly B&B in the hills outside Christiansted has topped the list for many travelers from its earliest days.

Cooper Island Beach Club, BVI. This favorite private-island retreat in the BVI is not the most luxurious—not by a long shot. But there's no better place to get away from it all without having to raid the kids' college fund.

Ritz-Carlton, St. Thomas, USVI. Built like a palatial Italian villa, this is the best Ritz-Carlton in the Caribbean; there's elegance everywhere.

Sugar Mill Hotel, Tortola, BVI. Many love this small hotel's romantic, tropical ambience, and the restaurant is one of the best on Tortola.

ISLAND FINDER

	ST. THOMAS	ST. JOHN	ST. CROIX	TORTOLA	VIRGIN GORDA	JOST VAN DYKE	ANEGADA
APPEAL							
Crowds	●	◐	◐	◐		◐	
Urban Development	●	◐	●	◐			
Family-friendly	●	●	◐	●	◐		◐
BEACHES							
Beautiful	◐	●	◐	◐	◐	●	●
Deserted		●	◐	◐	●	◐	●
ENTERTAINMENT							
Cultural and Historic Sights	●	◐	◐	◐			
Fine Dining	●	◐	◐	◐	◐		
Nightlife	◐	◐	◐	◐		●	
Shopping	●	◐	◐	◐			
Casinos	●	◐				◐	
LODGING							
Luxury Resorts	●	◐	◐	◐	●		
Moderately Priced Resorts	●		●	◐	◐	◐	◐
Small Inns	●	◐	●	◐			◐
NATURE							
Wildlife	◐	●	◐	◐	●	◐	◐
Ecotourism	◐	●	◐	◐	●		
SPORTS							
Golf	●		◐				
Scuba Diving	●	◐	●	●	●	◐	●
Snorkeling	●	●	◐	●	●	●	●
Fishing	●	◐	●	◐	●		◐

●: noteworthy; ◐: some; blank space: little or none

FREQUENTLY ASKED QUESTIONS

Is it safe to travel to the Virgin Islands? Crime certainly happens in the Virgin Islands, and there are sections of Charlotte Amalie, St. Thomas, and Christiansted, St. Croix, that you would not want to walk through even during the day. But, for the most part, crime in the USVI and BVI is much lower than in most large U.S. cities. Petty theft of belongings from your car or on the beach can be a problem in many islands, but in general crime in the BVI is somewhat less than in the USVI.

Are there any all-inclusive resorts in the Virgin Islands? Just one. The Sugar Bay Resort on St. Thomas is the only true all-inclusive resort in the Virgin Islands. Some of the private-island resorts in the BVI do offer full-meal or all-inclusive plans, but they are as far from the typical all-inclusive resort experience as you could possibly imagine. Few resorts (even those that do offer meal plans) include alcoholic drinks, as you'd find at an all-inclusive resort in the Dominican Republic or Jamaica.

How expensive is food in the Virgin Islands? You should expect to pay at least 30% more for groceries in the Virgin Islands than you would at home, and on some of the smaller islands, you'll pay an even larger premium. But there are good, U.S.–style supermarkets on St. Thomas and St. Croix, and decent markets on St. John and Tortola.

Can I bring a cooler of food with me? Many people pack a few staples in their checked luggage (especially if there is a particular brand you might not find in the supermarkets in the Virgin Islands). It's best not to bring fresh fruits and vegetables since they might be confiscated. And you can certainly pack a cooler of frozen or refrigerated food to bring with you to the U.S. Virgin Islands, but you'll have to check it in. Airlines no longer allow cold-packs in carry-on luggage (because they exceed the 3-ounce rule for liquids). And be extra careful about bringing frozen meat into the British Virgin Islands; you must file a $25 importation permit.

How much should I tip at a restaurant? Sometimes you'll see a service charge of about 10% on your restaurant bill (especially in the BVI); when this is the case, tip a little extra (about 5%). Otherwise, tip as you would at home, about 15%.

How much should I tip at my hotel or resort? Many hotels and resorts in the Virgin Islands add a hefty service charge of 10% to 15%, but that money doesn't always find its way to the staff. It's not inappropriate to leave $2 or $3 per day for the maid or to give $1 per bag to the bellhop. Tip taxi drivers in the USVI about 15% of the fare.

Do I need a passport to visit the U.S. Virgin Islands? No, you do not need a passport to visit the U.S. Virgin Islands; however, you will pass through customs, and you will also undergo an agricultural inspection. And you must also provide proof of citizenship (an original birth certificate with raised seal *plus* a government-issued photo ID) on your return.

What about entry into the British Virgin Islands? You do need a passport if you fly into the British Virgin Islands. If you travel to the BVI by *ferry* from the USVI, you can use one of the new, less expensive Passport Cards issued by the U.S. government, or you can use your regular valid passport. But a birth certificate and driver's license are no longer enough.

For more help on trip planning, see the Travel Smart chapter.

WHEN TO GO

The high season in the USBVI is traditionally winter—from December 15 to the week after the St. Thomas Carnival, usually the last week in April—when northern weather is at its worst. During this season you're guaranteed the most entertainment at resorts and the most people with whom to enjoy it. It's also the most fashionable, the most expensive, and the most popular time to visit—and most hotels are heavily booked. You must make reservations at least two or three months in advance for the very best places (sometimes a year in advance for the most exclusive spots). Hotel prices drop 20% to 50% after April 15; airfares and cruise prices also fall. Saving money isn't the only reason to visit the USBVI during the off-season. Summer is usually one of the prettiest times of the year; the sea is even calmer, and things move at a slower pace (except for the first two weeks of August on Tortola, when the BVI celebrate Carnival). The water is clearer for snorkeling and smoother for sailing in the Virgin Islands in May, June, and July.

Climate

Weather in the USBVI is a year-round wonder. The average daily temperature is about 80°F, and there isn't much variation from the coolest to the warmest months. Rainfall averages 40 to 44 inches per year. But in the tropics rainstorms tend to be sudden and brief, often erupting early in the morning and at dusk.

In May and June what's known as the Sahara Dust sometimes moves through, making for hazy spring days and spectacular sunsets.

Toward the end of summer hurricane season begins in earnest, with the first tropical wave passing by in June. Islanders pay close attention to the tropical waves as they form and travel across the Atlantic from Africa. In an odd paradox, tropical storms passing by leave behind the sunniest and clearest days you'll ever see. (And that's saying something in the land of zero air pollution.)

ON THE CALENDAR

The USBVI's top seasonal events are listed here, and any one of them could provide the stuff of lasting memories. Contact local tourism authorities for exact dates and for more information.

October–April
The **Candlelight Concert Series** at Whim Plantation is an ongoing classical music program—the only such program of its kind on St. Croix—that presents concerts on Friday and Saturday evenings throughout the year on the grounds of the historic plantation.

November
On Thanksgiving weekend, the **Annual Coral Bay Thanksgiving Regatta** brings together boat owners for a two-day race event sponsored by the Coral Bay Yacht Club.

December
St. Croix celebrates Carnival with its **Crucian Christmas Festival**, which starts in late December. After weeks of beauty pageants, food fairs, and concerts, the festival wraps up with a parade in early January.

February
Every February, St. Croix celebrates its natural bounty with the **St. Croix Agriculture and Food Fair**, also called "AgriFest." ⊕ *www.viagrifest.org*

In mid-February, the **Water Island Classical Music Festival** takes place at Paradise Point on Water Island. The free concerts are served by special ferry service from Crown Bay Marina. ⊕ *http://water-island-music.com*

On Valentine's Day, St. John always hosts the **Celebration of Love** at Trunk Bay, a free vow-renewal ceremony right on the beach.

March
Locals and yachties gather at Foxy's bar on Jost Van Dyke in the British Virgin Islands for the annual **St. Patrick's Day** celebration.

The annual **St. John Blues Festival** brings musicians from all over to play for five nights in Coral Bay and Cruz Bay.

March–April
During Easter weekend, St. Thomas Yacht Club hosts the **Rolex Cup Regatta,** which is part of the three-race Caribbean Ocean Racing Triangle (CORT) that pulls in yachties and their pals from all over. ⊕ *http://stthomasinternational regatta.com*

The internationally known **BVI Spring Regatta & Sailing Festival,** which includes the competition for the Nation's Challenge Cup, begins during the last week in March and continues into the first weekend in April, with parties and sailing competitions on Tortola and Virgin Gorda. ⊕ *www.bvispringregatta.org*

Join the fun at the **Virgin Gorda Festival,** which culminates with a parade on Easter Sunday.

April
In April, foodies will prosper when local restaurateurs get together to celebrate the **St. Croix Food and Wine Experience**, a four-day celebration of all things food related. One of the highlights is "A Taste of St. Croix," a special one-night event when the top restaurants on the island serve up their top dishes; the event often sells out the same day the highly coveted tickets become available. ⊕ *http://stxfoodand wine.com*

The **VI Carnival St. Thomas** takes place at the end of April for two weeks of fun and festivities featuring both cultural events

and entertainment. ⊕ *www.vicarnival. com*

May

Every May hordes of people head to Tortola for the three-day **BVI Music Festival** to listen to reggae, gospel, blues, and salsa music by musicians from around the Caribbean and the U.S. mainland. ⊕ *www.bvimusicfestival.com*

The **St. Croix Half Ironman Triathlon** attracts international-class athletes as well as amateurs every May for a 1-mile (2-km) swim, a 7-mile (12-km) run, and a 34-mile (55-km) bike ride; it includes a climb up the Beast on Route 69. ⊕ *www.stcroix triathlon.com*

Late May means that it's time for **Foxy's Wood Boat Regatta** on Jost Van Dyke, which has been sponsored by Foxy's and Tortola's West End Yacht Club for well over 30 years. The race brings together myriad older wooden boats for two days of racing excitement.

June–July

Events of the **St. John Festival** celebrating the island's heritage and history continue throughout the month of June—including beauty pageants and a food fair—culminating with an annual parade on Independence Day.

July

The St. Thomas Gamefishing Club hosts its **July Open Tournament** early in the month. There are categories for serious marlin anglers, just-for-fun fishermen, and even kids who want to try their luck from docks and rocks. ⊕ *www.abmt.vi/*

All three islands of the USVI celebrate Independence Day on **July 4** with fireworks, though the biggest celebration is on St. John.

August

Try your hand at sportfishing, as anglers compete to land the largest catch at the **BVI Sportfishing Tournament.**

August sees two weeks of joyful revelry during Tortola's **BVI Emancipation Festival** celebrations.

ST. THOMAS

WELCOME TO ST. THOMAS

TOP REASONS TO GO

★ **Shop till you drop:** Find great deals on duty-free jewelry, timepieces, and electronics along Charlotte Amalie's Main Street—but don't forget to pick up some locally made crafts as well.

★ **Tell fish stories:** Go in search of magnificent blue marlins and other trophy-worthy fish in the waters around St. Thomas from June through October.

★ **Get your sea legs:** Charter a yacht (or just take a regularly scheduled day sail) to cruise between the islands any time of year, or join the St. Thomas International Regatta in March. It's also a short hop over to the British Virgin Islands from St. Thomas.

★ **Hit the links:** Play through the "Devil's Triangle," an intimidating cliff-side trio of holes at Mahogany Run Golf Course.

★ **Take a dip:** Swim at Magens Bay, considered by many to be one of the most beautiful beaches in the world.

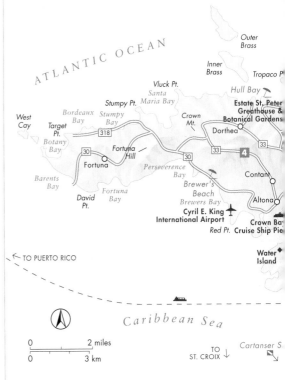

1 Charlotte Amalie. The capital of the USVI has the lion's share of the island's historic sights, not to mention good restaurants, excellent shopping, and some recommendable inns and hotels. Many ferries leave from the dock here, as does seaplane service. The island's main cruise terminal is also here.

2 East End. Most of the island's large beach resorts (not to mention some of the best beaches) are on the East End, about a 30-minute drive from Charlotte Amalie. Red Hook, the main ferry hub for St. Thomas, is also here.

2

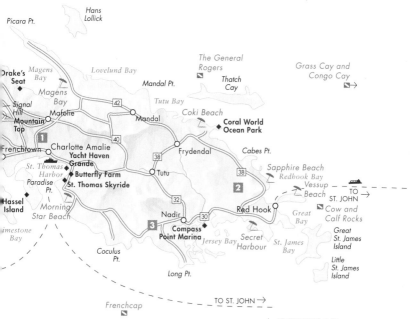

Picara Pt.

Hans Lollick

Drake's Seat

Magens Bay

Lovelund Bay

Mandal Pt.

The General Rogers

Grass Cay and Congo Cay

Thatch Cay

Signal Hill

Magens Bay

Mafolie

Mountain Top

42

Tutu Bay

Mandal

Coki Beach

Coral World Ocean Park

1

40

Charlotte Amalie

Yacht Haven Grande

Frydendal

Cabes Pt.

Frenchtown

St. Thomas Harbor

38

Butterfly Farm

St. Thomas Skyride

Sapphire Beach

Redhook Bay

Vessup Beach

Paradise Pt.

Tutu

38

2

ST. JOHN

TO

Hassel Island

Morning Star Beach

32

Nadir

Red Hook

Great Bay

Cow and Calf Rocks

Limestone Bay

Coculus Pt.

30

Compass Point Marina

Jersey Bay

Secret Harbour

St. James Bay

Great St. James Island

Long Pt.

Little St. James Island

Frenchcap

TO ST. JOHN →

GETTING ORIENTED

3 South Shore. There are a few beach resorts along the South Shore, as well as some restaurants.

4 West End. Aside from Frenchtown and Magens Bay, most of West End is residential, though the main airport is just west of Frenchtown. There are some less-visited beaches beyond Magens Bay, such as Hull Bay, as well as a few restaurants in the hills around Mafolie.

St. Thomas is 13 miles (21 km) long and less than 4 miles (6½ km) wide, but it's extremely hilly, and even an 8- or 10-mile (13- or 16-km) trip could take well over an hour. Don't let that discourage you, though; the mountain ridge that runs east to west through the middle and separates the island's Caribbean and Atlantic sides has spectacular vistas.

EATING AND DRINKING WELL IN THE VIRGIN ISLANDS

Take a mix of indigenous and imported ingredients—everything from papaya to salt cod. Blend this with the cooking styles of people like the ancient Amerindians, Africans, Europeans, East Indians, and Asians, and you have the melting pot that is traditional Virgin Islands cuisine.

Despite its American-flag status and the abundant fast-food and Continental-style restaurants that dominate the islands, the traditional cuisine of the Virgin Islands still maintains a foothold here. The best places to sample the authentic flavors of the islands are local restaurants, bakeries, and mobile food vans, as well as the many food fairs and fish fries that take place throughout the year. When you order an entrée—a "plate of food" as a meal is called—it will often be accompanied by a green salad and a choice of three starchy side dishes. It's no wonder that a favorite saying is, "Better belly bus' than good food waste."—Carol Bareuther

SNACKS

Be sure to try the popular **Caribbean pate** *(pah-teh)*, a triangular fried pastry stuffed with spicy ground beef, conch, or salted fish. And nothing beats **mango-ade, passion fruit punch,** or **soursop juice** to tame the heat (pates often boast a touch of fiery Scotch bonnet peppers among their ingredients). For a tamer snack, look for **johnny-cakes** (fried cornmeal cakes) or hush puppy–like **conch fritters.** Another tasty refresher is **coconut water,** the nectar of freshly cracked coconuts. **Dundersloe,** the Virgin Islands version of peanut brittle, is often sold by vendors outside of shopping centers.

FRUIT

Tropical fruits are abundant throughout the islands. Make sure to sample juicy, sweet mangoes, floral-scented papaya (great with a squeeze of lime), tart star fruit (bite into it or slice it up), and finger-long fig bananas, which are sweeter than stateside varieties. Other favorites include soursop, passion fruit, coconuts (both young and mature), guava, and pineapple.

VEGETABLES

Common vegetables include okra, spinach and other greens, sweet potatoes, eggplants, green plantains, and gnarly root vegetables like tannia, cassava, and boniato. *Kallaloo* is a popular soupy vegetable stew made with spinach and okra, seasoned with fresh herbs, and further flavored with crab, fish, or ham.

SEAFOOD

Popular fish varieties include snapper, grouper, yellowtail, mahimahi, and wahoo, which are often fried or grilled and served whole. Lobster and conch also are prevalent, the latter appearing in everything from ceviche salads to soups. The unofficial national dish for the Virgin Islands is "fish and fungi," simmered fish with okra-studded cornmeal mush.

MEAT

Meat plays a prominent role in soups on the islands. Goat water (mutton stew) and souse (pig-foot stew) make hearty

meals, and are typically served with dumplings or bread. Curried goat is a classic dish worth a taste. For something less spicy, try simply prepared chicken and rice.

STARCHES

Don't be thrown off by unexpected naming conventions. For example, "peas and rice" may be made with red beans, kidney beans, or black beans (no peas). Potato stuffing, a mix of mashed white potatoes, tomato sauce, and seasonings, isn't used to stuff anything. And "fungi" (fun-gee) is not mushrooms, but a polenta-like dish of African origin made from cornmeal studded with chopped okra. More straightforward are the fried plantains, and boiled sweet potatoes, yams, and tannia.

DRINKS

Rum, made from sugarcane, has a significant history in the Virgin Islands, dating back to the rise of sugarcane plantations in the mid-1700s. Rum is still produced here, and it's available in numerous styles (and flavors). For a lower-proof sipper, try *mauby*, a somewhat bitter, root beer–like drink traditionally used as folk medicine that is made from the bark of the mauby tree, which is steeped with sugar and spices and served ice-cold. For a morning eye-opener, some islanders recommend "bush tea," an herbal infusion of native plants.

By Carol M. Bareuther

Because it's the transportation hub of the Virgin Islands, most visitors land on hilly St. Thomas even if they don't linger. Visitors who stay longer may be drawn by the legendary shopping and the wide variety of water sports, activities, beaches, and accommodations. The bustling port of Charlotte Amalie is the main town, while Red Hook sits on the eastern tip. The west end of the island is relatively wild, and hotels and resorts rim the southern and eastern shores.

If you fly to the 32-square-mile (83-square-km) island of St. Thomas, you land at its western end; if you arrive by cruise ship, you come into one of the world's most beautiful harbors. Either way, one of your first sights is the town of Charlotte Amalie. From the harbor you see an idyllic-looking village that spreads into the lower hills. If you were expecting a quiet hamlet with its inhabitants hanging out under palm trees, you've missed that era by about 300 years. Although other islands in the USVI developed plantation economies, St. Thomas cultivated its harbor, and it became a thriving seaport soon after it was settled by the Danish in the 1600s.

The success of the naturally perfect harbor was enhanced by the fact that the Danes—who ruled St. Thomas with only a couple of short interruptions from 1666 to 1917—avoided involvement in some 100 years' worth of European wars. Denmark was the only European country with colonies in the Caribbean to stay neutral during the War of the Spanish Succession in the early 1700s. Accordingly, products of the Dutch, English, and French islands—sugar, cotton, and indigo—were traded through Charlotte Amalie, along with the regular shipments of slaves. When the Spanish wars ended, trade fell off, but by the end of the 1700s Europe was at war again, Denmark again remained neutral, and St. Thomas continued to prosper. Even into the 1800s, while the economies of St. Croix and St. John foundered with the market for sugarcane, St. Thomas's economy remained vigorous. This prosperity led to the development of shipyards, a well-organized banking system, and a large merchant class. In 1845 Charlotte Amalie had 101 large importing houses owned by the English, French, Germans, Haitians, Spaniards, Americans, Sephardim, and Danes.

Charlotte Amalie is still one of the world's most active cruise-ship ports. On almost any day at least one and sometimes as many as eight cruise ships are tied to the docks or anchored outside the harbor. Gently rocking in the shadows of these giant floating hotels are just about every other kind of vessel imaginable: sleek sailing mono- and multihulls that will take you on a sunset cruise complete with rum punch and a Jimmy Buffett sound track, private megayachts that spirit busy executives away, and barnacle-bottom sloops—with laundry draped over the lifelines—that are home to world-cruising gypsies. Huge container ships pull up in Sub Base, west of the harbor, bringing in everything from breakfast cereals to tires. Anchored right along the waterfront are down-island barges that ply the waters between the Greater Antilles and the Leeward Islands, transporting goods like refrigerators, VCRs, and disposable diapers.

The waterfront road through Charlotte Amalie was once part of the harbor. Before it was filled in to build the highway, the beach came right up to the back door of the warehouses that now line the thoroughfare. Two hundred years ago those warehouses were filled with indigo, tobacco, and cotton. Today the stone buildings house silk, crystal, linens, and leather. Exotic fragrances are still traded, but by island beauty queens in air-conditioned perfume palaces instead of through open market stalls. The pirates of old used St. Thomas as a base from which to raid merchant ships of every nation, though they were particularly fond of the gold- and silver-laden treasure ships heading to Spain. Pirates are still around, but today's versions use St. Thomas as a drop-off for their contraband: illegal immigrants and drugs.

GETTING HERE AND AROUND

AIR TRAVEL
American, Continental, Delta, JetBlue, Spirit, United, and US Airways fly to St. Thomas from the United States. Cape Air and Seaborne Airlines fly from San Juan.

BUS TRAVEL
On St. Thomas the island's large buses make public transportation a very comfortable—though slow—way to get from east and west to Charlotte Amalie and back (service to the north is limited). Buses run about every 30 minutes from stops that are clearly marked with Vitran signs. Fares are $1 between outlying areas and town and 75¢ for journeys within town. Some open-air safari vans also follow the bus routes, and these drivers charge the same fares as Vitran—hence their nickname "dollar buses."

CAR TRAVEL
You will want to rent a car if you are staying in a private villa, but if you are staying in a hotel on the beach, you can usually get by with taxis, though getting a taxi every day can be expensive. If you are a family

or group of four, then a car can be a more cost-effective solution since taxi rates are per person.

Traffic can be bad, especially in Charlotte Amalie at rush hour (7 to 9 and 4:30 to 6). If you need to get from an East End resort to the airport during these times, find the alternate route (starting from the East End, Route 38 to 42 to 40 to 33) that goes up the mountain and then drops you back onto Veterans Highway. All drivers should get a copy of *Road Map St. Thomas–St. John,* available on the island anywhere you find maps and guidebooks. In addition, most GPS units will work in the Virgin Islands and some car-rental agencies will rent out GPS devices.

CAR RENTALS

Major car-rental companies, including Avis, Budget, and Hertz have locations at the airport; Avis and Budget also have branch offices. Local rental companies include Dependable Car Rental and Discount Car Rental.

Contacts **Avis** ✉ *Cyril E. King Airport, 70 Lindbergh Bay, 4 miles west of Charlotte Amalie, Lindbergh Bay* ☎ *340/774-1468* ⊕ *www.avis.com* ✉ *Al Cohens Mall, Rte. 30, Havensight Cruise Ship Dock, Havensight* ☎ *340/777-8888* ✉ *Across from Windward Passage Hotel, 3400 Veterans Dr., at Seabourne Airlines terminal, Charlotte Amalie* ☎ *340/776-7329.* **Biz Rentals.** Scooters, motorcycles, and Jeep Wranglers for rent by the day or week. ✉ *Rte. 30, across from the main Havensight Mall gate, between Al Cohen Mall and Guardian Insurance Plaza, Havensight* ☎ *340/774-5840* ⊕ *www.rentamotion.com.* **Budget** ✉ *Cyril E. King Airport, 70 Lindbergh Bay, 4 miles west of Charlotte Amalie, Lindbergh Bay* ☎ *340/776-5774* ⊕ *www.budgetstt.com* ✉ *Havensight Cruise Ship Dock, Rte. 30, Havensight* ☎ *340/776-5774.* **Dependable Car Rental** ✉ *Estate Contant, 12 Lindbergh Bay, 1½ miles east of Cyril E. King Airport off Rte. 308, turning north at the Medical Arts Building, Lindbergh Bay* ☎ *340/774-2253, 800/522-3076* ⊕ *www.dependablecar.com.* **Discount Car Rental.** The main office of this local family-owned business is in Lindbergh Bay, but they pick up at the Cyril E. King Airport as well as from most resorts and hotels. ✉ *Cyril E. King Airport, 70 Lindbergh Bay, 4 miles west of Charlotte Amalie, adjacent to the entrance road of the airport* ☎ *340/776-4858, 877/478-2833* ⊕ *www.discountcar.vi.* **E-Z Car Rental** ✉ *Anchorage Beach Resort, Yacht Club Rd., off Rte. 322, on the far east end of St. Thomas and a 30-min drive from the airport* ☎ *340/775-6255, 800/524-2027.* **Hertz** ✉ *Cyril E. King Airport, Airport Rd., 8100 Lindbergh Bay, 4 miles west of Charlotte Amalie, Lindbergh Bay* ☎ *340/774-1879* ⊕ *www.hertz.com.*

FERRY TRAVEL

There's frequent service from St. Thomas to St. John and Tortola, and less frequent service to Virgin Gorda and Jost Van Dyke. Virgin Islands ferry schedules are published on the website of the Virgin Islands Vacation Guide & Community. There's also a ferry from Charlotte Amalie's waterfront to the Marriott Frenchman's Reef Hotel. In St. Thomas, ferries leave from both Charlotte Amalie and Red Hook. Remember that a passport is now required to travel between the USVI and BVI by ferry. Schedules change, so you should confirm current schedules with the ferry companies.

Contacts **Virgin Islands Vacation Information** ⊕ *www.vinow.com.*

TAXI TRAVEL

USVI taxis charge per person and have set prices. Drivers usually take multiple fares, especially from the airport, ferry docks, and the cruise-ship terminal. Most taxis are either safari-style or enclosed, air-conditioned vans. They can be hailed on the street (especially in town and near major shopping malls and attractions) and can also be called by telephone. There are taxi stands in Charlotte Amalie across from Emancipation Garden (in front of Little Switzerland, behind the post office) and along the waterfront. V.I. Taxi Association has exclusive rights to pick up customers at Cyril E. King Airport, Havensight Cruise Ship Dock, Marriott Frenchman's Reef Resort, Sugar Bay Resort, and Sapphire Beach Resort.

Contacts Dial A Ride St. Thomas. Six lift-equipped or lowered-floor minivans are available to take you to hotels with 24-hour notice. A one-time registration fee of $25 includes round-trip service between the airport and any property. After that, rates are comparable to standard taxis. One companion rides for free. ■ TIP→ They also give island tours; reserve one month in advance. ⊠ *Knud Hansen Complex, 1303 Hospital Ground, adjacent to Lionel Roberts Stadium* ☎ *340/776–1277.* **East End Taxi** ⊠ *Urman Victor Fredericks Marine Terminal, 6117 Red Hook Quarters, off Rte. 38 in Red Hook* ☎ *340/775–6974* ⊕ *eastend-taxi.cbt.cc.* **Islander Taxi Services** ⊠ *Fortress Storage, Building K Suite 2025, at the intersection of Rtes. 313 and 38, Sugar Estate* ☎ *340/774–4077* ⊕ *www. islandertaxiservice.com.* **Virgin Islands Taxi Association** ⊠ *68A Estate Contant, Charlotte Amalie* ☎ *340/774–4550, 340/774–7457* ⊕ *vitaxiassociation.com.*

ESSENTIALS

BANKS

The major banks on St. Thomas are First Bank, Banco Popular, and Scotia Bank, each of which has several branches in convenient locations.

HOTELS

You can let yourself be pampered at a luxurious resort, or, if your means are more modest, you can find cheaper hotels in lovely settings throughout the island. There are also guesthouses and inns with great views (if not a beach at your door) and great service at about half the cost of what you'll pay at the beachfront pleasure palaces. Many of these are west and north of Charlotte Amalie or in the overlooking hills—ideal if you plan to get out and mingle with the locals. There are also inexpensive lodgings (most right in town) that are perfect if you just want a clean room to return to after a day of exploring or beach-bumming. East End condominium complexes are popular with families. Although condos are pricey, they have full kitchens, and you can definitely save money by cooking for yourself—especially if you bring some of your own nonperishable foodstuffs. Though you may spend some time laboring in the kitchen, many condos ease your burden with daily maid service and on-site restaurants; a few also have resort amenities, including pools and tennis courts.

Hotel reviews have been shortened. For full information, visit Fodors. com.

RESTAURANTS

The beauty of St. Thomas and its sister islands has attracted a cadre of professionally trained chefs who know their way around fresh fish and local fruits. You can dine on everything from terrific cheap local dishes such as goat water (a spicy stew) and *fungi* (a cornmeal polenta-like side dish) to imports such as hot pastrami sandwiches and raspberries in crème fraîche.

WHAT IT COSTS IN U.S. DOLLARS			
$	**$$**	**$$$**	**$$$$**
Restaurants	under $13	$13–$20	$21–$30	over $30
Hotels	under $276	$276–$375	$376–$475	over $475

Restaurant prices are the average cost of a main course at dinner or, if dinner is not served, at lunch. Hotel prices are the lowest cost of a standard double room in high season.

SAFETY

To be safe, keep your hotel or vacation villa door locked at all times, stick to well-lighted streets at night, and use the same kind of street sense that you would in any unfamiliar territory. Don't wander the streets of Charlotte Amalie alone at night. If you plan to carry things around, rent a car—not an open-air vehicle—and lock possessions in the trunk. Keep your rental car locked wherever you park. Don't leave cameras, purses, and other valuables lying on the beach while you snorkel for an hour (or even for a minute), no matter how many people are nearby.

VISITOR INFORMATION

Contacts USVI Department of Tourism ⊠ *74B & 75 Kronprinsdens Gade, Charlotte Amalie* ☎ *340/774–8784, 800/372–8784* ⊕ *www.visitusvi.com.* **U.S. Virgin Islands Hotel and Tourism Association** ☎ *340/774–6835* ⊕ *www. virgin-islands-hotels.com.*

EXPLORING ST. THOMAS

To explore outside Charlotte Amalie, rent a car or hire a taxi. Your rental car should come with a good map and perhaps a GPS unit; if not, pick up the pocket-size *Road Map St. Thomas–St. John* at a tourist information center. Roads are marked with route numbers, but they're confusing and seem to switch numbers suddenly. Roads are also identified by signs bearing the St. Thomas–St. John Hotel and Tourism Association's mascot, Tommy the Starfish. More than 100 of these color-coded signs line the island's main routes. Orange signs trace the route from the airport to Red Hook; green signs identify the road from town to Magens Bay; Tommy's face on a yellow background points from Mafolie to Crown Bay through the north side; red signs lead from Smith Bay to Four Corners via Skyline Drive; and blue signs mark the route from the cruise-ship dock at Havensight to Red Hook. These color-coded routes are not marked on most visitor maps, however. Allow yourself a day to explore, especially if you want to stop to take pictures or to enjoy a light bite or refreshing swim. Most gas stations are on the island's more populated eastern side, so fill up before heading to the north side. And remember to drive on the left!

CHARLOTTE AMALIE

Look beyond the pricey shops, T-shirt vendors, and bustling crowds for a glimpse of the island's history. The city served as the capital of Denmark's outpost in the Caribbean until 1917, an aspect of the island often lost in the glitz of the shopping district.

Emancipation Gardens, right next to the fort, is a good place to start a walking tour. Tackle the hilly part of town first: head north up Government Hill to the historic buildings that house government offices and have incredible views. Several regal churches line the route that runs west back to the town proper and the old-time market. Virtually all the alleyways that intersect Main Street lead to eateries that serve frosty drinks, sandwiches, and West Indian fare. There are public restrooms in this area, too. Allow an hour for a quick view of the sights.

A note about the street names: in deference to the island's heritage, the streets downtown are labeled by their Danish names. Locals will use both the Danish name and the English name (such as Dronningens Gade and Norre Gade for Main Street), but most people refer to things by their location ("a block toward the Waterfront off Main Street" or "next to the Little Switzerland Shop"). You may find it more useful if you ask for directions by shop names or landmarks.

TOP ATTRACTIONS

99 Steps. This staircase "street," built by the Danes in the 1700s, leads to the residential area above Charlotte Amalie and to Blackbeard's Castle, a U.S. National Historic Landmark. If you count the stairs as you go up, you'll discover, as thousands have before you, that there are more than the name implies. ⊠ *Look for steps heading north from Government Hill.*

FAMILY **Fort Christian.** St. Thomas's oldest standing structure, this remarkable building was built between 1672 and 1680 and now has U.S. National Landmark status. Over the years, it was used as a jail, governor's residence, town hall, courthouse, and church. In 2005, a multimillion-dollar renovation project started to stabilize the structure and halt centuries of deterioration. The fort reopened for public tours in 2014. Inside you can visit the inner courtyard and rooms, and from the outside, you can see the four renovated faces of the famous 19th-century clock tower. ⊠ *Waterfront Hwy., east of shopping district* ☎ *340/774–5541* ⊕ *stthomashistoricaltrust.org.*

Hassel Island. East of Water Island in Charlotte Amalie harbor, Hassel Island is part of the Virgin Islands National Park. On it are the ruins of a British military garrison (built during a brief British occupation of the USVI during the 1800s) and the remains of a marine railway (where ships were hoisted into dry dock for repairs). Daily guided kayak tours to the island are available from VI Ecotours. The St. Thomas Historical

Trust also leads walking tours throughout the year. ⊠ *Charlotte Amalie harbor* ☎ *340/776–6201 Virgin Islands National Park main office* ⊕ *www.nps.gov/viis.*

Pissarro Building. Housing several shops and an art gallery, this was the birthplace and childhood home of the acclaimed 19th-century impressionist painter Camille Pissarro, who lived for most of his adult life in France. The art gallery on the second floor contains three original pages from Pissarro's sketchbook and two pastels by Pissarro's grandson, Claude. ⊠ *14 Dronningens Gade (Main St.), between Raadets Gade and Trompeter Gade.*

FAMILY **Roosevelt Park.** The former Coconut Park was renamed in honor of Franklin D. Roosevelt in 1945. It's a great place to put your feet up and people-watch. Five granite pedestals represent the five branches of the military, bronze urns commemorate special events and can be lighted, and inscribed bronze plaques pay tribute to the territory's veterans who died defending the United States. There's also a children's playground. ⊠ *Intersection of Norre Gade and Rte. 35, adjacent to the Memorial Moravian Church* ☎ *340/774–5541* ⊕ *www.stthomashistoricaltrust.org.*

Seven Arches Museum and Gallery. This restored 18th-century home is a striking example of classic Danish–West Indian architecture. There seem to be arches everywhere—seven to be exact—all supporting a "welcoming arms" staircase that leads to the second floor and the flower-framed front doorway. The Danish kitchen is a highlight: it's housed in a separate building away from the main house, as were all cooking facilities in the early days (for fire prevention). Inside the house you can see mahogany furnishings and gas lamps and brightly colored abstract canvases painted by the museum's curator, a local artist. ⊠ *Government Hill, 18A-B Dronningens Gade, 3 bldgs. east of Government House* ☎ *340/774–9295* ⊕ *www.sevenarchesmuseum.com* ⌦ *$5 donation* ⊗ *By appointment only.*

FAMILY **Water Island.** This island, the fourth-largest of the U.S. Virgin Islands, floats about a ¼ mile (½ km) out in Charlotte Amalie harbor. A ferry between Crown Bay Marina and the island operates several times daily Monday through Saturday 6:30–6 and Sunday and holidays 8–5 at a cost of $10 round-trip. (On cruise-ship days, a ferry goes directly from the West India Company dock, but only for cruise passengers on the bike trip.) From the ferry dock, it's a hike of less than a half-mile to Honeymoon Beach (though you have to go up a big hill), where Brad Pitt and Cate Blanchett filmed a scene of the movie *The Curious Case of Benjamin Button*. Get lunch from a food truck that pulls up on weekends. ⊠ *Charlotte Amalie harbor* ☎ *340/690–4159 for ferry information.*

WORTH NOTING

All Saints Episcopal Church. Built in 1848 from stone quarried on the island, the church has thick, arched window frames lined with the yellow brick that came to the islands as ballast aboard ships. Merchants left the bricks on the waterfront when they filled their boats with molasses, sugar, mahogany, and rum for the return voyage. The church was built in celebration of the end of slavery in the USVI.

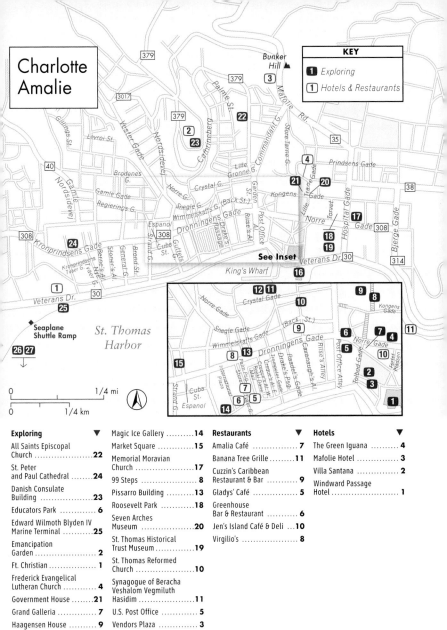

Charlotte Amalie

Fort Christian (1672–80), the oldest surviving structure in St. Thomas

✉ *13 Commandant Gade, near the Emancipation Garden post office* ☎ *340/774–0217* ☉ *Mon.–Sat. 9–3.*

Danish Consulate Building. Built in 1830, this structure once housed the Danish Consulate. Although the Danish consul general, Søren Blak, has an office in Charlotte Amalie, the Danish Consulate is now in the Scandinavian Center in Havensight Mall. ⚠ **This building is not open to the public.** ✉ *Take stairs north at corner of Bjerge Gade and Crystal Gade to Denmark Hill.*

Educators Park. A peaceful place amid the town's hustle and bustle, the park has memorials for three famous Virgin Islanders: educator Edith Williams, J. Antonio Jarvis (a founder of the *Daily News*), and educator and author Rothschild Francis. The last gave many speeches here. ✉ *Main St., across from Emancipation Garden post office.*

Edward Wilmoth Blyden IV Marine Terminal. Locally called Tortola Wharf, this is where you can catch the *Native Son* and other ferries to the BVI. The restaurant upstairs is a good place to watch the Charlotte Amalie harbor traffic and sip an iced tea. Next door is the Charles F. Blair Jr. Seaplane Terminal, where Seaborne Airlines offers service to St. Croix, the BVI, and Puerto Rico. ✉ *Veterans Dr., across from the Windward Passage Hotel* ☎ *340/774–1629* ⊕ *www.viport.com.*

Emancipation Garden. A bronze bust of a freed slave blowing a conch shell commemorates slavery's end in 1848—the garden was built to mark emancipation's 150th anniversary in 1998. The gazebo here is used for official ceremonies. Two other monuments show the island's Danish-American connection—a bust of Denmark's King Christian and a scaled-down model of the U.S. Liberty Bell. ✉ *Between Tolbod*

Gade and Fort Christian, next to Vendor's Plaza.

Frederick Evangelical Lutheran Church. This historic church has a massive mahogany altar, and its pews—each with its own door—were once rented to families of the congregation. Lutheranism is the state religion of Denmark, and when the territory was without a minister, the governor—who had his own elevated pew—filled in. ⊠ *7 Norre Gade, across from Emancipation Garden and the Grand Hotel* ☎ *340/776–1315* ⊕ *www.felc1666.org* ⊙ *Mon.–Sat. 9–4.*

> **BIG EVENT**
>
> April is a great time to visit St. Thomas, as the island comes alive for Carnival. The celebrations—steel-drum music, colorful costumes, and dancing in the streets—culminate the last weekend of the month.

Government House. Built in 1867, this neoclassical white brick-and-wood structure houses the offices of the governor of the Virgin Islands. Inside, the staircases are of native mahogany, as are the plaques, hand-lettered in gold with the names of the governors appointed and, since 1970, elected. Brochures detailing the history of the building are available, but you may have to ask for them. ⊠ *Government Hill, 21–22 Kongens Gade, across from the Emancipation Garden post office* ☎ *340/774–0001* ☏ *Free* ⊙ *Weekdays 8–5.*

Grand Galleria. This imposing building stands at the head of Main Street. Once the island's premier hotel, it has been converted into offices, shops, and a deli. ⊠ *43-46 Norre Gade, at intersection of Tolbod Gade, adjacent to Emancipation Garden* ☎ *340/774–7282* ⊙ *Weekdays 8–5, Sat. 9–noon.*

Haagensen House. This lovingly restored house was built in the early 1800s by Danish entrepreneur Hans Haagensen. It's surrounded by an equally impressive cookhouse, outbuildings, and terraced gardens. A lower-level banquet hall showcases antique prints and photographs. A guided tour includes this property, plus other restored 19th-century houses, a rum factory, amber museum, and finally, the lookout tower at Blackbeard's Castle. ⊠ *Government Hill, 29–30 Kongens Gade, behind Hotel 1829* ☎ *340/776–1234* ☏ *Tours $10* ⊙ *Mon.–Thurs. 9–2.*

Legislature Building. Its pastoral-looking lime-green exterior conceals the vociferous political wrangling of the Virgin Islands Senate. Constructed originally by the Danish as a police barracks, the building was later used to billet U.S. Marines, and much later it housed a public school. ■ TIP➔ You're welcome to sit in on sessions in the upstairs chambers. ⊠ *Waterfront Hwy. (Rte. 30), across from Fort Christian* ☎ *340/774–0880* ⊕ *www.legvi.org* ⊙ *Daily 8–5.*

Market Square. A cadre of old-timers gathers daily—especially by 4 am on Saturday mornings—at this 18th-century slave market, to sell local fruits such as mangoes and papayas, strange-looking root vegetables, and bunches of fresh herbs. Sidewalk vendors offer brightly colored fabrics, tie-dyed clothing, and handicrafts at good prices. ■ TIP➔ A smaller number of vendors set up shop here all week long. ⊠ *Main St., at Strand Gade* ☎ *340/774–5182* ⊙ *Weekdays 9–5, Sat. 5–5.*

Memorial Moravian Church. Built in 1884, this church was named to commemorate the 150th anniversary of the Moravian Church in the Virgin Islands. ⊠ *17 Norre Gade, next to Roosevelt Park* ☎ *340/776–0066* ⊕ *www.memorialmoravianvi.org* ☉ *Weekdays 8–5.*

Saints Peter and Paul Cathedral. This building was consecrated as a parish church in 1848, and serves as the seat of the territory's Roman Catholic diocese. The ceiling and walls are covered with a dozen murals depicting biblical scenes; they were painted in 1899 by two Belgian artists, Father Leo Servais and Brother Ildephonsus. The marble altar and walls were added in the 1960s. ⊠ *22-AB Kronprindsens Gade, 1 block west of Market Square* ☎ *340/774–0201* ⊕ *cathedralvi.com* ☉ *Mon.–Sat. 8–5.*

St. Thomas Historical Trust Museum. Tours of the museum take 30 minutes and include a wealth of pirate artifacts, as well as West Indian antique furniture, old-time postcards, and historic books. The Trust office, also located at the museum, is where you can book reservations for the one-hour historic Charlotte Amalie walking tour and three-hour Hassel Island tour, both of which have to be scheduled by appointment. ⊠ *West end of Roosevelt Park* ☎ *340/774–5541* ⊕ *www.stthomashistoricaltrust.org* ☉ *Tues. and Thurs. 10–2 or by appt.*

St. Thomas Reformed Church. This church has an austere loveliness that's amazing considering all it's been through. Founded in 1744, it's been rebuilt twice after fires and hurricanes. The unembellished cream-color hall is quite peaceful. The only other color is the forest green of the shutters and the carpet. Call ahead if you wish to visit at a particular time, as the doors are sometimes locked. Services are held at 9 am each Sunday. ⊠ *5 Crystal Gade at Nye Gade, 1½ blocks north of Main St.* ☎ *340/776–8255* ⊕ *www.stthomasreformedchurch.org* ☉ *Weekdays 9–5.*

Synagogue of Beracha Veshalom Vegmiluth Hasidim. The synagogue's Hebrew name translates as the Congregation of Blessing, Peace, and Loving Deeds. The small building's white pillars contrast with rough stone walls, as does the rich mahogany of the pews and altar. The sand on the floor symbolizes the exodus from Egypt. Since the synagogue first opened its doors in 1833, it has held a weekly service, making it the oldest synagogue building in continuous use under the American flag and the second-oldest (after the one on Curaçao) in the Western Hemisphere. Guided tours can be arranged. Brochures detailing the key structures and history are also available. Next door the Weibel Museum showcases Jewish history on St. Thomas. ⊠ *Synagogue Hill, 15 Crystal Gade* ✧ *From Main St., walk up Raadet's Gade (H. Stern is on the corner) to the top of the hill, turn left and synagogue is the 2nd bldg. on right* ☎ *340/774–4312* ⊕ *www.onepaper.com/synagogue* ☉ *Weekdays 9–4.*

U.S. Post Office. While you buy stamps, contemplate the murals of waterfront scenes by *Saturday Evening Post* artist Stephen Dohanos. His art was commissioned as part of the Works Project Administration in the 1930s. ⊠ *Tolbod Gade and Main St., 5046 Norre Gade, next to Emancipation Garden* ☎ *340/774–3750.*

FAMILY **Vendors Plaza.** Here merchants sell everything from T-shirts to African attire to leather goods. Look for local art among the ever-changing selections at this busy market. There is a group of hair-braiders here, too. ⊠ *Waterfront, west of Fort Christian* ☉ *Weekdays 8–6, weekends 9–1.*

Weibel Museum. In this museum next to the synagogue, 300 years of Jewish history on St. Thomas are showcased. The small gift shop sells a commemorative silver coin celebrating the anniversary of the Hebrew congregation's establishment on the island in 1796. There are also tropically inspired items, such as menorahs painted to resemble palm trees. ⊠ *Synagogue Hill, 15 Crystal Gade* ✛ *From Main St., walk up Raadet's Gade (H. Stern is on the corner) to the top of the hill, turn left and it's the 2nd bldg. on right* ☎ *340/774–4312* ⊕ *www.onepaper.com/ synagogue* ☖ *Free* ☉ *Weekdays 9–4.*

EAST END

Although the eastern end has many major resorts and spectacular beaches, don't be surprised if a cow, a herd of goats, or even a deer crosses your path as you drive through the relatively flat, dry terrain. You can pick up sandwiches from a deli in the Red Hook area if you want a picnic lunch.

TOP ATTRACTIONS

FAMILY
Fodor's Choice
★
Coral World Ocean Park. This interactive aquarium and water-sports center lets you experience a variety of sea life and other animals. There's a new two-acre dolphin habitat under construction, as well as several outdoor pools where you can pet baby sharks, feed stingrays, touch starfish, and view endangered sea turtles. During the Sea Trek Helmet Dive, you walk along an underwater trail wearing a helmet that provides a continuous supply of air. You can also try "snuba," a cross between snorkeling and scuba diving. Swim with a sea lion and have a chance at playing ball or getting a big, wet, whiskered kiss. You can also buy a cup of nectar and let the cheerful lorikeets perch on your hand and drink. The park also has an offshore underwater observatory, an 80,000-gallon coral reef exhibit (one of the largest in the world), and a nature trail with native ducks and tortoises. Daily feedings take place at most exhibits. ⊠ *Coki Point north of Rte. 38, 6450 Estate Smith Bay, Estate Frydendal* ☎ *340/775–1555* ⊕ *www.coralworldvi.com* ☖ *$19, Sea Lion Splash $126, Sea Lion Encounter $86, Sea Trek $79, Snuba $73, Shark and Turtle Encounters $53, Semi-Submarine $41* ☉ *Daily 9–4. Off-season (May–Oct.) hrs may vary, so call to confirm.*

WORTH NOTING

Red Hook. The IGY American Yacht Harbor marina here has fishing and sailing charter boats, a dive shop, and powerboat-rental agencies. There are also several bars and restaurants, including Molly Molone's, Fish Tails, Duffy's Love Shack, and the Caribbean Saloon. Ferries depart from Red Hook en route to St. John and the British Virgin Islands. ⊠ *Red Hook, intersection of Rtes. 38 and 32.*

SOUTH SHORE

TOP ATTRACTIONS

FAMILY **Skyride to Paradise Point.** Fly skyward in a 7-minute gondola ride to Paradise Point, an overlook with breathtaking views of Charlotte Amalie and the harbor. You'll find several shops, a bar, a restaurant, and a wedding gazebo. A ¼-mile (½-km) hiking trail leads to spectacular views of St. Croix. Wear sturdy shoes, as the trail is steep and rocky. You can also skip the $21 gondola ride and taxi to the top for $6 per person from the Havensight Dock. ⊠ *Rte. 30, across from Havensight Mall, Havensight* ☎ *340/774–9809* ⊕ *www.ridetheview.com* ⊡ *$21* ☉ *Thurs.–Tues. 9–5, Wed. 9–9.*

WORTH NOTING

FAMILY **Butterfly Garden.** Step into this 10,000-square-foot mesh enclosure and watch hundreds of colorful, exotic butterflies flutter all around you. A 25-minute tour takes you through their life cycle. Outside the enclosure, you can wander a garden of native plants designed to attract local butterflies and hummingbirds. The butterflies are most active in the morning. If you're a photographer, you'll probably prefer the afternoon, when the butterflies move more slowly and are more easily captured in pictures. ⊠ *9016 Havensight Mall, adjacent to West Indian Company cruise-ship dock, Havensight* ☎ *340/715–3366* ⊕ *www. butterflygardenvi.com* ⊡ *$12* ☉ *Nov.–Apr. 8:30–4 on days a cruise ship is at the Havensight Dock. Off-season (May–Oct.) hrs may vary, so call to confirm.*

Frenchtown. Popular for its bars and restaurants, Frenchtown is also the home of descendants of immigrants from St. Barthélemy (St. Barths). You can watch them pull up their brightly painted boats and display their equally colorful catch of the day along the waterfront. If you chat with them, you can hear speech patterns slightly different from those of other St. Thomians. Get a feel for the residential district of Frenchtown by walking west to some of the town's winding streets, where tiny wooden houses have been passed down from generation to generation. ⊠ *Turn south off Waterfront Hwy. (Rte. 30) at post office, Frenchtown*

French Heritage Museum. Next to Joseph Aubain Ballpark, the museum houses fishing nets, accordions, tambourines, mahogany furniture, photographs, and other artifacts illustrating the lives of the French descendants during the 18th through 20th centuries. Admission is free, but donations are accepted. ⊠ *Rue de St. Anne and Rue de St. Barthélemy, Frenchtown* ☎ *340/714–2583* ⊕ *www.frenchheritagemuseum. com* ⊡ *Free* ☉ *Mon.–Sat. 9–6.*

WEST END

The west end of the island is lusher and quieter—with fewer houses and less traffic. Here there are roller-coaster routes (made all the scarier because the roads have no shoulders) as well as incredible vistas. Leave time in the afternoon for a swim and enjoy a slice of pizza at Magens Bay before leaving. A day in the country will reveal the tropical pleasures that have enticed more than one visitor to become a resident.

TOP ATTRACTIONS

FAMILY **Mountain Top.** Head out to the observation deck—more than 1,500 feet above sea level—to get a bird's-eye view that stretches from Puerto Rico's out-island of Culebra in the west all the way to the British Virgin Islands in the east. There's also a restaurant, restrooms, and duty-free shops that sell everything from Caribbean art to nautical antiques, ship models, and touristy T-shirts. Kids will like talking to the parrots—and hearing them answer back. ⊠ *Head north off Rte. 33, look for signs, Mountain Top* ☎ *340/774–2400* ⊕ *www.mountaintopvi.com* 🎟 *Free* ⊙ *Daily 8–5.*

WORTH NOTING

Drake's Seat. Sir Francis Drake was supposed to have kept watch over his fleet, looking for enemy ships from this vantage point. The panorama is especially breathtaking (and romantic) at dusk, and if you arrive late in the day, you can miss the hordes of day-trippers on taxi tours who stop here to take pictures. ⊠ *Rte. 40, ¼ mile west of the intersection of Rtes. 40 and 35, Estate Zufriedenheit.*

Estate St. Peter Greathouse and Botanical Gardens. This unusual spot is perched on a mountainside 1,000 feet above sea level, with views of more than 20 islands and islets. You can wander through a gallery displaying local art, sip a complimentary rum punch while looking out at the view, or follow a nature trail that leads you past nearly 70 varieties of tropical plants, including 17 varieties of orchids. ⊠ *Rte. 40, directly across from Tree Limin' Extreme Zipline, Estate St. Peter* ☎ *340/774–4999* ⊕ *www.greathousevi.com* 🎟 *$8.*

Magic Ice Gallery. This is one cool gallery! Life-size ice carvings feature sea life, a pirate ship, a chapel, a bar (a complimentary drink is included in the tour), a slide you can ride down, and much more. Insulated ponchos with hoods and mittens are provided, but you don't get to keep them. ⊠ *Charlotte Amalie Waterfront, 21 Dronningens Gade, next to the Pizza Hut on the Waterfront* ☎ *340/422–6000* ⊕ *www.magicice.vi* 🎟 *$22* ⊙ *Weekends 10–5, weekdays 11–5.*

BEACHES

All 44 St. Thomas beaches are open to the public, although you can reach some of them only by walking through a resort. Hotel guests frequently have access to lounge chairs and floats that are off-limits to nonguests; for this reason, you may feel more comfortable at one of the beaches not associated with a resort, such as Magens Bay (which charges an entrance fee to cover beach maintenance) or Coki Beach. Whichever one you choose, remember to remove your valuables from the car and keep them out of sight when you go swimming.

EAST END

FAMILY **Coki Beach.** Funky beach huts selling local foods such as pates (fried
Fodor'sChoice turnovers with a spicy ground-beef filling), quaint vendor kiosks, and
★ a brigade of hair braiders and taxi men make this beach overlooking picturesque Thatch Cay feel like an amusement park. But this is the

best place on the island to snorkel and scuba dive. Fish, including grunts, snappers, and wrasses, are like an effervescent cloud you can wave your hand through. **Amenities:** food and drink; lifeguards; parking; showers; restrooms; water sports. **Best for:** partiers; snorkeling. ⊠ *Rte. 388, next to Coral World Ocean Park, Estate Smith Bay.*

FAMILY **Lindquist Beach.** The newest public beach in the Virgin Islands has a serene sense of wilderness that isn't found on the more crowded beaches. A lifeguard is on duty between 8 am and 5 pm and picnic tables and restrooms are available. Try snorkeling over the offshore reef. There's a $2 per person entrance fee. **Amenities:** lifeguards; parking; toilets. **Best For:** swimming; snorkeling. ⊠ *Rte. 38, at end of a dirt road, Estate Smith Bay* ☎ *340/777–6300.*

FAMILY **Sapphire Beach.** A steady breeze makes this beach a boardsailor's paradise. The swimming is great, as is the snorkeling, especially at the reef near Pettyklip Point. Beach volleyball is big on the weekends. Sapphire Beach Resort and Marina has a snack shop, a bar, and water-sports rentals. **Amenities:** parking; restrooms. **Best for:** snorkeling; swimming; windsurfing. ⊠ *Rte. 38, ½ mile north of Red Hook, Sapphire Bay.*

Secret Harbour. Placid waters make it easy to stroke your way out to a swim platform offshore from the Secret Harbour Beach Resort & Villas. Nearby reefs give snorkelers a natural show. There's a bar and restaurant, as well as a dive shop. **Amenities:** food and drink; parking; restrooms; water sports. **Best for:** snorkeling; sunset; swimming. ⊠ *Rte. 322, take first right off Rte. 322, Red Hook.*

Vessup Beach. This wild, undeveloped beach is lined with sea grape trees and century plants. It's close to Red Hook harbor, so you can watch the ferries depart. The calm waters are excellent for swimming. It's popular with locals on weekends. **Amenities:** parking; water sports. **Best for:** swimming. ⊠ *Off Rte. 322, Vessup Bay.*

SOUTH SHORE

Brewer's Beach. Watch jets land at the Cyril E. King Airport as you dip into the usually calm seas. Rocks at either end of the shoreline, patches of grass poking randomly through the sand, and shady tamarind trees 30 feet from the water give this beach a wild, natural feel. Civilization has arrived, in the form of one or two mobile food vans parked on the nearby road. Buy a fried-chicken leg and johnnycake or burgers and chips to munch on at the picnic tables. **Amenities:** food and drink; lifeguards; parking; restrooms. **Best for:** sunset; swimming. ⊠ *Rte. 30, west of University of the Virgin Islands.*

Morningstar Beach. Nature and nurture combine at this ¼-mile-long (½-km-long) beach between Marriott Frenchman's Reef and Morning Star Beach resorts, where the amenities include beachside bar service.

A concession rents floating mats, snorkeling equipment, sailboards, and Jet Skis. Swimming is excellent; there are good-size rolling waves year-round, but do watch the undertow. If you're feeling lazy, rent a lounge chair with umbrella and order a libation from one of two full-service beach bars. At 7 am and again at 5 pm, you can catch the cruise ships gliding majestically out to sea from the Charlotte Amalie harbor. **Amenities:** food and drink; parking; restrooms; water sports. **Best for:** partiers; surfing; swimming. ⊠ *Rte. 315 ⊹ 2 miles (3 km) southeast of Charlotte Amalie, past Havensight Mall and cruise-ship dock.*

> **WORD OF MOUTH**
>
> "Magens [Bay] beach on the north side of the island is gorgeous, but go on a non-ship day or early in the morning before shippers get there, or after 3 when they leave."
> —Virginia

WEST END

Hull Bay. Watch surfers ride the waves here from December to March, when huge swells roll in from north Atlantic storms. The rest of the year, tranquility prevails at this picturesque neighborhood beach. Enjoy hot pizza, barbecue ribs, and a game of darts at the Hull Bay Hideaway Bar & Restaurant, home of the annual Bastille Day Kingfish Tournament held each July. **Amenities:** food and drink; parking; water sports. **Best for:** swimming; snorkeling; partiers. ⊠ *Hull Bay, Rte. 37, at end of road on north side.*

FAMILY
Fodor's Choice
★

Magens Bay. Deeded to the island as a public park, this heart-shape stretch of white sand is considered one of the most beautiful in the world. The bottom of the bay is flat and sandy, so this is a place for sunning and swimming rather than snorkeling. On weekends and holidays the sounds of music from groups partying under the sheds fill the air. There's a bar, snack shack, and beachwear boutique; and bathhouses with restrooms, changing rooms, and saltwater showers are close by. Sunfish, kayaks, and paddleboards are the most popular rentals at the water-sports kiosk. East of the beach is Udder Delight, a one-room shop that serves a Virgin Islands tradition—a milk shake with a splash of Cruzan rum. (Kids can enjoy virgin versions, which have a touch of soursop, mango, or banana flavoring.) If you arrive between 8 am and 5 pm, you pay an entrance fee of $4 per person, $2 per vehicle; it's free for children under 12. **Amenities:** food and drink; lifeguards; parking (fee); showers; restrooms; water sports. **Best for:** partiers; swimming; walking. ⊠ *Magens Bay, Rte. 35, at end of road on north side of island* ☎ *340/777–6300* ⊕ *www.magensbayauthority.com.*

WHERE TO EAT

Restaurants are spread all over the island, although fewer are found in the west and northwest sections. Most restaurants out of town are easily accessible by taxi and have ample parking. If you dine in Charlotte

Amalie, take a taxi. Parking close to restaurants can be difficult to find, and walking around after dark isn't advisable for safety reasons.

Dining on St. Thomas is informal. Few restaurants require a jacket and tie. Still, at dinner in the snazzier places shorts and T-shirts are inappropriate; men would do well to wear slacks and a shirt with buttons. Dress codes on St. Thomas rarely require women to wear skirts, but you can never go wrong with something flowing.

CHARLOTTE AMALIE

$$$$ SPANISH Fodor's Choice ★

🍴 **Amalia Café.** A great place to take a break and get a bite while shopping, this open-air café tucked into the alleyway of Palm Passage is owned by Antiguan-born Randolph Maynard and his German wife Helga. They serve authentic Spanish cuisine. Try tapas such as mussels in brandy sauce, escargots with mushrooms and herb butter, or Galician-style octopus and baby eels served in a sizzling garlic sauce. Paella is a house specialty, as is the caramel flan. Ask for an inside table if the idea of passersby checking out your meal isn't too appetizing. *www.amaliacafe.com* [$] *Average main: $32* ✉ *Palm Passage, 24 Dronningens Gade, facing the Waterfront* ☎ *340/714–7373* 🌐 ⏲ *Closed Sun.*

$$$$ ECLECTIC Fodor's Choice ★

🍴 **Banana Tree Grille.** The eagle's-eye view of the Charlotte Amalie harbor from this breeze-cooled restaurant is as fantastic as the food. Linen tablecloths, china, and silver place settings combine with subdued lighting to make an elegant space. To start, try the flame-grilled oysters or crispy calamari dipped in tangy lemon aioli. The signature dish here—and worthy of its fame—is a grass-fed pasture-raised filet mignon topped with plump shrimp and served with velvety Bearnaise sauce and fresh asparagus. Arrive before 6 pm to watch the cruise ships depart from the harbor while you enjoy a drink at the bar. [$] *Average main: $40* ✉ *Bluebeard's Castle, Bluebeard's Hill, 1331 Estate Taamburg* ☎ *340/776–4050* 🌐 *www.bananatreegrille.com* ✍ *Reservations essential* ⏲ *Closed Mon. No lunch.*

$$ JAPANESE

🍴 **Beni Iguana's Sushi Bar & Restaurant.** Edible art is an apt description for the sushi and sashimi feast that draws visitors and locals alike. The 5-foot-tall reef tank will definitely put you in the mood for seafood. There are nearly 30 vegetarian and seafood rolls to choose from, including avocado, spicy crab, and red snapper. The real favorite here is steamed mussels in a house-made creamy sesame dressing dubbed "iguana sauce," which is, happily, not made from the spiny reptile that roams the island's hillsides and roadways. [$] *Average main: $15* ✉ *Havensight Mall, West Indian Dock Rd., Bldg. IX, facing the cruise-ship dock* ☎ *340/777–8744* 🌐 *beniiguanassushibar.com* ⏲ *Closed Sun.*

$$ CARIBBEAN

🍴 **Cuzzin's Caribbean Restaurant and Bar.** In a 19th-century livery stable on Back Street, this restaurant is hard to find but well worth it if you want to sample bona fide Virgin Islands cuisine. For lunch, order tender slivers of conch stewed in a rich onion-and-butter sauce, savory braised oxtail, or curried chicken. At dinner the island-style mutton, served in thick gravy and seasoned with locally grown herbs, offers a tasty treat that's deliciously different. Side dishes include peas and rice, boiled green bananas, fried plantains, and potato stuffing. [$] *Average main:*

DID YOU KNOW?

With its flat, sandy bottom, Magens Bay is one of the best swimming beaches on St. Thomas. After your outing, stop by Udder Delight east of the beach for a milk shake, rum-spiked or not.

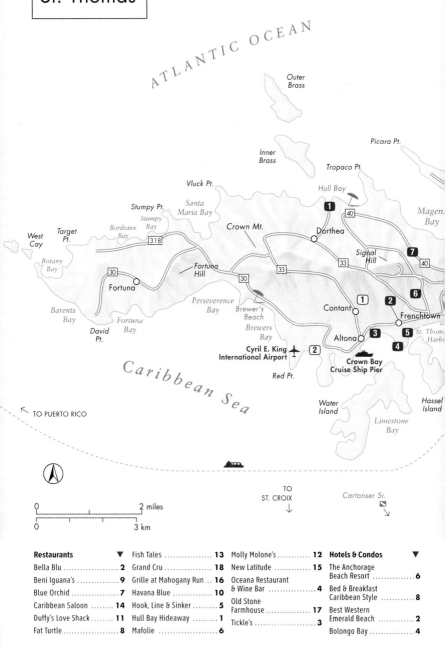

St. Thomas

ATLANTIC OCEAN

Outer Brass

Picara Pt.

Inner Brass

Tropaco Pt.

Vluck Pt.

Hull Bay

1

Stumpy Pt.

Santa Maria Bay

40

Magens Bay

Bordeaux Bay

Stumpy Bay

Crown Mt.

Dorthea

318

West Cay

Target Pt.

Botany Bay

30

Fortuna Hill

33

Signal Hill

7

33

40

Fortuna

30

Perseverence Bay

1

2

6

Brewer's Beach

Contant

Frenchtown

Barents Bay

Fortuna Bay

Brewers Bay

Altona

3

5

St. Thomas Harbor

David Pt.

Cyril E. King International Airport

2

4

Red Pt.

Crown Bay Cruise Ship Pier

Caribbean Sea

← TO PUERTO RICO

Water Island

Hassel Island

Limestone Bay

TO
ST. CROIX
↓

Cartanser Sr.

0   2 miles

0   3 km

KEY

🏖 *Beaches*
🚢 *Cruise Ship Terminal*
🔲 *Dive Sites*
⛴ *Ferry*
1 *Restaurants*
1 *Hotels*

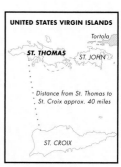

UNITED STATES VIRGIN ISLANDS

Tortola
ST. THOMAS   ST. JOHN

Distance from St. Thomas to St. Croix approx. 40 miles

ST. CROIX

Hans Lollick

Lovelund Bay

The General Rogers

Thatch Cay

Grass Cay and Congo Cay →

Mandal Pt.

Magens Bay

17

Tutu Bay

Coki Beach

Charlotte Amalie see detail map

16

42

Mandal

11

40

Frydendal

38

38

10

Cabes Pt.

18

9

Sapphire Beach

Redhook Bay

9

Tutu

32

Vessup Beach

TO → ST. JOHN

8

Morning Star Beach

8   7

Cow and Calf Rocks

Paradise Pt.

10

5

Red Hook

15

Great Bay

Great St. James Island

3

Nadir

30

6

11 · 14

4

Secret Harbour

St. James Bay

Coculus Pt.

Jersey Bay

Little St. James Island

Long Pt.

TO ST. JOHN →

🔲 *Frenchcap*

$15 ✉ 7 Wimmelskafts Gade (Back St.) ☎ 340/777–4711 🌐 cuzzinsvi.com 🕒 Closed Sun.

$$ CARIBBEAN Fodor's Choice ★

🍴 **Gladys' Cafe.** Even if the local specialties—conch in butter sauce, jerk pork, pan-fried yellowtail snapper—didn't make this a recommended café, it would be worth coming for Gladys's smile. Her cozy alleyway restaurant is rich in atmosphere with its mahogany bar and native stone walls, making dining a double delight. While you're here, pick up a $5 or $10 bottle of her special hot sauce. There are mustard-, oil and vinegar–, and tomato-based versions; the tomato-based sauce is the hottest. [$] *Average main: $14 ✉ Waterfront, 28A Dronningens Gade, west side of Royal Dane Mall ☎ 340/774–6604 🕒 No dinner ☞ Only Amex credit cards accepted.*

$$ AMERICAN FAMILY

🍴 **Greenhouse Bar and Restaurant.** Fun-lovers come to this waterfront restaurant to eat, listen to music, and play games, both video and pool. Even the most finicky eater should find something to please on the eight-page menu that offers burgers, salads, and pizza served all day long, along with peel-and-eat shrimp, Maine lobster, Alaskan king crab, and Black Angus prime rib for dinner. This is generally a family-friendly place, though the Two-for-Tuesdays happy hour and Friday-night live reggae music that starts thumping at 10 pm draw an occasionally rambunctious young-adult crowd. [$] *Average main: $18 ✉ Waterfront Hwy. at Storetvaer Gade ☎ 340/774–7998 🌐 www.thegreenhouserestaurant.com.*

$$ AMERICAN FAMILY Fodor's Choice ★

🍴 **Jen's Island Café and Deli.** This hole-in-the-wall eatery is the closest thing you can find to a New York–style Jewish deli. Choose the smoked salmon platter for breakfast or hot pastrami on rye at lunch. Plus, Jen's husband Stanley is a local commercial fisherman, so fresh fish like snapper served whole in a Creole sauce is a daily specialty. Homemade desserts such as mango cheesecake and key lime pie are yummy. **■ TIP→ There's no parking nearby, so come on foot or by cab.** [$] *Average main: $16 ✉ Grand Galleria, 43–46 Norre Gade, across from Emancipation Garden ☎ 340/777–4611 🌐 www.jensdeli.com 🕒 Closed Sun. No dinner.*

$$$$ ITALIAN

🍴 **Virgilio's.** For the island's best northern Italian cuisine, don't miss this intimate, elegant hideaway that's on a quiet side street. Eclectic art covers the two-story brick walls, and the sound of opera sets the stage for a memorable meal. Come here for more than 40 homemade pastas topped with superb sauces—capellini with fresh tomatoes and garlic or peasant-style spaghetti in a rich tomato sauce with mushrooms and prosciutto. House specialties include osso buco and tiramisu, which are expertly crafted by chef Ernesto Garrigos, who has prepared these two dishes on the Discovery Channel's *Great Chefs of the World* series. [$] *Average main: $34 ✉ 5150 Dronningens Gade ☎ 340/776–4920 🌐 www.virgiliosvi.com ✍ Reservations essential 🕒 Closed Sun.*

EAST END

$$$ AMERICAN

🍴 **Caribbean Saloon.** Sports on wide-screen TVs and live music on weekends are two added attractions at this hip sports bar that's in the center of the action in Red Hook. The menu ranges from finger-licking barbecue ribs to more sophisticated fare, such as the signature filet mignon

Where to Shop for Groceries

High food prices in Virgin Islands supermarkets are enough to dull anyone's appetite. According to a report by the U.S. Virgin Islands Department of Labor, food is significantly more expensive than on the mainland.

Although you'll never match the prices back home, you can shop around for the best deals. If you're traveling with a group, it pays to stock up on the basics at warehouse-style stores like Pricesmart (membership required) and Cost-U-Less. Even the nonbulk food items here are sold at lower prices than in the supermarkets or convenience stores. Good buys include beverages, meats, produce, and spirits.

After this, head to supermarkets such as Plaza Extra, Pueblo, and Food Center. Although the prices aren't as good as at the big-box stores, the selection is better.

Finally, if you want to splurge on top-quality meats, exotic produce and spices, and imported cheeses and spirits, finish off your shopping at high-end shops such as Moe's Fresh Market or Gourmet Gallery.

The Fruit Bowl is the place for fresh produce. The prices and selection are unbeatable.

For really fresh tropical fruits, vegetables, and seasoning herbs, visit the farmers' markets in Smith Bay (daily), at Market Square (daily), at Yacht Haven Grande (first and third Sunday of the month), and in Estate Bordeaux (second and fourth Sunday of every month).

---

wrapped in bacon and smothered in melted Gorgonzola cheese. There's always a catch of the day; the fishing fleet is only steps away. A late-night menu is available from 10 pm until 4 am. $ *Average main: $28* ✉ *American Yacht Harbor, Rte. 32, Bldg B., Red Hook* ☎ *340/775–7060* ⊕ *www.caribbeansaloon.com.*

$$ ✕ **Duffy's Love Shack.** If the floating bubbles don't attract you to this
ECLECTIC zany eatery, the lime-green shutters, loud rock music, and fun-loving waitstaff just might. It's billed as the "ultimate tropical drink shack," and the bartenders shake up such exotic concoctions as the Love Shack Volcano—a 50-ounce flaming extravaganza. The menu has a selection of burgers, tacos, burritos, and salads. Try the grilled-fish tacos or Caribbean Pu-Pu platter that includes conch fritters, coconut shrimp, and Puerto Rican–style *pinonos* (sweet plantains stuffed with savory meat or cheese and deep fried). $ *Average main: $15* ✉ *Red Hook Shopping Center, Rte. 32 and 6500 Red Hook Plaza, in the parking lot, Red Hook* ☎ *340/779–2080* ⊕ *www.duffysloveshack.com.*

$$$ ✕ **Fish Tales.** Watch fishermen walk up the dock here each afternoon and
SEAFOOD deliver fresh fish like tuna, wahoo, mahimahi, and "ole wife" (a local
FAMILY white fish) directly to the chef. The real deal is the daily Happy Hour from 3 to 6 pm, when you can order fresh oysters on the half shell for $14 per dozen or $7 per half-dozen. Save room for the signature Fisherman's Platter—a half-pound each of Alaskan king crab legs, Dungeness crab, shrimp, and Andouille sausage—which you can order for lunch or dinner. Farm-raised catfish, three types of Po Boys (shrimp, oyster,

and scallop), and housemade key lime pie are all winners. There's also a children's menu. [$] *Average main: $26* ⊠ *Rte. 32, next to the Red Hook Ferry Terminal, Red Hook* ☎ *340/714–3188* ⊕ *www.fishtalesvi.com.*

$$$
IRISH
FAMILY

✕ **Molly Molone's.** This dockside eatery has a devoted following among local boaters, who swear by the traditional American and Irish fare. Opt for eggs Benedict or platefuls of Irish sausages and eggs for breakfast, or fork into fish-and-chips, Irish stew, or bangers and mash (sausage and mashed potatoes) for lunch or dinner. ⚠ **Beware: the resident iguanas will beg for table scraps—bring your camera.** [$] *Average main: $24* ⊠ *American Yacht Harbor, Bldg. D, Rte. 32, Red Hook* ☎ *340/775–1270* ⊕ *mollymalonesstthomas.com.*

$$$
CREOLE

✕ **The New Latitude 18.** Gravel floors, plastic chairs, cloth-covered wooden tables, and an open-air view to the small marina give way to a great menu of dishes that blend down-home style with Caribbean flavors. There's a ribeye steak smothered in cream sauce, spaghetti and meatballs, and six styles of burgers, plus stuffed crab and bite-sized chunks of deep-fried shark as appetizers. Live bands on the weekends always draw a big crowd of yachties and U.S. mainland expats. [$] *Average main: $28* ⊠ *9C Vessup Ln., next to Vessup Beach, East End* ☎ *340/777–4552* ⊕ *latitude18stt.com.*

$$$$
ECLECTIC
Fodor's Choice
★

✕ **Old Stone Farmhouse.** Dine in the splendor of a beautifully restored plantation house. Come early and sidle up to the beautiful mahogany bar, where you can choose from an extensive wine list. Then, start with a first course of heirloom tomato gazpacho, move on to Wagyu beef and local lobster surf and turf or perfectly seared scallops; and finish with a thick rich pineapple crème brûlée. Exotic meats such as camel and kangaroo are available on the special Butcher's Block entrée selections. Personalized attention makes dining here a delight. [$] *Average main: $36* ⊠ *Rte. 42, 1 mile (1½ km) west of entrance to Mahogany Run Golf Course, Estate Lovenlund* ☎ *340/777–6277* ⊕ *oldstonefarmhouse.com* ⚑ *Reservations essential* ⊗ *Closed Mon.*

SOUTH SHORE

$$$
ECLECTIC

✕ **Fat Turtle.** Graze on local lobster, burgers, and salads, as well as pizza baked in a stone-floored oven while gazing at the million-dollar megayachts docked right next to this hip seaside eatery. Even if you aren't hungry, stop here on Friday nights for the DJ Dance Party and Laser Light Show that starts at 10 pm. [$] *Average main: $21* ⊠ *5403 Yacht Haven Grande, Charlotte Amalie* ☎ *340/714–3566.*

$$$
MEDITERRANEAN

✕ **Grande Cru.** At this nautically themed wine bar and restaurant, you can either graze on small plates such as ahi tuna carpaccio, jumbo lump crab and marscapone crepes, and graham cracker–coated calamari, or have a larger entrée like grilled organic Scottish salmon or pepper-crusted prime rib. Even if you aren't hungry, stop here for the mixologist martinis, wines by the glass, rich ambience, and backdrop views of million-dollar megayachts. [$] *Average main: $21* ⊠ *Long Bay, 5403 Yacht Haven Grande, immediately to the east of the Esplanade, Charlotte Amalie* ☎ *340/774–87263* ⊕ *www.grandecruvi.com* ⊗ *Closed Sun.*

$$$$ ECLECTIC Fodor's Choice ★ 🍴 **Havana Blue.** The cuisine here is described as Latin America meets Pacific Rim, but however you describe it, the dining experience is outstanding. A glowing wall of water meets you as you enter this beachfront eatery, and then you're seated at a table laid with linen and silver that's illuminated in a soft blue light radiating from above. Be sure to sample the mango mojito, made with fresh mango, crushed mint, and limes. Tapas-style entrées include slow-roasted pulled-pork Cuban sliders, seared tuna with Szechuan peppercorn, and shiitake spring rolls. Hand-rolled cigars and aged rums finish the night off in true Latin style. For something really special, request an exclusive table for two set on Morning Star Beach—you get a seven-course tasting menu, champagne, and your own personal waiter, all for $350 for two. [$] *Average main: $36* ✉ *Marriott Morningstar Beach Resort, Rte. 315, 2nd fl., above front desk, Estate Bakkeroe* ☎ *340/715–2583* 🌐 *www.havanabluerestaurant.com* ✍ *Reservations essential* ⏲ *No lunch.*

WEST END

$$$ AUSTRIAN 🍴 **Bella Blu.** In a quaint building in Frenchtown, this place has an ever-changing display of local art on the walls and delicious specials to match. The Austrian-inspired menu includes six varieties of schnitzel and boasts a Caribbean flair with fresh-fish dishes such as house specialty snapper Provençal. Lunchtime attracts a business crowd that breaks bread and brokers deals at the same time. Fork into omelets, pancakes, or waffles during Saturday's Jazz Brunch from 10 am to 3 pm. [$] *Average main: $26* ✉ *Frenchtown Mall, 24-A Honduras St., across from the ballpark, Frenchtown* ☎ *340/774–4349* 🌐 *www.bellabludining.com* ✍ *Reservations essential* ⏲ *Closed Sun.*

$$$$ CARIBBEAN 🍴 **Blue Orchid.** Come for sunset cocktails on the observation deck and stay for the ultra-fresh food at this contemporary restaurant set on the beautifully landscaped grounds of an 18th-century guesthouse. Chef Sally Darash builds a creative menu around locally grown fruits and vegetables and freshly caught seafood. A great example is the tortilla-crusted yellow snapper served with black bean tomato salsa and fresh cilantro chili rice. [$] *Average main: $32* ✉ *3A–18 Estate St. Peter, off Rte. 40, Estate St. Peter* ☎ *340/774–4999* 🌐 *blueorchidvi.com* ✍ *Reservations essential* ⏲ *Closed Sun.*

$$$$ STEAKHOUSE 🍴 **Grille at Mahogany Run.** You don't have to play golf to break bread at what is undeniably the best steak house on the island. Fork into hand-cut certified Angus prime rib, NY striploin, and ribeye, or a choice of fresh fish grilled with a variety of eight compound butters or sauces. There's burgers, brisket, and bison chili for lunch, while Sunday brunch serves up a homestyle selection of steak and eggs, shrimp and grits, and chicken and biscuits. Order a cup of Seattle-sourced Dillanos-brand coffee any time of day. [$] *Average main: $36* ✉ *Off Rte. 42, 1 Mahogany Run N., 1 mile east of the intersection of Rtes. 42 and 35, Estate Lovenlund* ☎ *340/777–6250* 🌐 *www.mahoganyrungolf.com/dining* ⏲ *Closed Mon.*

$$$ SEAFOOD FAMILY 🍴 **Hook, Line and Sinker.** Anchored on the breezy Frenchtown waterfront and close to the pastel-painted boats of the local fishing fleet, this harbor-view eatery serves high-quality fish dishes. The almond-crusted

yellowtail snapper is a house specialty. Spicy jerk-seasoned swordfish and grilled tuna topped with a yummy mango-rum sauce are also good bets. This is one of the few independent restaurants serving Sunday brunch. [$] *Average main: $24* ✉ *Frenchtown Mall, 2 Honduras St., at the head of the Frenchtown Marina docks, Frenchtown* ☎ *340/776–9708* 🌐 *www.hooklineandsinkervi.com.*

$ AMERICAN FAMILY
🍴 **Hull Bay Hideaway.** Here you can find live bands (think rock and roll, country and western, and reggae), pool tables, dart tournaments, burgers, fish tacos, chicken or shrimp Caesar salads, and a fully stocked bar just steps away from the beach. This family-friendly open-air bar and restaurant is the unofficial home of the Northside French commercial fishing fleet and home of the Annual Bastille Day Kingfish Tournament in July. [$] *Average main: $12* ✉ *10-1 Estate Hull Bay, Rte. 37, at the end of the road, Estate Hull Bay* ☎ *340/777–1898* 🌐 *www.hullbayhideaway.com.*

$$$$ CARIBBEAN
🍴 **Mafolie Restaurant.** Enjoy a romantic meal with an iconic bird's-eye view of the Charlotte Amalie harbor. For starters, there's *kallaloo* soup (shrimp and crab in a thick, creamy spinach broth), and entrées include chicken with mango and chili, and seafood jambalaya. Side dishes definitely offer a taste of the tropics: boiled green bananas, mashed breadfruit, and sweet potato–and-coconut dumplings. Key lime pie is the most sublime dessert. [$] *Average main: $39* ✉ *7091 Estate Mafolie, Off Rte. 35, Charlotte Amalie* ☎ *340/774–2790* 🌐 *mafolie.com.*

$$$$ ECLECTIC
🍴 **Oceana Restaurant and Wine Bar.** In the old Russian consulate greathouse at the tip of the Frenchtown peninsula, this restaurant offers superb views along with fresh seafood dishes expertly prepared by longtime Virgin Islands chef Patricia LaCourte and her staff. Specialties include Bouillabaisse brimming with Caribbean lobster, shrimp, mussels, and clams in a tomato-saffron broth; and an entrée duo of grilled bacon-wrapped beef filet with garlic shrimp. After dinner, take a five-minute stroll to nearby Frenchtown where several bars offer live music on the weekends. [$] *Average main: $62* ✉ *Villa Olga, 8A Honduras, Frenchtown* ✣ *Turn off Rte. 30 into Frenchtown, at intersection of Post Office. Take first right, with ballfield on left, then take next left and immediately next left; follow this road a half-mile to the end* ☎ *340/774–4262* 🌐 *www.oceanavi.com* ✍ *Reservations essential* ⏲ *No dinner Sun.*

$$ AMERICAN FAMILY
🍴 **Tickles Dockside Pub.** Nautical types as well as the local working crowd come here for casual fare with homey appeal: chicken-fried steak, meat loaf with mashed potatoes, and baby back ribs. Hearty breakfasts feature eggs and pancakes, and lunch is a full array of burgers, salads, sandwiches, and soups. From November through April, the adjacent marina is full of enormous yachts, which make for some great eye candy while you dine. [$] *Average main: $17* ✉ *Crown Bay Marina, 8168 Crown Bay Marina, Suite 308, off Rte. 304, Estate Contant* ☎ *340/777–8792* 🌐 *ticklesdocksidepub.com.*

WHERE TO STAY

The island's first hotels were all based in Charlotte Amalie, the hub of action at the time. Most people choose lodgings here to be close to the airport, to experience the charm of the historic district, or for convenience when on business. Over the years, tourism has trickled eastward, and today the major hotel chains have perched their properties on the beach. Those who want a self-contained resort that feels like an island unto itself head here. The location of these resorts makes island-hopping to St. John or the British Virgin Islands a breeze. Private villas dot the island, especially in the less populated north.

PRIVATE VILLAS AND CONDOMINIUMS

St. Thomas has a wide range of private villas, from modest two-bedroom houses to luxurious five-or-more-bedroom mansions. Most will require that you book for seven nights during high season, five in low season. A minimum stay of up to two weeks is often required during the Christmas season.

You can arrange private villa rentals through various agents that represent luxury residences and usually have both websites and brochures that show photos of the properties they represent. Some are suitable for travelers with disabilities, but be sure to ask specific questions regarding your own needs.

Calypso Realty ☎ *340/774–1620, 800/747–4858* ⊕ *www.calypsorealty. com.*

McLaughlin-Anderson Luxury Caribbean Villas. Handling rental villas throughout the U.S. Virgin Islands, British Virgin Islands, and Grenada, McLaughlin-Anderson has a good selection of complexes in St. Thomas's East End. ☎ *340/776–0635, 800/537–6246* ⊕ *www. mclaughlinanderson.com.*

CHARLOTTE AMALIE

Accommodations in town and near town offer the benefits of being close to the airport, shopping, and a number of casual and fine-dining restaurants. The downside is that this is the most crowded and noisy area of the island. Crime can also be a problem. Don't go for a stroll at night in the heart of town. Use common sense, and take the same precautions you would in any major city. Properties along the hillsides are less likely to have crime problems; plus, they command a steady breeze from the cool trade winds. This is especially important if you're visiting in summer and early fall.

$ ⬚ **The Green Iguana.** Atop Blackbeard's Hill, this value-priced small hotel
HOTEL   offers the perfect mix of gorgeous harbor views, proximity to shopping (a five-minute walk), and secluded privacy provided by the surrounding showy trees and bushy hibiscus. **Pros:** personalized service; near the center of town; laundry on premises. **Cons:** need a car to get around; town may be noisy at night depending on seasonal events. $ *Rooms from: $150* ✉ *1002 Blackbeard's Hill* ☎ *340/776–7654, 855/473–4733* ⊕ *www.thegreeniguana.com* ↘ *9 rooms* ○ *No meals.*

$ ⊡ **Mafolie Hotel.** The view and the value are the selling points of this
B&B/INN   hotel perched 800 feet above Charlotte Amalie's harbor. **Pros:** fantastic
views; nice restaurant and bar; family-run establishment. **Cons:** tiny
pool; on a busy street; need a car to get around. $ *Rooms from: $210*
⊠ *7091 Estate Mafolie, off Rte. 35* ☎ *340/774–2790, 800/225–7035*
⊕ *www.mafolie.com* ⊄ *22 rooms* ⦿ *Breakfast.*

$ ⊡ **Villa Santana.** Built by exiled General Antonio López Santa Anna of
HOTEL   Mexico, this 1857 landmark provides a panoramic view of the harbor
Fodor'sChoice   and plenty of West Indian charm, which will make you feel as if you're
★   living in a charming slice of Virgin Islands history. **Pros:** historic charm;
plenty of privacy. **Cons:** not on a beach; no restaurant; need a car to get
around. $ *Rooms from: $170* ⊠ *2602 Bjerge Gade, 2D Denmark Hill*
☎ *340/776–1311* ⊕ *www.villasantana.com* ⊄ *6 rooms* ⦿ *No meals.*

$ ⊡ **Windward Passage Hotel.** Business travelers, tourists on their way
HOTEL   to the British Virgin Islands, and laid-back vacationers who want the
convenience of being able to walk to duty-free shopping, sights, and
restaurants, stay at this harborfront hotel. **Pros:** walking distance to
Charlotte Amalie; nice harbor views; across from BVI ferry terminal.
Cons: basic rooms; on a busy street; no water sports, but dive shop is on
property. $ *Rooms from: $220* ⊠ *Waterfront Hwy.* ☎ *340/774–5200,*
800/524–7389 ⊕ *www.windwardpassage.com* ⊄ *140 rooms, 11 suites*
⦿ *No meals.*

EAST END

You can find most of the large, luxurious beachfront resorts on St.
Thomas's East End. The downside is that these properties are about
a 30-minute drive from town and a 45-minute drive from the airport
(substantially longer during peak hours). On the upside, these properties
tend to be self-contained; plus, there are a number of good restaurants,
shops, and water-sports operators in the area. Once you've settled in,
you don't need a car to get around.

$$$ ⊡ **The Anchorage Beach Resort.** A beachfront setting and homey con-
RENTAL   veniences that include full kitchens and washer-dryer units are what
FAMILY   attract families to these two- and three-bedroom suites on Cowpet Bay
next to the St. Thomas Yacht Club. **Pros:** on the beach; good amenities.
Cons: small pool; noisy neighbors; need a car to get around; petty theft
is a problem in the neighborhood. $ *Rooms from: $395* ⊠ *Rte. 317,*
Estate Nazareth ☎ *800/874–7897* ⊕ *www.antillesresorts.com* ⊄ *11*
suites ⦿ *No meals.*

$ ⊡ **Bed & Breakfast Caribbean Style.** Couples will enjoy the romantic feel
B&B/INN   of these private, waterfront, individually decorated condos and the per-
sonal attention of owner and longtime island resident Juliana Van Don-
gen. **Pros:** waterfront location; homey rooms; romantic atmosphere.
Cons: no water sports; need a car to get around; mosquitoes can be
a problem. $ *Rooms from: $100* ⊠ *6918 Vessup Ln., Estate Vessup*
Bay ⊹ *Rte. 317 at Cabrita Point* ☎ *340/715–1117, 800/593–1390*
⊕ *cstylevi.com* ⊄ *4 1-bedroom condos* ⦿ *Breakfast.*

$ ⊡ **Pavilions and Pools Villa Hotel.** Perfect for couples craving privacy, the
RENTAL   villas here have full kitchens, lots of space, and sunken garden showers.

Pros: intimate atmosphere; friendly host; private pools. **Cons:** on a busy road; long walk to beach; rooms could use a bit of refurbishment. [$] *Rooms from: $260* ✉ *6400 Estate Smith Bay, off Rte. 38, Estate Smith Bay* ☎ *340/775–6110, 800/524–2001* 🌐 *www.pavilionsandpools.com* ⇨ *25 1-bedroom villas* 🍴 *Breakfast.*

$$ RESORT **Point Pleasant Resort.** Hilltop suites give you an eagle's-eye view of the East End and beyond, and those in a building adjacent to the reception area offer incredible sea views. **Pros:** lush setting; convenient kitchens; pleasant pools. **Cons:** steep climb from beach; need a car to get around; some rooms need refurbishing. [$] *Rooms from: $320* ✉ *6600 Estate Smith Bay, off Rte. 38, Estate Smith Bay* ☎ *340/775–7200, 800/524–2300* 🌐 *www.pointpleasantresort.com* ⇨ *128 suites* 🍴 *No meals.*

$$$$ RESORT FAMILY Fodor's Choice ★ **Ritz-Carlton, St. Thomas.** Everything sparkles at the island's most luxurious resort, from the in-room furnishings and amenities to the infinity pool, white-sand beach, and turquoise sea beyond. **Pros:** gorgeous views; great water-sports facilities; beautiful beach; airport shuttle. **Cons:** service can sometimes be spotty for such an upscale (and pricey) hotel; food and drink can lack flair and are expensive ($19 hamburger, $12 piña colada); half-hour or more drive to town and airport. [$] *Rooms from: $610* ✉ *6900 Estate Great Bay, off Rte. 317, Estate Great Bay* ☎ *340/775–3333, 800/241–3333* 🌐 *www.ritzcarlton.com* ⇨ *255 rooms, 20 suites, 2 villas, 81 condos* 🍴 *No meals.*

$$ RENTAL **Secret Harbour Beach Resort.** There's not a bad view from these low-rise studio, one-, and two-bedroom condos, which are either beachfront or perched on a hill overlooking an inviting cove. **Pros:** beautiful beach and great snorkeling; good restaurant; secluded location. **Cons:** some rooms are small; car needed to get around; condo owners are territorial about beach chairs. [$] *Rooms from: $340* ✉ *Rte. 317* ☎ *340/775–6550, 800/524–2250* 🌐 *www.secretharbourvi.com* ⇨ *49 suites* 🍴 *Breakfast.*

SOUTH SHORE

The south shore of St. Thomas connects to the east end of the island via a beautiful road that rambles along the hillside, with frequent peeks between the hills for views of the ocean, and, on a clear day, of St. Croix some 40 miles (60 km) to the south. The resorts here are on their own beaches. They offer several opportunities for water sports, as well as land-based activities, fine dining, and evening entertainment.

$$$ RESORT **Bolongo Bay Beach Resort.** All the rooms at this family-run resort tucked along a 1,000-foot-long palm-lined beach have balconies with ocean views; down the beach are 12 studio and two-bedroom condos with full kitchens. **Pros:** family-run property; on the beach; water sports abound. **Cons:** a bit run-down; on a busy road; need a car to get around. [$] *Rooms from: $385* ✉ *Rte. 30, Box 715, Estate Bolongo* ☎ *340/775–1800, 800/524–4746* 🌐 *www.bolongobay.com* ⇨ *65 rooms, 12 condos* 🍴 *No meals.*

$$$ RESORT FAMILY **Frenchman's Reef & Morning Star Marriott Beach Resort.** Set majestically on a promontory overlooking the east side of Charlotte Amalie's harbor, Frenchman's Reef is a high-rise full-service superhotel; Morning Star is the even more upscale boutique property that's closer

to the fine white-sand beach. **Pros:** beachfront location; good dining options; plenty of activities. **Cons:** musty smell on lower levels; long walk between resorts; a crowded-cruise-ship feel. $ *Rooms from: $430* ✉ *Rte. 315, Estate Bakkeroe* ☎ *340/776–8500, 800/233–6388* ⊕ *www. marriott.com* ⤳ *479 rooms, 27 suites; 220 2- and 3-bedroom time-share units* ⦿| *No meals.*

WEST END

A few properties are in the hills overlooking Charlotte Amalie to the west or near Frenchtown, which is otherwise primarily residential.

$ ⍐| **Best Western Emerald Beach Resort.** You get beachfront ambience at this
HOTEL reasonably priced mini resort tucked beneath the palm trees, but the tradeoff is that it's directly across from a noisy airport runway. **Pros:** beachfront location; good value; great Sunday brunch. **Cons:** airport noise until 10 pm; on a busy road; limited water sports. $ *Rooms from: $220* ✉ *8070 Lindbergh Bay, Lindbergh Bay* ☎ *340/777–8800, 800/780–7234* ⊕ *www.emeraldbeach.com* ⤳ *90 rooms* ⦿| *Breakfast.*

$ ⍐| **Island View Guesthouse.** Perched 545 feet up the face of Crown Moun-
B&B/INN tain, this small, homey inn has hands-on owners who can book tours or offer tips about the best sightseeing spots. **Pros:** spectacular views; friendly atmosphere; good value. **Cons:** small pool; need a car to get around. $ *Rooms from: $115* ✉ *Rte. 332, Estate Contant* ☎ *340/774–4270, 800/524–2023* ⊕ *www.islandviewstthomas.com* ⤳ *12 rooms, 10 with bath* ⦿| *Breakfast.*

NIGHTLIFE AND PERFORMING ARTS

On any given night, especially in season, you can find steel-pan orches-tras, rock and roll, piano music, jazz, broken-bottle dancing (actual dancing atop broken glass), disco, and karaoke. Pick up a free copy of the bright-yellow *St. Thomas–St. John This Week* magazine when you arrive (it can be found at the airport, in stores, and in hotel lobbies). The back pages list who's playing where. The Friday edition of the *Daily News* carries complete listings for the upcoming weekend.

NIGHTLIFE

CHARLOTTE AMALIE

BARS

Greenhouse Bar and Restaurant. Once this popular eatery puts away the salt-and-pepper shakers after 10 pm, it becomes a rock-and-roll club with a DJ or live reggae bands bringing the weary to their feet six nights a week. ✉ *Waterfront Hwy. at Storetvaer Gade* ☎ *340/774–7998* ⊕ *www.thegreenhouserestaurant.com.*

CLOSE UP

Mocko Jumbie Magic

Mocko Jumbies, the island's other-worldly stilt walkers, trace their roots back to West Africa. The steps of the stilt walkers held religious significance in West Africa, but today's West Indian version is more secular—bending backward to gravity-defying lengths and high kicking to the pulsating beat of drums, bells, and whistles.

Today satins and sequins have replaced costumes made of grasses, shells, and feathers. Festive headpieces—braids of feathers, glittering crowns, tall hats, and even spiky horns—attract plenty of attention from onlookers. A mask completes the outfit, assuring that the dancer's identity is concealed from spectators, thus maintaining the magic of the Mocko Jumbie.

Beyond Carnival celebrations, the Mocko Jumbie is so popular that it's a mainstay at many hotels. Mocko Jumbie dancers also perform at store openings, when cruise ships dock, or even at weekend beach jams. Old-fashioned or newfangled, Mocko Jumbies will always be loved best for driving away "jumbie spirits," as they say in the islands.

EAST END
BARS
Duffy's Love Shack. At this island favorite, a live band and dancing under the stars are the big draws for locals and visitors alike. ⊠ *Red Hook Plaza, Rte. 32, Red Hook* ☎ *340/779–2080* ⊕ *www.duffyslove shack.com.*

Latitude 18. This popular hot spot hosts an ever-changing lineup of live bands from the island and from the U.S. mainland. Open-mic night is every Thursday. ⊠ *Vessup Bay, 9C Vessup Ln., Red Hook* ☎ *340/777–4552.*

SOUTH SHORE
BARS
Epernay Bistro & Wine Bar. Sometimes you need nothing more than small tables for easy chatting and wine and champagne by the glass. You can also mix and mingle with island celebrities here. The action at this intimate nightspot runs from 4 pm until the wee hours Monday through Saturday. ⊠ *Frenchtown Mall, 24-A Honduras St., Frenchtown* ☎ *340/774–5348.*

Iggies Beach Bar. Bolongo Bay's beachside bar offers karaoke on Saturday nights, so you can sing along to the sounds of the surf or the latest hits here. There are live bands on weekends, and you can dance inside or kick up your heels under the stars. On Wednesday it's Carnival Night, complete with steel-pan music, a limbo show, and a West Indian buffet. ⊠ *Bolongo Bay Beach Club & Villas, Rte. 30, Estate Bolongo* ☎ *340/775–1800* ⊕ *www.iggiesbeachbar.com.*

PERFORMING ARTS

SOUTH SHORE

THEATER

FAMILY **Pistarckle Theater.** This theater in the Tillett Gardens complex is air-conditioned and has more than 100 seats; it hosts a half dozen productions annually, plus a children's summer drama camp. ⊠ *Tillett Gardens, Rte. 38, across from Tutu Park Shopping Mall, Estate Tutu* ☎ *340/775–7877* ⊕ *pistarckletheater.com.*

Reichhold Center for the Arts. St. Thomas's major performing arts center has an amphitheater, and its more expensive seats are covered by a roof. Throughout the year there's an entertaining mix of local plays, dance exhibitions, and music of all types. ⊠ *Rte. 30, across from Brewers Beach, Estate Lindbergh Bay* ☎ *340/693–1559* ⊕ *www.reichhold center.com.*

SHOPPING

Fodor's Choice St. Thomas lives up to its billing as a duty-free shopping destination.
★ Even if shopping isn't your idea of how to spend a vacation, you still may want to slip in on a quiet day (check the cruise-ship listings—Monday and Sunday are usually the least crowded) to browse. Among the best buys are liquor, linens, china, crystal (most stores will ship), and jewelry. The amount of jewelry available makes this one of the few items for which comparison shopping is worth the effort. Local crafts include shell jewelry, carved calabash bowls, straw brooms, woven baskets, and dolls. Creations by local doll maker Sally George—like her school-uniformed West Indian children and Mocko Jumbie dolls—have been little goodwill ambassadors, bought by visitors around the world. Spice mixes, hot sauces, and tropical jams and jellies are other native products.

On St. Thomas, stores on Main Street in Charlotte Amalie are open weekdays and Saturday 9 to 5. The hours of the shops in the Havensight Mall (next to the cruise-ship dock) and the Crown Bay Commercial Center (next to the Crown Bay cruise-ship dock) are the same, though occasionally some stay open until 9 on Friday, depending on how many cruise ships are anchored nearby. You may also find some shops open on Sunday if cruise ships are in port. Hotel shops are usually open evenings as well.

There's no sales tax in the USVI, and you can take advantage of the $1,600 duty-free allowance per family member (remember to save your receipts). Although you can find the occasional salesclerk who will make a deal, bartering isn't the norm.

CHARLOTTE AMALIE

The prime shopping area in Charlotte Amalie is between Post Office and Market squares; it consists of two parallel streets that run east–west (Waterfront Highway and Main Street) and the alleyways that connect them. Particularly attractive are the historic **A.H. Riise Alley, Royal Dane Mall, Palm Passage,** and pastel-painted **International Plaza.**

Vendors Plaza, on the waterfront side of Emancipation Gardens in Charlotte Amalie, is a central location for vendors selling handmade earrings, necklaces, and bracelets; straw baskets and handbags; T-shirts; fabrics; African artifacts; and local fruits. Look for the many brightly colored umbrellas.

ART GALLERIES

Camille Pissarro Art Gallery. This second-floor gallery, at the birthplace of St. Thomas's famous artist, offers a fine collection of original paintings and prints by local and regional artists. ⊠ *14 Main St.* ☏ *340/774–4621.*

Gallery St. Thomas. The gallery in this charming space has a nice collection of fine art and collectibles, including paintings, wood sculptures, glass, and jewelry that are from or inspired by the Virgin Islands. ⊠ *Palm Passage, 5143 Palm Passage, Suite A-13* ☏ *340/777–6363* ⊕ *gallerystthomas.com.*

CAMERAS AND ELECTRONICS

Boolchand's. This store sells brand-name cameras, audio and video equipment, and binoculars. ⊠ *31 Main St., 5124 Dronningens Gade* ☏ *340/776–0794* ⊕ *www.boolchand.com* ☉ *Closed Sun. (if no cruise ship is in port).*

Royal Caribbean. Find a wide selection of cameras, camcorders, stereos, watches, and clocks at this store. ⊠ *33 Main St.* ☏ *340/776–4110* ⊕ *www.royalcaribbeanvi.com* ⊠ *Havensight Mall, off Rte. 30, Bldg. A, Havensight* ☏ *340/776–8890.*

CHINA AND CRYSTAL

The Crystal Shoppe at A.H. Riise. This retailer specializes in all that glitters, from Swarovski and Waterford crystal to figurines by Hummel, Daum, and Royal Copenhagen, and china by Belleek, Kosta Boda, and several Limoges factories. There's also a large selection of Lladró figurines. ⊠ *37 Main St., at Riise's Alley* ☏ *340/777–2222, 800/323–7232* ⊕ *www.ahriise.com.*

Little Switzerland. This popular Caribbean chain carries crystal from Baccarat, Waterford, and Orrefors; and china from Kosta Boda, Rosenthal, and Wedgwood. There's also an assortment of Swarovski cut-crystal animals, gemstone globes, and many other affordable collectibles. It also does a booming mail-order business. ⊠ *5 Dronningens Gade, across from Emancipation Garden* ☏ *340/776–2010* ⊕ *www.littleswitzerland. com* ⊠ *Havensight Mall, 9002 Havensight Shop Ctr., Rte. 30, Suite D, Havensight* ☏ *340/776–2198.*

CLOTHING

FAMILY **Fresh Produce Sportswear.** This clothing store doesn't sell lime-green mangoes, peachy-pink guavas, or sunny-yellow bananas, but you will find these fun, casual colors on its clothing for children and adults. This is one of 30 stores nationwide to stock all of the California-created, tropical-feel line of women's separates. The dresses, shirts, slacks, and skirts are in small to plus sizes, and bags and hats and other accessories

Charlotte Amalie is filled with back alleys and interesting shops.

are also available. ✉ *Riise's Alley, 5189 Dronningens Gade, across from the Rolex store* ☎ *340/774–0807* ⊕ *www.freshproduceclothes.com.*

FAMILY **Local Color.** This St. Thomas chain has clothes for men, women, and children among its brand names, which include Jams World, Fresh Produce, and Urban Safari. You can also find St. John artist Sloop Jones's colorful, hand-painted island designs on cool dresses, T-shirts, and sweaters. The tropically oriented accessories include big-brimmed straw hats, bold-color bags, and casual jewelry. ✉ *Waterfront Hwy., at Raadets Gade* ☎ *340/776–5860* ⊕ *www.localcolorvi.com* ✉ *Route 315, at Coco Joe's restaurant at the Morning Star Marriott Beach Resort* ✉ *Havensight Mall, Rte. 30, Bldg. 7, 2 stores north of post office.*

Tommy Hilfiger. This outlet for the popular designer specializes in classic American jeans and sportswear, as well as trendy bags, belts, ties, socks, caps, and wallets. ✉ *Waterfront Hwy. at Trompeter Gade* ☎ *340/777–1189* ⊕ *www.tommy.com.*

White House/Black Market. This store boasts sophisticated clothing for women. You'll find just the right party or evening-wear look in dresses, tops, and bottoms made out of everything from sequins to shimmering and satiny fabrics. Check out the perpetual sale rack in the back for the best deals. ✉ *5316 Yacht Haven Grande, Suite 116* ☎ *340/776–5566* ⊕ *www.whitehouseblackmarket.com.*

FOODSTUFFS

FAMILY **Belgian Chocolate Factory.** This store makes its beautiful chocolates before your eyes. Specialties include triple-chocolate rum truffles. You can find imported chocolates here as well. Both the homemade and imported delectables come in decorative boxes, so they make great gifts.

✉ *Hibiscus Alley, 5093 Dronningens Gade, Suite 3* ☎ *340/777–5247* ⊕ *www.thebelgianchocolatefactory.com.*

HANDICRAFTS

Native Arts and Crafts Cooperative. This crafts market is made up of a group of more than 40 local artists—including schoolchildren, senior citizens, and people with disabilities—who create the handcrafted items for sale here: African-style jewelry, quilts, calabash bowls, dolls, soaps, carved-wood figures, woven baskets, straw brooms, note cards, and cookbooks. ✉ *48B Tolbod Gade, across from Emancipation Garden* ☎ *340/777–1153.*

JEWELRY

Cardow Jewelers. You can get gold in several lengths, widths, sizes, and styles, along with jewelry made of diamonds, emeralds, and other precious gems from this small chain's main store. You're guaranteed 40% to 60% savings off U.S. retail prices, or your money will be refunded within 30 days of purchase. ✉ *5195 Dronningens Gade, across from Emancipation Garden* ☎ *340/776–1140* ⊕ *www.cardow. com* ✉ *Marriott Frenchman's Reef Resort, Rte. 315, Estate Bakkeroe* ☎ *340/774–0434.*

Diamonds International. At this large chain with several outlets on St. Thomas, just choose a diamond, emerald, or tanzanite gem and a mounting, and you can have your dream ring set in an hour. Famous for having the largest inventory of diamonds on the island, this shop welcomes trade-ins, has a U.S. service center, and includes diamond earrings with every purchase. ✉ *31 Main St.* ☎ *340/774–3707* ⊕ *www. diamondsinternational.com* ✉ *3A Main St.* ☎ *340/774–1516* ✉ *1 Dronningens Gade* ☎ *340/775–1202.*

H. Stern Jewelers. The World Collection of jewels set in modern, fashionable designs and an exclusive sapphire watch have earned this Brazilian jeweler a stellar reputation. There is another location in Havensight. ✉ *5332 Dronningens Gade* ☎ *340/776–1146* ⊕ *www. hstern.net* ✉ *Marriott Frenchman's Reef Resort, Rte. 315, Estate Bakkeroe* ☎ *340/776–3550.*

Jewels. This jewelry store sells name-brand jewelry and watches in abundance. Designer jewelry lines include David Yurman, Bulgari, Chopard, and Penny Preville. The selection of watches includes Jaeger le Coultre, Tag Heuer, Breitling, Movado, and Gucci. ✉ *Main St., at Riise's Alley* ☎ *248/809–5560* ⊕ *www.jewelsonline.com* ✉ *Havensight Mall, Rte. 30, Bldg. 2, Havensight.*

Rolex Watches at A.H. Riise. A.H. Riise is the official Rolex retailer of the Virgin Islands, and this shop offers one of the largest selections of these fine timepieces in the Caribbean. An After Sales Service Center helps you keep your Rolex ticking for a lifetime. ✉ *37 Main St., at Riise's Alley* ☎ *340/777–6789* ⊕ *www.ahriise.com.*

Trident Jewels and Time. Fine gems and exquisite timepieces are the draw at this second-generation family-owned boutique. You'll find loose diamonds, sapphires, emeralds, and tanzanite as well as name-brand watches such as Ulysse Nardin, Harry Winston, Franck Muller,

Bovet, Jaquet Droz, Bell & Ross, U-Boat, and Graham. ⊠ *9 Main St.* ☎ *340/776–7152* ⊕ *www.trident-jewels.com.*

LEATHER GOODS

Coach. This designer leather store has a full line of fine leather handbags, belts, gloves, and more for women, plus briefcases and wallets for men. Accessories for both sexes include organizers, travel bags, and cell-phone cases. ⊠ *Yacht Haven Grande, 5328 Yacht Haven Grande, Suite 104* ☎ *340/776–1930* ⊕ *www.coach.com.*

Zora's. This store specializes in fine, made-to-order leather sandals. There's also a selection of locally made backpacks, purses, and briefcases in durable, brightly colored canvas. ⊠ *34 Norre Gade, across from Roosevelt Park* ☎ *340/774–2559* ⊕ *www.zoraofstthomas.com.*

LINENS

Fabric in Motion. Fine Italian linens share space with Liberty London's silky cottons, colorful batiks, cotton prints, ribbons, and accessories in this small shop. ⊠ *7 Store Tvaer Gade* ☎ *340/774–2006.*

Mr. Tablecloth. This store has prices to please, and the friendly staff here will help you choose from the floor-to-ceiling selection of linens, which include Tuscan lace tablecloths and Irish linen pillowcases. ⊠ *6–7 Main St.* ☎ *340/774–4343* ⊕ *mrtablecloth-vi.com.*

LIQUOR AND TOBACCO

A.H. Riise Liquors and Tobacco. This giant duty-free liquor outlet carries a large selection of tobacco (including imported cigars), as well as cordials, wines, and rare vintage Armagnacs, cognacs, ports, and Madeiras. It also stocks fruits in brandy and barware from England. Enjoy rum samples at the tasting bar. The prices are among the best in St. Thomas. ⊠ *37 Main St., at Riise's Alley* ☎ *340/777–2222* ⊕ *www.ahriise.com.*

EAST END

Red Hook has **American Yacht Harbor,** a waterfront shopping area with a dive shop, a tackle store, clothing and jewelry boutiques, a bar, and a few restaurants.

Don't forget **St. John.** A ferry ride (an hour from Charlotte Amalie or 20 minutes from Red Hook) will take you to the charming shops of **Mongoose Junction** and **Wharfside Village,** which specialize in unusual, often island-made articles.

ART GALLERIES

The Color of Joy Art & Framing. This gallery offers locally made arts and crafts, including pottery, batik, hand-painted linen-and-cotton clothing, glass plates and ornaments, and watercolors by owner Corinne Van Rensselaer. There are also original prints by many local artists. Framing is available. ⊠ *Rte. 322, about 100 yards west of Ritz-Carlton, Red Hook* ☎ *340/775–4020* ⊕ *www.thecolorofjoyvi.com.*

CLOTHING

FAMILY   **Keep Left.** This is a friendly shop with something for everyone in the family, including Patagonia dresses, Quiksilver swimwear, Columbia shirts, Skechers shoes, and Body Glove bathing suits for women. There are also Naish SUP boards, Island SurfBoards, and Wavezone skimboards for sale. ⊠ *American Yacht Harbor, Rte. 32, 6100 Red Hook Quarters, Suite B2-9, Red Hook* ☎ *340/775–9964* ⊕ *keepleftstthomas.com.*

FOODSTUFFS

Food Center. This supermarket sells fresh produce, meats, and seafood. There's also an on-site bakery and deli with hot and cold prepared foods, which are the big draw here, especially for those renting villas, condos, or charter boats in the East End area. ⊠ *Rte. 32, 1 mile west of Red Hook, Estate Frydenhoj* ☎ *340/777–8806* ⊕ *www.food centervi.com.*

Moe's Fresh Market. This gourmet market near the ferry to St. John has the best deli cheeses, prepared-to-order subs, and selection of organic foods, coffees, and wines on the island. ⊠ *Rte. 32, 6502 Smith Bay Road, Red Hook* ☎ *340/693–0254* ⊕ *moesvi.com.*

Pueblo Supermarket. This Caribbean chain carries stateside brands of most products—but at higher prices because of shipping costs to the islands. ⊠ *Sub Base, ½ mile (¾ km) east of Crown Bay Marina* ☎ *340/774–4200* ⊠ *Rte. 30, 1 mile (1½ km) north of Havensight Mall* ☎ *340/774–2695.*

JEWELRY

Jewels. Designer jewelry available in this major chain include David Yurman, Bulgari, Chopard, and Penny Preville. The selection of watches is also extensive. ⊠ *Ritz-Carlton St. Thomas, Rte. 322, Estate Nazareth* ☎ *248/809–5560* ⊕ *www.jewelsonline.com.*

SOUTH SHORE

West of Charlotte Amalie, the pink-stucco **Nisky Center,** on Harwood Highway about ½ mile (¾ km) east of the airport, is more of a home-town shopping center than a tourist area.

At the Crown Bay cruise-ship pier, the **Crown Bay Center,** off the Harwood Highway in Sub Base about ½ mile (¾ km) west of Frenchtown, has quite a few shops, but they only tend to be open on days when a cruise ship is docked at the Crown Bay Cruise Ship Pier.

Havensight Mall, next to the cruise-ship dock, may not be as charming as downtown Charlotte Amalie, but it does have more than 60 shops. It also has an excellent bookstore, a bank, a pharmacy, a gourmet grocery, and smaller branches of many downtown stores. The shops at **Port of $ale,** adjoining Havensight Mall (its buildings are pink instead of brown), sell discount goods. Next door to Port of $ale is the **Yacht Haven Grande** complex, a stunning megayacht marina with beautiful, safe walkways and many upscale shops.

East of Charlotte Amalie on Route 38, **Tillett Gardens** is an oasis of artistic endeavor across from the Tutu Park Shopping Mall. The late Jim and Rhoda Tillett converted this Danish farm into an artists' retreat in 1959. Today you can watch artisans produce silk-screen fabrics, candles, pottery, and other handicrafts. Something special is often happening in the gardens as well: the Classics in the Gardens program is a classical music series presented under the stars, Arts Alive is a semiannual

DID YOU KNOW?

Mocko jumbie stilt-walkers are a mainstay of Caribbean festivals and celebrations. They originated in West Africa and first appeared in the Caribbean in Trinidad.

2

arts-and-crafts fair held in November and May, and the Pistarckle Theater holds its performances here from November through April.

Tutu Park Shopping Mall, across from Tillett Gardens, is the island's one and only enclosed mall. More than 50 stores and a food court are anchored by Kmart and Plaza Extra grocery store. Archaeologists have discovered evidence that Arawak Indians once lived near the grounds.

ART GALLERIES

Mango Tango. This gallery sells and displays works by popular local artists—originals, prints, and note cards. There's a one-person show at least one weekend a month. ⊠ *Al Cohen's Plaza, ½ mi (¾ km) east of Charlotte Amalie, Raphune Hill* 🕾 *340/777–3060* ✉ *Yacht Haven Grande, Rte. 38, Crown Bay* 🕾 *340/777–3060.*

CAMERAS AND ELECTRONICS

Boolchand's. This store sells brand-name cameras, audio and video equipment, and binoculars. There's also a location on Main Street, Charlotte Amalie. ⊠ *Havensight Mall, Rte. 30, Bldg. II, Suite C, Havensight* 🕾 *340/776–0302* ⊕ *www.boolchand.com.*

Royal Caribbean. Royal Caribbean stocks a wide selection of cameras, camcorders, stereos, watches, and clocks and has several outlets, both in Charlotte Amalie and elsewhere on St. Thomas. ⊠ *Havensight Mall, Rte. 30, Bldg. A, Havensight* 🕾 *340/776–8890* ⊕ *www.royalcaribbeanvi.com* ✉ *Yacht Haven Grande, Ste. 100, Charlotte Amalie* 🕾 *340/779–6364* ✉ *Crown Bay Commercial Center, Rte. 30, Crown Bay* 🕾 *340/779–6372.*

CHINA AND CRYSTAL

Little Switzerland. The major Caribbean duty-free chain carries crystal from Baccarat, Waterford, and Orrefors; and china from Kosta Boda, Rosenthal, and Wedgwood, among others. There's also an assortment of Swarovski cut-crystal animals, gemstone globes, and many other affordable collectibles. It also does a booming mail-order business; ask for a catalog. ⊠ *Havensight Mall, 9002 Havensight Shop Ctr., Rte. 30, Suite D, Havensight* 🕾 *340/776–2198* ⊕ *www.littleswitzerland.com.*

Scandinavian Center. Find the best of Scandinavia here, including Royal Copenhagen, Georg Jensen, Kosta Boda, and Orrefors. Owners Søren and Grace Blak make regular buying trips to northern Europe and are a great source of information on crystal. Online ordering is available if you want to add to your collection once home. ⊠ *Havensight Mall, Rte. 30, Bldg. III, last store closest to cruise-ship dock, Havensight* 🕾 *340/777–8620, 877/454–8377* ⊕ *www.scandinaviancenter.com* ✉ *Crown Bay Center, Route 305, Crown Bay.*

CLOTHING

FAMILY **Local Color.** Local Color has clothes for men, women, and children among its brand-name wear such as Jams World, Fresh Produce, and Urban Safari. There's also St. John artist Sloop Jones's colorful, hand-painted island designs on cool dresses, T-shirts, and sweaters. Find tropically oriented accessories such as big-brim straw hats, bold-color bags, and casual jewelry. ⊠ *Havensight Mall, Rte. 30, Havensight* 🕾 *340/776–5860.*

White House/Black Market. This boutique sells sophisticated clothing for women. You'll find just the right party or evening wear look in dresses, tops and bottoms made out of everything from sequins to shimmering and satiny fabrics. Check out the perpetual sale rack in the back for the best deals. ⊠ *Yacht Haven Grande, 5316 Yacht Haven Grande, Ste. 116, Charlotte Amalie* ☎ *340/776–5566* ⊕ *www.whitehouseblack market.com.*

FOODSTUFFS

Cost-U-Less. This is the Caribbean equivalent of Costco and Sam's Club and it sells everything from soup to nuts—in giant sizes and case lots—without a membership fee. The meat-and-seafood department, however, has family-size portions. There's a well-stocked fresh-produce section and a case filled with rotisserie chicken and baked goods. ⊠ *Rte. 38, ¼ mile (½ km) west of Rte. 39 intersection, Annas Retreat* ☎ *340/777–3588* ⊕ *www.costuless.com.*

Fruit Bowl. This grocery store is the best place on the island to go for fresh fruits and vegetables. There are many ethnic, vegetarian, and health-food items as well as a fresh meat area, seafood department, and salad bar. ⊠ *Wheatley Center, intersection of Rtes. 38 and 313, Charlotte Amalie* ☎ *340/774–8565* ⊕ *www.thefruitbowlvi.com.*

Gourmet Gallery. This is where visiting megayacht owners (or their staff) go to buy their caviar. There's also an excellent and reasonably priced wine selection, as well as specialty ingredients for everything from tacos to curries to chow mein. A full-service deli offers imported meats, cheeses, and in-store prepared foods that are perfect for a picnic. ⊠ *Crown Bay Marina, Rte. 304, Estate Contant* ☎ *340/776–8555* ⊕ *gourmetgallery.net* ⊠ *Havensight Mall, Bldg. VI, Rte. 30, Havensight* ☎ *340/774–4948.*

Plaza Extra. This large, U.S.–style supermarket sells everything you need from produce to meat, including fresh seafood, an excellent deli, and a bakery. There's a liquor department, too. ⊠ *Tutu Park Shopping Mall, Rte. 38, Estate Tutu* ☎ *340/775–5646* ⊕ *www.plazaextra.com.*

FAMILY **PriceSmart.** This giant emporium carries everything from electronics to housewares in its members-only warehouse-size store. The meat, poultry, and seafood departments are especially popular. A small café in front sells pizzas, hot dogs, and the cheapest bottled water on the island—just $1 a pop. ⊠ *4400 Estate Charlotte Amalie, Rte. 38 west of Fort Mylner, Estate Tutu* ☎ *340/777–3430* ⊕ *www.pricesmart.com.*

JEWELRY

Cardow Jewelers. This store is a chain—with gold in several lengths, widths, sizes, and styles—along with diamonds, emeralds, and other precious gems. You're guaranteed 40% to 60% savings off U.S. retail prices or your money will be refunded within 30 days of purchase. ⊠ *Crown Bay Center, Rte 305, Crown Bay* ☎ *340/776–2038* ⊕ *www.cardow.com.*

Diamonds International. At this major chain shop with several outlets on St. Thomas, just choose a diamond, emerald, or tanzanite gem and a mounting, and you can have your dream ring set in an hour. Famous

2

for having the largest inventory of diamonds on the island, this shop welcomes trade-ins, has a U.S. service center, and offers free diamond earrings with every purchase. ⊠ *Havensight Mall, Rte. 30, Bldg. II, Havensight* ☎ *340/776–0040* ⊕ *www.diamondsinternational.com* ⊠ *Crown Bay Center, Rte. 305, Crown Bay* ☎ *340/779–7057.*

H. Stern Jewelers. This Brazilian jeweler is known for the modern settings and designs of its offerings. The jewelry vault design center is located on Main Street, Charlotte Amalie. ⊠ *Havensight Mall, Bldg. II, Rte. 30, Havensight* ☎ *340/776–1223* ⊕ *www.hstern.net.*

Jewels. Head here for name-brand jewelry and designer watches in abundance. Locations also at Havensight Mall, Crown Bay Center, and the Ritz-Carlton, St. Thomas. ⊠ *38 Dronnigans Gade (Main St.), Charlotte Amalie* ☎ *248/809–5560* ⊕ *www.jewelsonline.com.*

LIQUOR AND TOBACCO

Al Cohen's Discount Liquor. This warehouse of a store holds an extremely large wine and liquor selection. ⊠ *Rte. 30, across from the main entrance to Havensight Mall, Havensight* ☎ *340/774–3690.*

Duty Free St. Thomas. This giant duty-free liquor outlet offers a large selection of tobacco (including imported cigars), as well as cordials, wines, and rare vintage Armagnacs, cognacs, ports, and Madeiras. It also stocks fruits in brandy and barware from England. Enjoy rum samples at the tasting bar. Prices are among the best in St. Thomas. ⊠ *Havensight Mall, Rte. 30, Bldg. II, Havensight* ☎ *340/776–2303, 800/315–1600* ⊕ *www.dfstthomas.com* ⊠ *A.H. Riise Mall, 37 Main St., Charlotte Amalie* ☎ *340/777–2222, 800/524–2037* ⊕ *www.ahriise.com.*

Tobacco Discounters. This duty-free outlet carries a full line of discounted brand-name cigarettes, cigars, and tobacco accessories. ⊠ *9100 Port of $ale Mall, Rte. 30, next to Havensight Mall, Havensight* ☎ *340/774–2256.*

SPORTS AND THE OUTDOORS

AIR TOURS

Caribbean Buzz Helicopters. Near to the UVI field, Caribbean Buzz Helicopters offers a minimum 30-minute tour that includes St. Thomas, St. John, and Jost Van Dyke. It's a nice ride if you can afford the splurge (tours are from $600 for up to three people), but in truth, you can see most of the aerial sights from Paradise Point, and there's no place you can't reach easily by car or boat. ⊠ *Jet Port, 8202 Lindbergh Bay, Charlotte Amalie* ☎ *340/775–7335* ⊕ *www.caribbean-buzz.com.*

BOATING AND SAILING

Calm seas, crystal waters, and nearby islands (perfect for picnicking, snorkeling, and exploring) make St. Thomas a favorite jumping-off spot for day- or weeklong sails or powerboat adventures. With more than 100 vessels from which to choose, St. Thomas is the charter-boat center of the U.S. Virgin Islands. You can go through a broker to book a sailing vessel with a crew or contact a charter company directly. Crewed charters start at approximately $3,200 per person per week, while bareboat charters can start at as little as $2,400 per person for a 50- to 55-foot sailboat (but this doesn't include provisioning, fuel, and optional add-ons like water-toy rentals), which can comfortably accommodate up to six people. If you want to rent your own boat, hire a captain. Most local captains are excellent tour guides.

Single-day charters are also a possibility. You can hire smaller boats for the day, including the services of a captain if you wish to have someone take you on a guided snorkel trip around the islands.

Island Yachts. The sailboats and powerboats from Island Yachts are available for charter with or without crews. ⊠ *6100 Red Hook Quarter, 18B, Red Hook* ☎ *340/775–6666, 800/524–2019* ⊕ *www.iyc.vi.*

Magic Moments. *Luxury* is the word at Magic Moments, where crews aboard the 45-foot *Sea Ray* and 52-foot *Sunseeker* offer pampered island-hopping snorkeling cruises for $475 per person (children ages 2–10 are half price). Nice touches include a wine-and-lobster lunch and icy-cold eucalyptus-infused washcloths for freshening up. ⊠ *American Yacht Harbor, 6501 Red Hook Plaza, Suite #201, Docks B and C, Red Hook* ☎ *340/775–5066* ⊕ *www.yachtmagicmoments.com.*

Nauti Nymph. A large selection of 28- to 35-foot powerboats and power catamarans are available from this company. Rates, which vary from $700 to $945 a day, include snorkeling gear, water skis, and outriggers, but not fuel. You can hire a captain for $140 more per day. ⊠ *American Yacht Harbor Marina, 6501 Red Hook Plaza, Suite 201, Dock C, Red Hook* ☎ *540/775–5066, 800/734–7345* ⊕ *www.nautinymph.com.*

Stewart Yacht Charters. Run by longtime sailor Ellen Stewart, this company is skilled at matching clients with yachts and crews for week-long charter holidays. ⊠ *6501 Red Hook Plaza, Suite 20, Red Hook* ☎ *340/775–1358, 800/432–6118* ⊕ *www.stewartyachtcharters.com.*

VIP Yacht Charters. Forty-eight- to 59-foot powerboats, including a selection of stable trawlers, are available for bareboat charter. Professional captains available at request, for an extra charge. ⊠ *Compass Point Marina, 6300 Estate Frydenhoj, south off Rte. 32, Suite 27, Estate Frydenhoj* ☎ *340/774–9224, 866/847–9224* ⊕ *www.vipyachts.com.*

BICYCLING

Water Island Adventures. In this company's fun biking trip, you first take a ferry ride from Crown Bay to Water Island and then jump on a Cannondale for 90 minutes of biking over rolling hills on dirt and paved roads. (On cruise-ship days, a direct ferry goes from the West India Company Docks, but this is only for cruise passengers who have booked the bike tour.) Explore the remains of the Sea Cliff Hotel, reputedly the inspiration for Herman Wouk's book *Don't Stop the Carnival,* and then take a cooling swim at beautiful Honeymoon Beach. Helmets, water, guides, and ferry fare are included in the $85 cost. Bike rentals are available on days when no tours are scheduled: call for details. ⊠ *Water Island* ☎ *340/626–9815, 340/690–4019* ⊕ *www.waterislandadventures.com.*

DIVING AND SNORKELING

Popular dive sites include such wrecks as the *Cartanser Sr.*, a beautifully encrusted World War II cargo ship sitting in 35 feet of water, and the *General Rogers*, a Coast Guard cutter resting at 65 feet. Here you can find a gigantic resident barracuda. Reef dives offer hidden caves and archways at **Cow and Calf Rocks**, coral-covered pinnacles at **Frenchcap**, and tunnels where you can explore undersea from the Caribbean to the Atlantic at **Thatch Cay, Grass Cay,** and **Congo Cay.** Many resorts and charter yachts offer dive packages. A one-tank dive starts at $110; two-tank dives are $130 and up. Call the USVI Department of Tourism to obtain a free eight-page guide to Virgin Islands dive sites. There are plenty of snorkeling possibilities, too.

Admiralty Dive Center. Boat dives, rental equipment, and a retail store are available from this dive center. You can also get multiple-tank packages if you want to dive over several days. ⊠ *Windward Passage Resort, Waterfront Hwy. (Rte. 30), Charlotte Amalie* ☎ *340/777–9802, 888/900–3483* ⊕ *www.admiraltydive.com.*

Blue Island Divers. This full-service dive shop offers both day and night dives to wrecks and reefs and specializes in custom dive charters. ⊠ *Crown Bay Marina, Rte. 304, Estate Contant* ☎ *340/774–2001* ⊕ *www.blueislanddivers.com.*

B.O.S.S. Underwater Adventure. As an alternative to traditional diving, try an underwater motor scooter called BOSS, or Breathing Observation Submersible Scooter. A 3½-hour tour, including snorkel equipment, rum punch, and towels, is $140 per person. ⊠ *Crown Bay Marina, Rte. 304, Charlotte Amalie* ☎ *340/777–3549* ⊕ *www.bossusvi.com.*

FAMILY **Coki Dive Center.** Snorkeling and dive tours in the fish-filled reefs off Coki Beach are available from this PADI Five Star outfit, as are classes, including one on underwater photography. It's run by the avid diver Peter Jackson. ⊠ *Rte. 388, at Coki Point, Estate Frydendal* ☎ *340/775–4220* ⊕ *www.cokidive.com.*

Snuba of St. Thomas. In snuba, a snorkeling and scuba-diving hybrid, a 20-foot air hose connects you to the surface. The cost is $74. Children must be eight or older to participate. ⊠ *Rte. 388, at Coki Point, Estate Smith Bay* ☎ *340/693–8063* ⊕ *www.visnuba.com.*

St. Thomas Diving Club. This PADI Five Star center offers boat dives to the reefs around Buck Island and nearby offshore wrecks as well as multiday dive packages. ⊠ *Bolongo Bay Beach Resort, Rte. 30, Estate Bolongo* ☎ *340/776–2381* ⊕ *www.stthomasdivingclub.com.*

FISHING

Fishing here is synonymous with blue marlin angling—especially from June through October. Four 1,000-pound-plus blues, including three world records, have been caught on the famous North Drop, about 20

miles (32 km) north of St. Thomas. A day charter for marlin with up to six anglers costs from $1,600 to $1,900 for the day. If you're not into marlin fishing, try hooking sailfish in winter, dolphin (the fish, not the mammal) in spring, and wahoo in fall. Inshore trips for four hours range from $650 to $800. To find the trip that will best suit you, walk down the docks at either American Yacht Harbor or Sapphire Beach Marina in the late afternoon and chat with the captains and crews.

Abigail III. Captain Red Bailey's *Abigail III* specializes in marlin fishing. It operates out of the Sapphire Condominium Resort's marina. ⊠ *Estate Smith Bay, Rte. 38, ¼ mile northwest of Red Hook, Sapphire Bay* ☎ *340/775–6024* ⊕ *www.visportfish.com.*

Charter Boat Center. This is a major source for sail- and powerboat as well as sportfishing charters. Sportfishing charters include full-day trips for marlin as well as full, three-quarter, and half days for offshore and inshore species such as tuna, wahoo, dolphin (mahimahi), snapper, and kingfish. ⊠ *American Yacht Harbor, 6300 Smith Bay 16-3, Red Hook* ☎ *340/775–7990.*

FAMILY **Double Header Sportfishing.** This company offers trips out to the North Drop on its 40-foot sportfisher and half-day reef and bay trips aboard its two speedy 35-foot center consoles. ⊠ *Sapphire Bay Marina, Rte. 38, Sapphire Bay* ☎ *340/777–7317* ⊕ *www.doubleheadersportfishing.net.*

Marlin Prince. Captain Eddie Morrison, one of the most experienced charter operators in St. Thomas, specializes in fly-fishing for blue marlin from his 45-foot Viking boat. ⊠ *American Yacht Harbor, 6100 Red Hook Quarters #2, slip A-16, Red Hook* ☎ *340/693–5929* ⊕ *www. marlinprince.com.*

GOLF

Mahogany Run Golf Course. The Mahogany Run Golf Course is the only course in St. Thomas and it attracts golfers who are drawn by its spectacular view of the British Virgin Islands and the challenging three-hole Devil's Triangle of holes 13–15. This Tom and George Fazio–designed course is not particularly long, but in addition to the scenery, you will experience lots of natural flora and fauna. There's a fully stocked pro shop, snack bar, and open-air clubhouse. Walking is not permitted and the course enforces a dress code. It's open daily, and there are frequently informal weekend tournaments. ⊠ *Rte. 42, Estate Lovenlund* ☎ *340/777–6006, 800/253–7103* ⊕ *www.mahoganyrungolf.com* ⌂ *$165 for 18 holes; $115 for 9 holes during peak winter season* ⋔ *18 holes, 6022 yards, par 70.*

GUIDED TOURS

VI Taxi Association St. Thomas City-Island Tour. The VI Taxi Association gives a two-hour tour for two people in an open-air safari bus or enclosed van. Aimed at cruise-ship passengers, this $29 tour includes stops at Drake's Seat and Mountain Top. Other tours include a three-hour trip to Coki Beach with a shopping stop in downtown Charlotte Amalie for $35 per person; a three-hour trip to the Coral World Ocean Park for $45 per person; and a five-hour beach tour to St. John for $75 per person. For $60 for two, you can hire a taxi for a customized three-hour drive around the island. Make sure to see Mountain Top, as the view is wonderful. ☎ *340/774–4550* ⊕ *vitaxiassociation.com.*

SEA EXCURSIONS

Landlubbers and seafarers alike will enjoy the wind in their hair and salt spray in the air while exploring the waters surrounding St. Thomas. Several businesses can book you on a snorkel-and-sail to a deserted cay for a half day that starts at $90 per person or a full day that begins at $140 per person. An excursion over to the British Virgin Islands starts at $145 per person, not including customs fees. A luxury daylong motor-yacht cruise complete with gourmet lunch is $450 or more per person.

Adventure Center. For a soup-to-nuts choice of sea tours including a stand-up paddleboard (SUP) safari, full- and half-day sails, and sunset cruises, contact the Adventure Center. ⊠ *Marriott's Frenchman's Reef Hotel, Rte. 315, Estate Bakkeroe* ☎ *340/774–2992, 866/868–7784* ⊕ *www.adventurecenters.net.*

Charter Boat Center. The specialty here is day trips to the British Virgin Islands aboard 42-foot 12-passenger motoryachts *Stormy Petrel* and *Pirate's Penny.* There's also day- or weeklong sailing charters. ⊠ *American Yacht Harbor, 6300 Smith Bay 16-3, Red Hook* ☎ *340/775–7990.*

Treasure Isle Cruises. Jimmy Loveland at Treasure Isle Cruises can set you up with everything from a half-day sail to a seven-day Caribbean cruise. ⊠ *Rte. 32, Estate Nadir* ☎ *340/775–9500* ⊕ *www.treasureisle cruises.com.*

SEA KAYAKING

FAMILY **Virgin Islands Ecotours.** Fish dart, birds sing, and iguanas lounge on the
Fodor's Choice limbs of dense mangrove trees deep within a marine sanctuary on St.
★ Thomas's southeast shore. With Virgin Islands Ecotours you can learn about the islands' natural history in a guided kayak-snorkel tour to Patricia Cay or via an inflatable-boat tour to Cas Cay for snorkeling and hiking. Both are 2½ hours long. VI Ecotours also offers three- and five-hour guided kayak tours to St. Thomas's Mangrove Lagoon, Hassel Island, Henley Cay, and St. John's Caneel Bay. All trips include free snorkel instruction with snacks on three-hour trips and lunch on five-hour trips. The historic Hassel Island tour includes a visit to some of the historic forts and military structures on the island, a short hike to a breathtaking vista, and a swim off a deserted beach. ⊠ *Mangrove Lagoon, Rte. 32, 2 miles (3 km) east of the intersection of Rtes. 32 and 30, Estate Nadir* ☎ *340/779–2155, 877/845–2925* ⊕ *www.viecotours. com* ⌨ *From $69 per person.*

ST. JOHN

WELCOME TO ST. JOHN

TOP REASONS TO GO

★ **Beach-hopping:** Fill your cooler with cold drinks, grab the snorkeling gear, and stash your beach chair in the back of your car for a day spent at the beaches along St. John's North Shore Road.

★ **Hiking Reef Bay:** Opt for a trip with a ranger in Virgin Islands National Park. A safari bus takes you to the trailhead, and a boat brings you back.

★ **Snorkeling at Trunk Bay:** Trunk Bay is St. John's most popular snorkeling spot, and for good reason: a snorkeling trail teaches you about the local marine life.

★ **Relaxing in a villa:** There are about 1,000 vacation villas across the island in all sizes, prices, and locations; most will give you all the comforts of home.

★ **Exploring Cruz Bay:** Spend a half day poking around Cruz Bay's varied stores, shopping for that perfect gift for the folks back home.

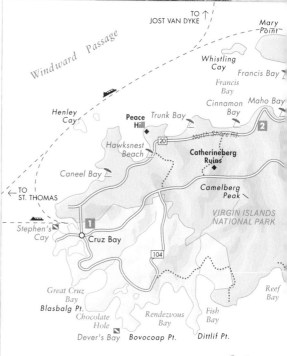

1 Cruz Bay and Environs. St. John's main town is where you go for both dining and nightlife. Most of the shopping is here, as well as the ferry dock, where all island visitors arriving by ferry land. Its environs include the area around the Westin Resort and Villas, Fish Bay, and Gifft Hill.

2 North Shore. Caneel Bay Resort and the Cinnamon Bay campground can all be found along North Shore Road. Some of the island's best beaches, including those at Cinnamon and Trunk Bay, are accessible here.

3 Coral Bay and Environs. The island's second town is about a half-hour drive from Cruz Bay. You'll find a collection of businesses here, including a half-dozen-plus places to eat and a slew of vacation villas. If you head to the northern edge of Coral Bay, the East

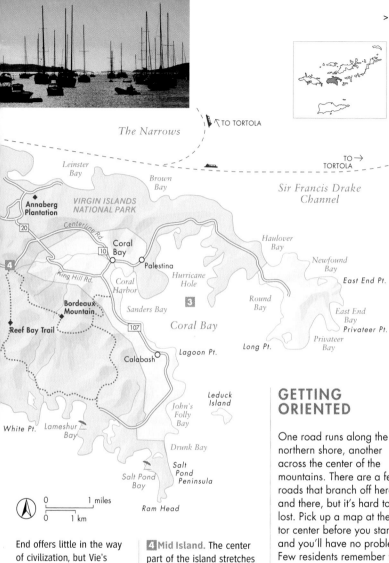

The Narrows

↑ TO TORTOLA

TO →
TORTOLA

3

Leinster
Bay

Brown
Bay

Sir Francis Drake
Channel

◆ Annaberg
Plantation

VIRGIN ISLANDS
NATIONAL PARK

Centerline Rd.

20

Coral
Bay

10

Haulover
Bay

Newfound
Bay

East End Pt.

4

King Hill Rd.

Palestina

Coral
Harbor

Hurricane
Hole

East End
Bay

Bordeaux
Mountain

Sanders Bay

3

Round
Bay

Privateer Pt.

Reef Bay Trail

107

Coral Bay

Privateer
Bay

Calabash

Lagoon Pt.

Long Pt.

Leduck
Island

John's
Folly
Bay

White Pt.

Lameshur
Bay

Drunk Bay

0   1 miles
0   1 km

Salt
Pond
Bay

Salt
Pond
Peninsula

Ram Head

End offers little in the way of civilization, but Vie's Snack Shack is a good place to stop for lunch if you want to enjoy the deserted beach here. On the southern edge, Salt Pond Bay Beach has some interesting tide pools to explore, and Lameshur Bay Beach is one of the island's better snorkeling spots.

4 Mid Island. The center part of the island stretches along Centerline Road (Rte. 10) from outside Cruz Bay past Reef Bay to Bordeaux. There are a couple of spots to take in the views, and a stop at the Catherineberg Ruins makes a nice break.

GETTING ORIENTED

One road runs along the northern shore, another across the center of the mountains. There are a few roads that branch off here and there, but it's hard to get lost. Pick up a map at the visitor center before you start out and you'll have no problems. Few residents remember the route numbers, so have your map in hand if you stop to ask for directions. There are lunch spots at Cinnamon Bay and in Coral Bay, or you can do what the locals do—find a secluded spot for a picnic. The grocery stores in Cruz Bay sell Styrofoam coolers just for this purpose.

Updated by
Lynda Lohr

Only 3 miles (5 km) from St. Thomas but still a world apart, St. John is the least developed of the U.S. Virgin Islands. While two-thirds of its tropical hills remain protected as national parkland, a bit of hustle and bustle has come to Cruz Bay, the island's main town. Accommodations range from world-class luxury resorts to top-notch vacation villas to back-to-basics campgrounds.

St. John's heart is Virgin Islands National Park, a treasure that takes up a full two-thirds of St. John's 20 square miles (53 square km). The park was spearheaded by Laurance S. Rockefeller and Frank Stick and was finally handed over to the Department of the Interior in 1956. The park helps keep the island's interior in its pristine and undisturbed state, but if you go at midday you'll probably have to share your stretch of beach with others, particularly at Trunk Bay.

The island is booming, and it can get a tad crowded at the ever-popular Trunk Bay Beach during the busy winter season; parking woes plague the island's main town of Cruz Bay, but you won't find traffic jams or pollution. It's easy to escape from the fray: just head off on a hike or go early or late to the beach. The sun won't be as strong, and you may have that perfect crescent of white sand all to yourself.

St. John doesn't have a grand agrarian past like her sister island, St. Croix, but if you're hiking in the dry season, you can probably stumble upon the stone ruins of old plantations. The less adventuresome can visit the repaired ruins at the park's Annaberg Plantation and Caneel Bay Resort.

In 1675 Jorgen Iverson claimed the unsettled island for Denmark. By 1733 there were more than 1,000 slaves working more than 100 plantations. In that year the island was hit by a drought, hurricanes, and a plague of insects that destroyed the summer crops. With famine a real threat and the planters keeping them under tight rein, the slaves revolted on November 23, 1733. They captured the fort at Coral Bay, took control of the island, and held on to it for six months. During this period, about 20% of the island's total population was killed, the tragedy affecting both black and white residents in equal percentages. The rebellion was eventually put down with the help of French troops from Martinique. Slavery continued until 1848, when slaves in St. Croix marched on Frederiksted to demand their freedom from the Danish government. This time it was granted. After emancipation, St. John fell into decline, its inhabitants eking out a living on small farms. Life continued in much the same way until the national park opened in 1956 and tourism became an industry.

Of the three U.S. Virgin Islands, St. John, which has 5,000 residents, has the strongest sense of community, which is primarily rooted in a desire to protect the island's natural beauty. Despite the growth, there are still many pockets of tranquility. Here you can truly escape the pressures of modern life for a day, a week—perhaps forever.

GETTING HERE AND AROUND

AIR TRAVEL

St. John does not have an airport, so you will need to fly into St. Thomas and then take a ferry over.

BUS TRAVEL

Modern Vitran buses on St. John run from the Cruz Bay ferry dock through Coral Bay to the far eastern end of the island at Salt Pond, making numerous stops in between. The fare is $1 to any point, but the service is slow and not always reliable.

CAR TRAVEL

You will almost certainly need a car if you are staying in a villa or in Coral Bay, but you might be able to get by with taxis if you are staying elsewhere. The terrain in St. John is very hilly, the roads are winding, and the blind curves numerous. Major roads are well paved, but once you get off a specific route, dirt roads filled with potholes are common. For such driving, a four-wheel-drive vehicle is your best bet. Be aware that you can't bring all rental cars over to St. John from St. Thomas. Even more important, the barge service is very busy, so you can't always get a space.

St. John has only two gas stations, both at the Cruz Bay end of the island so make sure you're not near empty when you set out for Coral Bay.

■TIP➜ Parking in Cruz Bay is difficult, but if you can't find a spot, there's plenty of room at the lot near the public tennis courts. Your best bet is to rent a car from a company that allows you to park in its lot. Make sure you ask before you sign on the dotted line if you plan to spend time in Cruz Bay.

CAR RENTALS

All the car-rental companies in St. John are locally owned, and most are just a short walk from the ferry dock in Cruz Bay. Those located a bit farther away will pick you up.

Contacts Best ⊠ *Near library, Cruz Bay, St. John* ☎ *340/693–8177.* **Cool Breeze** ⊠ *1 block east of the passenger ferry dock, Cruz Bay, St. John* ☎ *340/776–6588* ⊕ *www.coolbreezecarrental.com.* **Courtesy** ⊠ *Near St.*

Ursula's Church, Cruz Bay, St. John ☎ *340/776–6650* ⊕ *www.courtesycarrental. com.* **Delbert Hill Taxi & Jeep Rental Service** ⊠ *King St., Cruz Bay, St. John* ☎ *340/776–6637* ⊕ *www.delberthillcarrental.com.* **Denzil Clyne** ⊠ *North Shore Rd., Across from creek, Cruz Bay, St. John* ☎ *340/776–6715.* **O'Connor Car Rental** ⊠ *Rte. 104, Near the roundabout, Cruz Bay, St. John* ☎ *340/776–6343* ⊕ *www.oconnorcarrental.com.* **St. John Car Rental** ⊠ *Bay St., near Wharf- side Village, Cruz Bay, St. John* ☎ *340/776–6103* ⊕ *www.stjohncarrental. com.* **Spencer's Jeep** ⊠ *Boulon Center Rd., near creek, Cruz Bay, St. John* ☎ *340/693–8784, 888/776–6628.*

FERRY TRAVEL

There's frequent daily service from both Red Hook and Charlotte Ama- lie on St. Thomas to Cruz Bay (the more frequent ferry is the one from Red Hook). There's also frequent service from Cruz Bay to Tortola and less frequent service to the other British Virgin Islands, includ- ing Jost Van Dyke (some via Tortola). Virgin Islands ferry schedules are published on the website of the Virgin Islands Vacation Guide & Community. The actual schedules change, so you should check with the ferry companies to determine the current schedules. Remember that a passport is now required to travel between the USVI and BVI by ferry.

Contacts Virgin Islands Vacation Guide and Community ⊕ *www.vinow.com.*

TAXI TRAVEL

Taxis meet ferries arriving in Cruz Bay. Most drivers use vans or open- air safari buses. You can find them congregated at the dock and at hotel parking lots. You can also hail them anywhere on the road. Almost all trips will be shared, and prices are per person. Paradise Taxi will pick you up if you call, but most drivers don't provide that service. If you need one to pick you up at your rental villa, ask the villa manager to call or arrange a ride in advance.

Contacts Paradise Taxi ⊠ *Waterfront, Cruz Bay, St. John* ☎ *340/714–7913.*

ESSENTIALS

BANKS

St. John has one full-service bank plus several bank ATM machines. First Bank provides full services at its location one block up from the ferry dock. Banco Popular has a convenient ATM machine one block from the ferry dock. Scotia Bank has an ATM at the Marketplace Shop- ping Center on Route 107.

HOTELS

St. John doesn't have many beachfront hotels, but that's a small price to pay for all the pristine sand. The island's two excellent resorts— Caneel Bay Resort and the Westin St. John Resort & Villas—*are* on the beach. Most villas are in the residential south-shore area, a 15-minute drive from the north-shore beaches. If you head east you come to the laid-back community of Coral Bay, where there are growing numbers of villas and cottages. If you're looking for West Indian village charm, there are a few inns in Cruz Bay. Your choice of accommodations also includes condominiums and cottages near town; one campground at the edge of beautiful beaches (bring bug repellent); eco-resorts; and luxurious villas, often with a pool or a hot tub (sometimes both) and a stunning view.

Hotel reviews have been shortened. For full information go to Fodors. com.

RESTAURANTS

The cuisine on St. John seems to get better every year, with culinary school–trained chefs vying to see who can come up with the most imaginative dishes. There are restaurants to suit every taste and budget—from the elegant establishments at Caneel Bay Resort (where men may be required to wear a jacket at dinner) to the casual in-town eateries of Cruz Bay. For quick lunches, try the West Indian food stands in Cruz Bay Park and across from the post office. Some restaurants close for vacation in September and even October. If you have your heart set on a special place, call ahead to make sure it's open during these months.

WHAT IT COSTS IN U.S. DOLLARS			
	$	$$	$$$	$$$$
Restaurants	under $13	$13–$20	$21–$30	over $30
Hotels	under $276	$276–$375	$376–$475	over $475

Restaurant prices are the average cost of a main course at dinner or, if dinner is not served, at lunch. Hotel prices are the lowest cost of a standard double room in high season.

SAFETY

Although crime is not as prevalent on St. John as it is on St. Thomas and St. Croix, it does exist. Keep your hotel or vacation villa door locked at all times, even during the day if you are, say, out by the pool. Stick to well-lighted streets at night, and use the same kind of street sense that you would in any unfamiliar territory. It's not a good idea to walk around Cruz Bay late at night. If you don't have a car, plan on taking a taxi, which you should arrange in advance.

TOUR OPTIONS

On St. John taxi drivers provide tours of the island, making stops at various sites, including Trunk Bay and Annaberg Plantation, for about $25 a person. Rangers at the V.I. National Park Visitors Center give several guided tours on- and offshore (some requiring reservations).

Contacts **V.I. National Park Visitors Center** ⊠ *North Shore Rd., at creek, Cruz Bay, St. John* ☎ *340/776–6201* ⊕ *www.nps.gov/viis.*

VISITOR INFORMATION

Contacts **USVI Division of Tourism** ⊠ *Henry Samuel St., next to post office, Cruz Bay, St. John* ☎ *340/776–6450* ⊕ *www.visitusvi.com.* **Virgin Islands Hotel & Tourism Association** ☎ *340/774–6835* ⊕ *www.virgin-islands-hotels.com.*

EXPLORING ST. JOHN

CRUZ BAY AND ENVIRONS

St. John's main town may be compact (it consists of only several blocks), but it's definitely a hub: the ferries from St. Thomas and the British Virgin Islands pull in here, and it's where you can get a taxi or rent a car to travel around the island. There are plenty of shops in which to browse, a number of watering holes where you can stop for a breather, many restaurants, and a grassy square with benches where you can sit back and take everything in. Look for the current edition of the handy, amusing "St. John Map" featuring Max the Mongoose.

WORTH NOTING

Elaine Ione Sprauve Library. On the hill just above Cruz Bay is the Enighed Estate greathouse, built in 1757. *Enighed* is Danish for "concord" (unity or peace). The house and its outbuildings (a sugar factory and horse-driven mill) were destroyed by fire and hurricanes, and the house sat in ruins until 1982. The library offers Internet access for $2 an hour. ⊠ *Rte. 104, make a right past St. Ursula's Church* ☎ *340/776–6359* 🖾 *Free* ☉ *Weekdays 9–5.*

V.I. National Park Visitors Center. To pick up a useful guide to St. John's hiking trails, see various large maps of the island, and find out about current Park Service programs, including guided walks and cultural demonstrations, stop by the park visitor center. ⊠ *North Shore Rd., near creek* ☎ *340/776–6201* ⊕ *www.nps.gov/viis* ☉ *Daily 8–4:30.*

NORTH SHORE

TOP ATTRACTIONS

Fodor'sChoice **Annaberg Plantation.** In the 18th century, sugar plantations dotted the
★ steep hills of this island. Slaves and free Danes and Dutchmen toiled to harvest the cane that was used to create sugar, molasses, and rum for export. Built in the 1780s, the partially restored plantation at Leinster Bay was once an important sugar mill. Although there are no official visiting hours, the National Park Service has regular tours, and some well-informed taxi drivers will show you around. Occasionally you may see a living-history demonstration—someone making johnnycakes or weaving baskets. For information on tours and cultural events, contact the V.I. National Park Visitors Center. ⊠ *Leinster Bay Rd., Annaberg* ☎ *340/776–6201* ⊕ *www.nps.gov/viis* 🖾 *Free* ☉ *Daily dawn–dusk.*

WORTH NOTING

Peace Hill. It's worth stopping here, just past the Hawksnest Bay overlook, for great views of St. John, St. Thomas, and the BVI. On the flat promontory is an old sugar mill. ⊠ *Off Rte. 20, Denis Bay.*

Cruz Bay

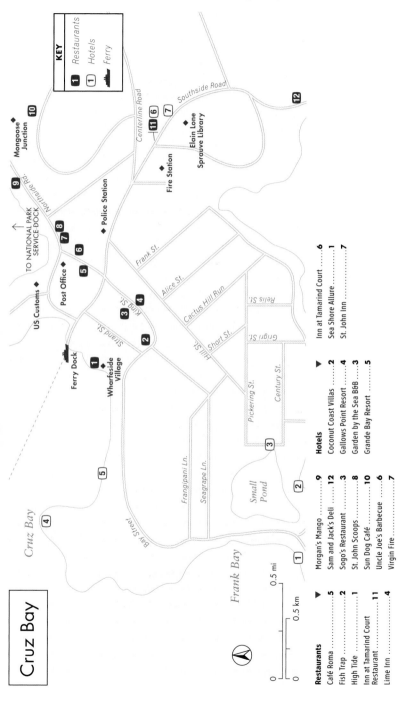

KEY

🔲 Restaurants

1️⃣ Hotels

⛴ Ferry

Restaurants ▶

Café Roma	**5**
Fish Trap	**2**
High Tide	**1**
Inn at Tamarind Court Restaurant	**11**
Lime Inn	**4**
Morgan's Mango	**9**
Sam and Jack's Deli	**12**
Sogo's Restaurant	**3**
St. John Scoops	**8**
Sun Dog Café	**10**
Uncle Joe's Barbecue	**6**
Virgin Fire	**7**

Hotels ▶

Coconut Coast Villas	**2**
Gallows Point Resort	**4**
Garden by the Sea B&B	**3**
Grande Bay Resort	**5**
Inn at Tamarind Court	**6**
Sea Shore Allure	**1**
St. John Inn	**7**

Mongoose Junction ◆

Elaine Ione Sprauve Library ◆

Fire Station ◆

Police Station ◆

TO NATIONAL PARK SERVICE DOCK ←

US Customs ◆

Post Office ◆

Wharfside Village ◆

Ferry Dock

Cruz Bay

Frank Bay

Small Pond

Centerline Road

Southside Road

Northside Rd.

Frank St.

Alice St.

Cactus Hill Run

Short St.

Strand St.

King St.

Bay Street

Frangipani Ln.

Seagrape Ln.

Pickering St.

Century St.

Hill St.

Grigri St.

Rells St.

0.5 mi

0.5 km

3

Sugar mill ruins at Annaberg Plantation

MID ISLAND

TOP ATTRACTIONS

Fodor's Choice ★ **Reef Bay Trail.** This is one of the most interesting hikes on St. John, but unless you're a rugged individualist who wants a physical challenge (and that describes a lot of people who stay on St. John), you can probably get the most out of the trip if you join a hike led by a park service ranger. A ranger can identify the trees and plants on the hike down, fill you in on the history of the Reef Bay Plantation, and tell you about the petroglyphs on the rocks at the bottom of the trail. A side trail takes you to the plantation's greathouse, a gutted but mostly intact structure with vestiges of its former beauty. Take the safari bus from the park's visitor center. A boat takes you from the beach at Reef Bay back to the visitor center, saving you the uphill climb. It's a good idea to make reservations for this trip, especially during the winter season. They can be made at the Friends of the Park store, in Mongoose Junction. ⌂ *Rte. 10, Reef Bay* ☎ *340/779–8700 for reservations* ⊕ *www.nps.gov/viis* ⌷ *$30 includes a safari bus ride to the trailhead, a guided tour, and a boat ride back to the visitor center* ☉ *Tours at 9:30 am; days change seasonally.*

WORTH NOTING

Catherineberg Ruins. At this fine example of an 18th-century sugar and rum factory, there's a storage vault beneath the windmill. Across the road, look for the round mill, which was later used to hold water. In the 1733 slave revolt Catherineberg served as headquarters for the Amina warriors, a tribe of Africans captured into slavery. ⌂ *Catherineberg Rd., off Rte. 10, Catherineberg.*

CORAL BAY AND ENVIRONS

WORTH NOTING

Coral Bay. This laid-back community at the island's dry, eastern end is named for its shape rather than for its underwater life—the word *coral* comes from *krawl*, Dutch for "corral." Coral Bay is growing fast, but it's still a small, neighborly place. You'll probably need a four-wheel-drive vehicle if you plan to stay at this end of the island, as some of the rental houses are up unpaved roads that wind around the mountain. If you come just for lunch, a regular car will be fine. ⊠ *Coral Bay.*

BEACHES

St. John is blessed with many beaches, and all of them fall into the good, great, and don't-tell-anyone-else-about-this-place categories. Those along the north shore are all within the national park. Some are more developed than others—and many are crowded on weekends, holidays, and in high season—but by and large they're still pristine. Beaches along the south and eastern shores are quiet and isolated.

NORTH SHORE

Cinnamon Bay Beach. This long, sandy beach faces beautiful cays and abuts the national park campground. You can rent water-sports equipment here—a good thing, because there's excellent snorkeling off the point to the right; look for the big angelfish and large schools of purple triggerfish. Afternoons on Cinnamon Bay can be windy—a boon for windsurfers but an annoyance for sunbathers—so arrive early to beat the gusts. The Cinnamon Bay hiking trail begins across the road from the beach parking lot; ruins mark the trailhead. There are actually two paths here: a level nature trail (signs along it identify the flora) that loops through the woods and passes an old Danish cemetery, and a steep trail that starts where the road bends past the ruins and heads straight up to Route 10. Restrooms are on the main path from the commissary to the beach and scattered around the campground. **Amenities:** food and drink; parking; showers; toilets; water sports. **Best for:** snorkeling; swimming; walking; windsurfing. ⊠ *North Shore Rd., Rte. 20, about 4 miles (6 km) east of Cruz Bay, Cinnamon Bay* ⊕ *www.nps.gov/viis.*

Francis Bay Beach. Because there's little shade, this beach gets toasty warm in the afternoon when the sun comes around to the west, but the rest of the day it's a delightful stretch of white sand. The only facilities are a few picnic tables tucked among the trees and a portable restroom, but folks come here to watch the birds that live in the swampy area behind the beach. The park offers bird-watching hikes here on Friday morning; sign up at the visitor center in Cruz Bay. To get here, turn left at the Annaberg intersection. **Amenities:** parking; toilets. **Best for:** snorkeling; swimming; walking. ⊠ *North Shore Rd., Rte. 20, ¼ mile (½ km) from Annaberg intersection, Francis Bay* ⊕ *www.nps.gov/viis.*

Hawksnest Beach. Sea grapes and waving palm trees line this narrow beach, and there are restrooms, cooking grills, and a covered shed for

St. John Archaeology

Archaeologists continue to unravel St. John's past through excavations at Trunk Bay and Cinnamon Bay, both prime tourist destinations within Virgin Islands National Park.

Work began back in the early 1990s, when the park wanted to build new bathhouses at the popular Trunk Bay. In preparation for that project, the archaeologists began to dig, turning up artifacts and the remains of structures that date to AD 900. The site was once a village occupied by the Taíno, a peaceful group that lived in the area for many centuries. A similar but not quite as ancient village was discovered at Cinnamon Bay.

By the time the Taíno got to Cinnamon Bay—they lived in the area from about AD 1000 to 1500—their society had developed to include chiefs, commoners, workers, and slaves. The location of the national park's busy Cinnamon Bay campground was once a Taíno temple that belonged to a king or chief. When archaeologists began digging in 1998, they uncovered several dozen *zemis*, which are small clay gods used in ceremonial activities, as well as beads, pots, and many other artifacts.

Near the end of the Cinnamon Bay dig archaeologists turned up another less ancient but still surprising discovery. A burned layer indicated that a plantation slave village had also stood near Cinnamon Bay campground; it was torched during the 1733 revolt because its slave inhabitants had been loyal to the planters. Since the 1970s, bones from slaves buried in the area have been uncovered at the water's edge by beach erosion.

picnicking. A patchy reef just offshore means snorkeling is an easy swim away, but the best underwater views are reserved for ambitious snorkelers who head farther to the east along the bay's fringes. Watch out for boat traffic—a channel guides dinghies to the beach, but the occasional boater strays into the swim area. It's the closest drivable beach to Cruz Bay, so it's often crowded with locals and visitors. **Amenities:** parking; toilets. **Best for:** snorkeling; swimming. ⊠ *North Shore Rd., Rte. 20, about 2 miles (3 km) east of Cruz Bay, Hawksnest Bay* ⊕ *www.nps.gov/viis.*

Maho Bay Beach. Maho Bay Beach is a gorgeous strip of sand that sits right along the North Shore Road. It's a popular place, particularly on weekends, when locals come out in droves to party at the picnic tables at the south end of the beach. Snorkeling along the rocky edges is good, but the center is mostly sea grass. If you're lucky, you'll cross paths with turtles. **Amenities:** parking; toilets. **Best for:** snorkeling; swimming. ⊠ *North Shore Rd., Rte. 20, Maho Bay* ⊕ *www.nps.gov/viis.*

Fodor's Choice **Trunk Bay Beach.** St. John's most-photographed beach is also the pre-
★ ferred spot for beginning snorkelers because of its underwater trail. (Cruise-ship passengers interested in snorkeling for a day flock here, so if you're looking for seclusion, arrive early or later in the day.) Crowded or not, this stunning beach is one of the island's most beautiful. There are changing rooms with showers, bathrooms, a snack bar, picnic tables, a gift shop, phones, lockers, and snorkeling-equipment rentals. The

parking lot often overflows, but you can park along the road as long as the tires are off the pavement. **Amenities:** food and drink; lifeguards; parking; toilets; water sports. **Best for:** snorkeling; swimming; windsurfing. ✉ *North Shore Rd., Rte. 20, about 2½ miles (4 km) east of Cruz Bay, Trunk Bay* 🌐 *www.nps.gov/viis* 🎫 *$4.*

CORAL BAY AND ENVIRONS

Lameshur Bay Beach. This sea grape–fringed beach is toward the end of a partially paved road on the southeast coast. The reward for your long drive is good snorkeling and a chance to spy on some pelicans. The beach has a couple of picnic tables, rusting barbecue grills, and a portable restroom. The ruins of the old plantation are a five-minute walk down the road past the beach. The area has good hiking trails, including a trek (more than a mile) up Bordeaux Mountain before an easy walk to Yawzi Point. **Amenities:** parking; toilets. **Best for:** snorkeling; swimming; walking. ✉ *Off Rte. 107, about 1½ mile (2½ km) from Salt Pond, Lameshur Bay* 🌐 *www.nps.gov/viis.*

Salt Pond Bay Beach. If you're adventurous, this rocky beach on the scenic southeastern coast—next to rugged Drunk Bay—is worth exploring. It's a short hike down a hill from the parking lot, and the only facilities are an outhouse and a few picnic tables scattered about. Tide pools are filled with all sorts of marine creatures, and the snorkeling is good, particularly along the bay's edges. A short walk takes you to a pond where salt crystals collect around the edges. Hike farther uphill past cactus gardens to Ram Head for see-forever views. Leave nothing valuable in your car, as thefts are common. **Amenities:** parking; toilets. **Best for:** snorkeling; swimming; walking. ✉ *Rte. 107, about 3 miles (5 km) south of Coral Bay, Salt Pond Bay* 🌐 *www.nps.gov/viis.*

WHERE TO EAT

With the exception of the grown-on-the-island greens, which you can find in salads at a wide variety of local restaurants, and an occasional catch of local fish, almost all the food served here is imported from the mainland. This means that you may find prices on restaurant menus and supermarket shelves on the high side, since the shipping costs are passed along to the consumer.

During the summer, call ahead to confirm restaurant hours; some restaurants close for a month or so.

CRUZ BAY AND ENVIRONS

$$$$ ASIAN ✗ **Asolare.** Contemporary Asian cuisine dominates the menu at this elegant open-air eatery in an old St. John house. Come early and relax over drinks while you enjoy the sunset lighting up the harbor. Start with the sesame-crusted goat cheese salad, then move on to entrées such as applewood-smoked tenderloin with wasabi, or pan-roasted cod with a red curry sauce. If you still have room for dessert, try the mimosa-poached pears with honey. [$] *Average main: $36* ✉ *Rte. 20 on*

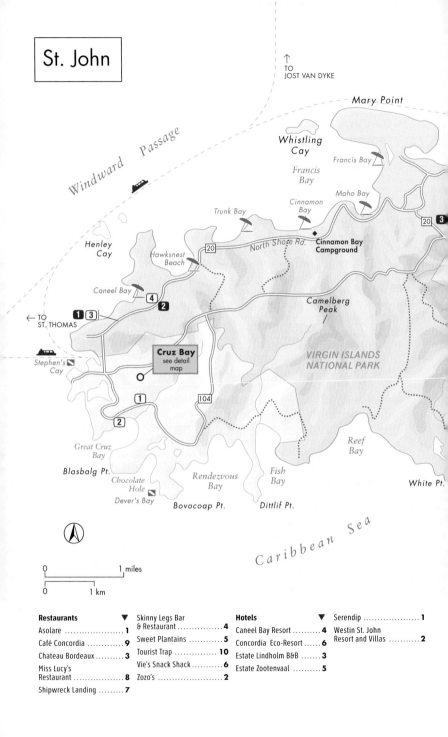

St. John

TO
JOST VAN DYKE

Mary Point

Whistling Cay

Francis Bay

Francis Bay

Windward Passage

Cinnamon Bay

Maho Bay

20 **3**

Trunk Bay

North Shore Rd. **Cinnamon Bay Campground**

Henley Cay

Hawksnest Beach

20

← TO ST. THOMAS

Camelberg Peak

Caneel Bay **4** **2**

1 **3**

Stephen's Cay

Cruz Bay see detail map

VIRGIN ISLANDS NATIONAL PARK

1

104

2

Great Cruz Bay

Reef Bay

Blasbalg Pt.

Chocolate Hole

Rendezvous Bay

Fish Bay

White Pt.

Dever's Bay

Bovocoap Pt.

Dittlif Pt.

Caribbean Sea

0 _____ 1 miles
0 _____ 1 km

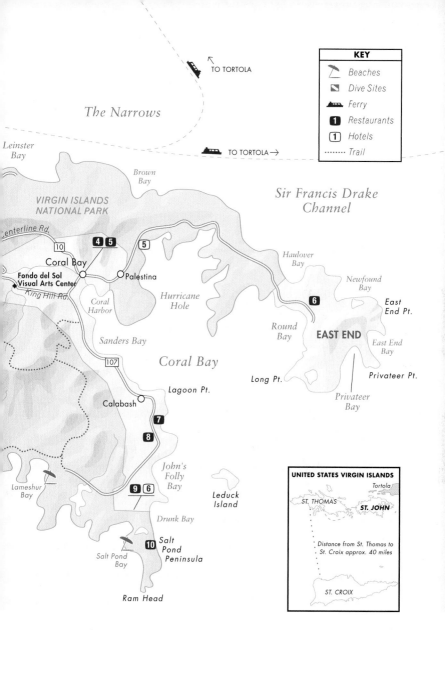

Caneel Hill, Estate Lindholm ☎ *340/779–4747* 🌐 *www.asolarestjohn.com* 🕒 *No lunch.*

$$$ ITALIAN FAMILY 🍴 **Café Roma.** This second-floor restaurant in the heart of Cruz Bay is *the* place for traditional Italian cuisine: lasagna, spaghetti and meatballs, and seafood manicotti. Small pizzas are available at the table, but larger ones are for takeout or at the bar. Tiramisu is a dessert specialty. This casual place can get crowded in winter, so show up early. [$] *Average main: $27* ✉ *Vesta Gade* ☎ *340/776–6524* 🌐 *www.stjohn-caferoma.com* 🕒 *No lunch.*

$$$$ AMERICAN FAMILY 🍴 **Fish Trap Restaurant and Seafood Market.** The main dining room here is open to the breezes and buzzes with a mix of locals and visitors, but the back room has air-conditioning. Start with a tasty appetizer such as conch fritters or fish chowder (a creamy combination of snapper, white wine, paprika, and spices). You can always find steak and chicken dishes, as well as the interesting fish of the day. [$] *Average main: $33* ✉ *Bay and Strand Sts., next to Our Lady of Mount Carmel Church* ☎ *340/693–9994* 🌐 *www.thefishtrap.com* 🕒 *Closed Mon. No lunch.*

$$$ ECLECTIC FAMILY 🍴 **High Tide.** This casual spot right at Cruz Bay Beach serves everything from hamburgers and mahimahi sandwiches to surf 'n turf and Caribbean lobster. The kids' menu includes favorites like chicken tenders and grilled-cheese sandwiches. [$] *Average main: $29* ✉ *Wharfside Village, Strand St.* ☎ *340/714–6169* 🌐 *www.hightidevi.com.*

$$ ECLECTIC 🍴 **Inn at Tamarind Court Restaurant.** There's a different chef—each with a unique style—here every night, which makes for an eclectic menu. On Tuesday, Caribbean cuisine brings out locals and visitors. On other nights you might find Southwestern, Japanese, or Italian cooking, depending on who's in the kitchen. [$] *Average main: $19* ✉ *Inn at Tamarind Court, Rte. 104* ☎ *340/776–6378* 🌐 *www.innattamarindcourt.com* 🕒 *No lunch.*

$$$ ECLECTIC 🍴 **Lime Inn.** The vacationers and mainland transplants who call St. John home like to flock to this alfresco spot for the congenial hospitality and good food, including all-you-can-eat shrimp on Wednesday night. Fresh lobster is the specialty, and the menu also includes shrimp-and-steak dishes and rotating chicken and pasta specials. [$] *Average main: $30* ✉ *Lemon Tree Mall, King St.* ☎ *340/776–6425* 🌐 *www.limeinn.com* 🕒 *No lunch Sat. Closed Sun.*

$$$ CARIBBEAN 🍴 **Morgan's Mango.** A visit to this alfresco eatery requires you to climb a long flight of stairs, but the food is well worth the effort. Although fish is the specialty—try the voodoo snapper topped with a fruity salsa—the chef also creates a vegetarian platter with black beans, fried plantains, and a mound of sweet potatoes. [$] *Average main: $25* ✉ *Across from V.I. National Park Visitors Center, North Shore Rd.* ☎ *340/693–8141* 🌐 *www.morgansmango.com* 🕒 *No lunch.*

$ DELI Fodor's Choice ★ 🍴 **Sam and Jack's Deli.** The sandwiches are scrumptious, but this deli also dishes up wonderful to-go meals that just need heating. If the truffle–wild mushroom ravioli is on the menu, don't hesitate to order it—it's a winner. There are a few seats inside, but most folks opt to eat at the tables in front of the deli. [$] *Average main: $12* ✉ *Marketplace Shopping Center, Rte. 104* ☎ *340/714–3354* 🌐 *www.samandjacksdeli.com* 🕒 *Closed Sun. No dinner.*

$ FAST FOOD 🍴 **St. John Scoops.** While you can get the usual chocolate and vanilla ice cream as well as smoothies at this tiny spot, owner Colette Rethage also dishes up frozen treats blended with alcoholic beverages. Try the champagne sorbet, espresso martini, peach margarita, or that tropical favorite, the rum-laced Painkiller. [$] *Average main: $6* ✉ *Mongoose Junction shopping center, North Shore Rd.*

$$ CARIBBEAN 🍴 **Sogo's.** Sogo's, which can be found in the heart of busy Cruz Bay, serves up delightful, traditional West Indian fare. The menu includes such dishes as kingfish, mutton, and curried goat that you won't find at other restaurants. Less adventurous eaters might like the jerk chicken or the conch fritters. [$] *Average main: $18* ✉ *King St.* ☎ *340/779–4404* 🕒 *Closed Sun.*

$$ ECLECTIC Fodor's Choice ★ 🍴 **Sun Dog Café.** There's an unusual assortment of dishes at this charming alfresco restaurant, which you'll find tucked into a courtyard in the upper reaches of the Mongoose Junction shopping center. Kudos to the white pizza with artichoke hearts, roasted garlic, mozzarella cheese, and capers. The Jamaican jerk chicken salad and the black-bean quesadilla are also good choices. [$] *Average main: $19* ✉ *Mongoose Junction Shopping Center, North Shore Rd.* ☎ *340/693–8340* 🌐 *www.sundogcafe.com* 🕒 *No dinner Sun.*

$$ BARBECUE FAMILY 🍴 **Uncle Joe's Barbecue.** Juicy ribs and tasty chicken legs dripping with house barbecue sauce make for one of St. John's best dining deals. An ear of corn, rice, and a generous scoop of macaroni salad, potato salad, or cole slaw round out the plate. This casual spot crowds the edge of a busy sidewalk in the heart of Cruz Bay. Even though there are a few open-air tables for "dining in," the ambience is more than a tad on the pedestrian side, so takeout is a better bet. [$] *Average main: $15* ✉ *North Shore Rd., across from post office* ☎ *340/693–8806.*

$$$ CARIBBEAN 🍴 **Virgin Fire.** "Contemporary Caribbean" is how owner Michael Barry markets what's on his menu. The tamarind barbecue ribs with pickled mango slaw, jerk pork tenderloin porterhouse with grilled fresh pineapple, and mahimahi with a coconut-ginger sauce fit that description to a tee. Finish with a wedge of key lime pie. [$] *Average main: $26* ✉ *Mongoose Junction Shopping Center, North Shore Rd.* ☎ *340/777–3473* 🌐 *www.virginfirevi.com.*

$$$$ ITALIAN Fodor's Choice ★ 🍴 **Zozo's at the Sugar Mill.** Creative takes on old standards coupled with lovely presentations draw crowds to this restaurant at Caneel Bay Resort. Start with crispy fried calamari served with a pesto mayonnaise. The chef dresses up roasted mahimahi with a pistachio crust and serves it with grilled polenta and a sweet pepper chutney. The slow-simmered osso buco comes with prosciutto-wrapped asparagus and saffron risotto. The sunset views will take your breath away. [$] *Average main: $43* ✉ *Caneel Bay Resort, Rte. 20, Caneel Bay* ☎ *340/693–9200* 🌐 *www.zozos.net* 🕒 *No lunch.*

MID ISLAND

$$$ AMERICAN 🍴 **Chateau Bordeaux.** Your hamburgers and sweet-potato fries come with a side of fabulous views of Coral Bay and the British Virgin Islands. Breakfast is the star here, especially the Amaretto pancakes. This restaurant also serves salads made with local greens and fish sandwiches.

Dinner features Caribbean lobster. $ *Average main: $21* ⊠ *Rte. 10, Bordeaux, St. John* ☎ *340/776–6611* ⊕ *www.chateaubordeaux.net* ⊘ *No dinner Fri.–Mon. Closed Sun.*

CORAL BAY AND ENVIRONS

$$$
ECLECTIC
Fodor'sChoice
★

✕ **Café Concordia.** A stellar view and delightful food are good reasons to drive all the way out to Concordia for dinner. The menu changes daily, but the snapper with key lime butter is a good bet. The ever-popular Sunday brunch includes house-made granola with yogurt as well as croissant French toast with fresh fruit. $ *Average main: $24* ⊠ *Concordia Eco-Resort, off Rte. 107, Estate Concordia* ☎ *340/693–5855* ⊕ *www.concordiaeco-resort.com.*

$$$
CARIBBEAN

✕ **Miss Lucy's Restaurant.** Sitting seaside at remote Friis Bay, Miss Lucy's dishes up Caribbean food with a contemporary flair. Dishes such as tender conch fritters, a spicy West Indian stew called *kallaloo*, and fried fish make up most of the menu, but you also find a generous paella filled with seafood, sausage, and chicken on the menu. Sunday brunches are legendary, and if you're around when the moon is full, stop by for the monthly full-moon party. The handful of small tables near the water are the nicest, but if they're taken or the mosquitoes are swarming, the indoor tables do nicely. $ *Average main: $25* ⊠ *Rte. 107, Friis Bay* ☎ *340/693–5244* ⊘ *Closed Mon. No dinner Sun.*

$$$
AMERICAN

✕ **Shipwreck Landing.** A favorite with locals and visitors, this alfresco restaurant serves up tasty food in a casual setting. Opt for the tables closest to the road for the best breezes and water views. The menu includes lots of seafood, but the chicken and beef dishes ensure that everyone's satisfied. If it's a day when the chef has prepared homemade soup, try at least a cup. For lunch, the grilled mahimahi sandwich is always a good bet. $ *Average main: $22* ⊠ *Rte. 107, Freeman's Ground* ☎ *340/693–5640* ⊕ *www.shipwrecklandingstjohn.com.*

$
AMERICAN

✕ **Skinny Legs Bar and Restaurant.** Sailors who live aboard boats anchored offshore and an eclectic coterie of residents and visitors gather for lunch and dinner at this funky spot in the middle of a boatyard and shopping complex. It's a great place for burgers, fish sandwiches, and whatever sports are on the satellite TV. $ *Average main: $11* ⊠ *Rte. 10* ☎ *340/779–4982* ⊕ *www.skinnylegs.com.*

$$$
CARIBBEAN
FAMILY

✕ **Sweet Plaintains.** The food here is a sophisticated take on Caribbean cuisine. The fish of the day—it could be mahimahi or swordfish—is always especially good. Or try one of the curries if you don't want seafood. For a real local taste, start with the saltfish cakes served with shredded cabbage and mango puree. The coconut flan for dessert is another Caribbean favorite. $ *Average main: $26* ⊠ *Rte. 107* ☎ *340/777–4653* ⊕ *www.sweetplantains-stjohn.com* ⊘ *Closed Sun. and Tues. No lunch.*

$
ECLECTIC

✕ **Tourist Trap.** Lobster rolls in traditional crustless buns are the main event at this roadside eatery—really just a roadside shack—but the fish sandwiches, hot dogs with homemade chili, barbecue pork sandwiches, and nachos with homemade roasted tomatillo sauce make for a tasty lunch or snack. $ *Average main: $12* ⊠ *Rte. 107, Concordia*

☎ *340/774–0912* 🌐 *www.wedontneednostinkingwebsite.com* ⏲ *Closed Sun. and Mon. No dinner.*

$ CARIBBEAN 🍴 **Vie's Snack Shack.** Stop by Vie's when you're out exploring the island. Although it's just a shack by the side of the road, Vie's serves up some great cooking. The garlic chicken legs are crisp and tasty, and the conch fritters are really something to write home about. Plump and filled with fresh herbs, a plateful will keep you going for the rest of the afternoon. Save room for a wedge of coconut pie—called a tart in this neck of the woods. [$] *Average main: $12* ✉ *Rte. 10, Hansen Bay* ☎ *340/693–5033* 🌐 *www.hansenbaycampground.com* 💳 *No credit cards* ⏲ *Closed Sun. and Mon. No dinner.*

WHERE TO STAY

St. John attracts so many different kinds of travelers because accommodations come in all price ranges. Folks on a budget can sleep at Cinnamon Bay Campground. Cruz Bay has a few moderately priced guesthouses and no-frills vacation villas. Those with fatter wallets will have no trouble finding a room at the island's resorts or luxury vacation villas.

CONDOMINIUM RESORTS AND COTTAGES

St. John does have several resort-style condo complexes. Many of the island's condos are just minutes from the hustle and bustle of Cruz Bay, but you can find more scattered around the island.

PRIVATE CONDOS AND VILLAS

Here and there between Cruz Bay and Coral Bay are about 1,000 private villas and condos (prices range from $ to $$$$). With pools or hot tubs, full kitchens, and living areas, these lodgings provide a fully functional home away from home. They're perfect for couples and extended groups of family or friends. You need a car, since most lodgings are in the hills and very few are at the beach. Villa managers usually pick you up at the dock, arrange for your rental car, and answer questions upon arrival as well as during your stay. Prices drop in the summer season, which is generally after April 15. Some companies begin off-season pricing a week or two later, so be sure to ask.

If you want to be close to Cruz Bay's restaurants and boutiques, a villa in the Chocolate Hole and Great Cruz Bay areas will put you a few minutes away. The Coral Bay area has a growing number of villas, but you'll be about 20 minutes from Cruz Bay. Beaches string out along the north shore, so you won't be more than 15 minutes from the water no matter where you stay.

RENTAL AGENTS

Carefree Get-Aways. This company manages vacation villas on the island's southern and western edges. ☎ *340/779–4070, 888/643–6002* 🌐 *www.carefreegetaways.com.*

Caribbean Villas & Resorts. Caribbean Villas handles condo rentals for Cruz Views and Gallow's Point Resort, as well as for many private villas. ☎ *340/776–6152, 800/338–0987* 🌐 *www.caribbeanvilla.com.*

Caribe Havens. Specializing in the budget market, Caribe Havens has properties scattered around the island. ✉ *Box 455, Cruz Bay* ☎ *340/776–6518* 🌐 *www.caribehavens.com.*

Catered to Vacation Homes. Specializing in luxury villas, this company has listings mainly in the middle of the island and on the western edge. ✉ *Marketplace Suite 206, 5206 Enighed, Cruz Bay* ☎ *340/776–6641, 800/424–6641* 🌐 *www.cateredto.com.*

Cloud 9 Villas. Most of the offerings are in the East End, Gifft Hill, and Chocolate Hole areas. ☎ *340/774–9633* 🌐 *www.cloud9villas.com.*

Island Getaways. Options from Island Getaways are mainly villas in the Rendezvous, Chocolate Hole, and Coral Bay areas. ☎ *340/693–7676, 888/693–7676* 🌐 *www.islandgetawaysinc.com.*

On-Line Vacations. On-Line Vacations books villas for most management companies and is based on St. John. ☎ *340/776–6036, 888/842–6632* 🌐 *www.onlinevacations.com.*

Private Homes for Private Vacations. This company handles villa rentals across the island. ✉ *7605 Mamey Peak Rd., Coral Bay* ☎ *340/776–6876* 🌐 *www.privatehomesvi.com.*

Seaview Vacation Homes. As the name implies, this company's specialty are houses with views of the ocean: they are in the Chocolate Hole, Great Cruz Bay, and Fish Bay areas. ☎ *340/776–6805, 888/625–2963* 🌐 *www.seaviewhomes.com.*

Star Villas. Star has cozy villas just outside Cruz Bay. ☎ *340/776–6704* 🌐 *www.starvillas.com.*

St. John Ultimate Villas. St. John Ultimate Villas manages villas across the island. ☎ *340/776–4703, 888/851–7588* 🌐 *www.stjohnultimatevillas.com.*

Vacation Vistas. This company's villas are mainly in the Chocolate Hole, Great Cruz Bay, and Rendezvous areas. ☎ *340/776–6462* 🌐 *www.vacationvistas.com.*

Windspree. Windspree's stock is mainly in and around Coral Bay. ✉ *7924 Emmaus, Coral Bay* ☎ *340/693–5423, 888/742–0357* 🌐 *www.windspree.com.*

CRUZ BAY AND ENVIRONS

$$ RENTAL 🏨 **Coconut Coast Villas.** This small condominium complex with studio, two-, and three-bedroom apartments is a 10-minute walk from Cruz Bay, but is insulated from the town's noise in a sleepy suburban neighborhood. **Pros:** good snorkeling; full kitchens; walk to Cruz Bay. **Cons:** small beach; some uphill walks; nearby utility plant can be noisy. [$] *Rooms from: $289* ✉ *Near pond, Turner Bay* ☎ *340/693–9100, 800/858–7989* 🌐 *www.coconutcoast.com* 🛏 *9 units* 🍴 *No meals.*

$$ B&B/INN 🏨 **Estate Lindholm Bed and Breakfast.** Built among old stone ruins on a lushly planted hill overlooking Cruz Bay, Estate Lindholm has an enchanting setting. **Pros:** lush landscaping; gracious host; pleasant decor. **Cons:** can be noisy; some uphill walks; on a busy road. [$] *Rooms*

from: $365 ✉ Rte. 20, at Caneel Hill ☎ 340/776–6121, 800/322–6335 🌐 www.estatelindholm.com 🛏 14 rooms 🍴 Breakfast.

$$$$ RENTAL 🏨 **Gallows Point Resort.** You're a short walk from restaurants and shops at this waterfront location just outside Cruz Bay, but once you step into your condo, the hustle and bustle are left behind. **Pros:** walk to shopping; excellent restaurant; comfortably furnished rooms. **Cons:** some rooms can be noisy; mediocre beach; insufficient parking. [$] *Rooms from: $495 ✉ Bay St. ☎ 340/776–6434, 800/323–7229 🌐 www.gallowspointresort.com 🛏 60 units 🍴 No meals.*

$ B&B/INN 🏨 **Garden by the Sea Bed and Breakfast.** Located in a middle-class residential neighborhood, this cozy bed-and-breakfast is an easy walk from Cruz Bay. **Pros:** homey atmosphere; great breakfasts; breathtaking view from deck; near a bird-filled salt pond. **Cons:** noise from nearby power substation; some uphill walks; basic amenities. [$] *Rooms from: $250 ✉ Near pond, Enighed ☎ 340/779–4731 🌐 www.gardenbythesea.com 🛏 3 rooms 💳 No credit cards 🍴 Breakfast.*

$$$ RENTAL 🏨 **Grande Bay Resort.** Located just a few minutes' walk from Cruz Bay's restaurants and shops, this modern condominium complex puts you close to the town's hustle and bustle. **Pros:** close to restaurants and shops; modern decor; walking distance to the ferry. **Cons:** need car or taxi to reach island attractions and the best beaches; beach across the street is minimal. [$] *Rooms from: $405 ✉ Bay St. ☎ 340/693–4668 🌐 www.grandebayresortusvi.com 🛏 64 condos 🍴 Breakfast.*

$ B&B/INN 🏨 **Inn at Tamarind Court.** If money is a concern—and you don't want to go camping—opt for the Inn at Tamarind Court. **Pros:** walk to restaurants and shops; good breakfasts; convivial atmosphere. **Cons:** on a busy road; bland decor; need a car to get around. [$] *Rooms from: $148 ✉ Rte. 104 ☎ 340/776–6378, 800/221–1637 🌐 www.tamarindcourt.com 🛏 20 rooms 🍴 Breakfast.*

$$$$ RENTAL 🏨 **Sea Shore Allure.** Located at the water's edge in a residential neighborhood, Sea Shore Allure combines attractive and modern decor with an easy, and safe, walk to Cruz Bay's restaurants and shops. **Pros:** lovely decor; waterfront location; close to town. **Cons:** need car or taxi to get to beach; road passes through modest but safe local neighborhood. [$] *Rooms from: $510 ✉ Pond Mouth Rd., Turner Bay ☎ 340/779–2880, 855/779–2880 🌐 www.seashoreallure.com 🛏 8 units 🍴 No meals.*

$ RENTAL 🏨 **Serendip.** This complex offers modern apartments on lush grounds with lovely views and makes a great pick for a budget stay in a residential locale. **Pros:** comfortable accommodations; good views; nice neighborhood. **Cons:** no beach; need car to get around; nearby construction. [$] *Rooms from: $240 ✉ Off Rte. 104, Enighed ☎ 340/776–6646, 888/800–6445 🌐 www.serendipstjohn.com 🛏 10 apartments 🍴 No meals.*

$ B&B/INN 🏨 **St. John Inn.** A stay here gives you a bit of style at what passes for budget prices in St. John. **Pros:** walk to restaurants and shops; convivial atmosphere; pretty pool. **Cons:** need a car to get around; noisy location; insufficient parking. [$] *Rooms from: $200 ✉ Off Rte. 104 ☎ 340/693–8688, 800/666–7688 🌐 www.stjohninn.com 🛏 11 units 🍴 Breakfast.*

3

$$$$ ⬚ **Westin St. John Resort and Villas.** The island's largest resort provides a
RESORT   nice beachfront location and enough activities to keep you busy. **Pros:**
FAMILY   entertaining children's programs; pretty pool area; many activities.
Cons: mediocre beach; long walk to some parts of the resort; need
car to get around. [$] *Rooms from: $729* ✉ *Rte. 104, Great Cruz Bay*
☎ *340/693–8000, 888/627–7206* ⊕ *www.westinresortstjohn.com* ⤳ *96
rooms, 200 villas* ⦿ *No meals.*

NORTH SHORE

$$$ ⬚ **Caneel Bay Resort.** If you dream of spending your days on gorgeous
RESORT   beaches, paddling kayaks to and fro, and enjoying languorous din-
Fodor'sChoice   ners with your feet in the sand, there's no finer laid-back–luxury resort
★   on St. John. **Pros:** seven lovely beaches; gorgeous rooms; lots of ame-
nities. **Cons:** staff can be chilly; isolated location; pricey; no TVs or
phones (just a warning for tech-junkies). [$] *Rooms from: $459* ✉ *Rte.
20, Caneel Bay* ☎ *340/776–6111, 855/226–3358* ⊕ *www.caneelbay.
com* ⤳ *166 rooms* ⦿ *Breakfast.*

CORAL BAY AND ENVIRONS

$ ⬚ **Concordia Eco-Resort.** This off-the-beaten-path resort is on the remote
RENTAL   Salt Pond peninsula. **Pros:** good views; ecofriendly environment; beach
Fodor'sChoice   nearby. **Cons:** need car to get around; lots of stairs. [$] *Rooms from:*
★   *$195* ✉ *Off Rte. 107, Concordia* ☎ *340/693–5855, 800/392–9004*
⊕ *www.concordiaeco-resort.com* ⤳ *9 condos, 8 studios, 25 tents* ⦿ *No
meals.*

$$ ⬚ **Estate Zootenvaal.** Comfortable and casual, this small cottage col-
RENTAL   ony gives you the perfect place to relax. **Pros:** quiet beach; private;
near restaurants. **Cons:** some traffic noise; no air-conditioning in some
units. [$] *Rooms from: $290* ✉ *Rte. 10, Hurricane Hole, Zootenvaal*
☎ *340/776–6321* ⊕ *www.estatezootenvaal.com* ⤳ *4 units* ⦿ *No meals.*

NIGHTLIFE

St. John isn't the place to go for glitter and all-night partying. Still, after-
hours Cruz Bay can be a lively little town in which to dine, drink, dance,
or flirt. Notices posted on the bulletin board outside the Connections
telephone center—up the street from the ferry dock—or listings in the
island's newspaper (*Tradewinds*) will keep you apprised of local events.

CRUZ BAY AND ENVIRONS

Woody's. Folks like to gather here, where the sidewalk tables provide a
close-up view of Cruz Bay action. ✉ *Near First Bank* ☎ *340/779–4625*
⊕ *www.woodysseafood.com.*

Local St. John Celebrations

Although the U.S. Virgin Islands mark all of the same federal holidays as the mainland, they have a few of their own. Transfer Day, on March 31, commemorates Denmark's sale of the territory to the United States in 1917. Emancipation Day, on July 3, marks the date slavery was abolished in the Danish West Indies in 1848. Liberty Day, on November 1, honors David Hamilton Jackson, who secured freedom of the press and assembly from King Christian X of Denmark.

While you're on St. John, don't hesitate to attend local events like the annual Memorial Day and Veterans Day celebrations. These small parades give a poignant glimpse into island life. The St. Patrick's Day Parade is another blink-and-you'll-miss-it event. It's fun to join the islanders who come out decked in green. The annual Friends of Virgin Islands National Park meeting in January is another place to mix and mingle with the locals.

CORAL BAY AND ENVIRONS

Skinny Legs Bar and Restaurant. Landlubbers and old salts listen to music and swap stories at this popular casual restaurant and bar on the far side of the island. ⊠ *Rte. 10, Coral Bay* ☎ *340/779–4982* ⊕ *www.skinny legs.com.*

SHOPPING

CRUZ BAY AND ENVIRONS

Luxury goods and handicrafts can be found on St. John. Most shops carry a little of this and a bit of that, so it pays to poke around. The main Cruz Bay shopping district runs from **Wharfside Village,** just around the corner from the ferry dock, to **Mongoose Junction,** an inviting shopping center on North Shore Road. (The name of this upscale shopping mall, by the way, is a holdover from a time when those furry island creatures gathered at a nearby garbage bin.) Out on Route 104, the **Marketplace** has the island's only pharmacy. It also has a good selection of kid's beach toys. On St. John, store hours run from 9 or 10 to 5 or 6. Wharfside Village and Mongoose Junction shops in Cruz Bay are often open into the evening.

ART GALLERIES

Fodor'sChoice
★
Bajo el Sol. This gallery sells works by owner Livy Hitchcock, plus pieces from a roster of the island's best artists. You can also shop for oils, pastels, watercolors, and turned wood pieces. ⊠ *Mongoose Junction Shopping Center, North Shore Rd.* ☎ *340/693–7070* ⊕ *www. bajoelsolgallery.com.*

Caravan Gallery. Caravan sells affordable jewelry, unique gifts, and artifacts that its owner, Radha Speer, has traveled the world to find. The more you look, the more you see—Caribbean larimar jewelry, unusual sterling pieces, and tribal art cover the walls and tables, making this a great place to browse. ✉ *Mongoose Junction Shopping Center, North Shore Rd.* ☎ *340/779–4566* ⊕ *www.caravangallery.com.*

Coconut Coast Studios. This waterside shop, a five-minute walk from the center of Cruz Bay, showcases the work of Elaine Estern. She specializes in undersea scenes. ✉ *Frank Bay* ☎ *340/776–6944* ⊕ *www.coconut coaststudios.com.*

BOOKS

Friends of the Park Store. Find CDs, books, flip-flops made of coconut husks and recycled rubber, and more at this store run by the nonprofit group that raises money for Virgin Islands National Park. It's a great spot to buy educational materials for kids and books about the island. ✉ *Mongoose Junction Shopping Center, North Shore Rd.* ☎ *340/779–8700* ⊕ *www.friendsvinp.org.*

National Park Headquarters Bookstore. The bookshop at Virgin Islands National Park Visitor Center sells several good histories of St. John, including *St. John Back Time* by Ruth Hull Low and Rafael Lito Valls and, for intrepid explorers, longtime resident Pam Gaffin's *Feet, Fins and Four-Wheel Drive.* ✉ *Visitor Center, North Shore Rd.* ☎ *340/776–6201* ⊕ *www.nps.gov/viis.*

CLOTHING

Big Planet Adventure Outfitters. You knew when you arrived that someplace on St. John would cater to the outdoor enthusiasts who hike up and down the island's trails. This store sells flip-flops and Reef footwear, along with colorful and durable cotton clothing and accessories by Billabong. The store also sells children's clothes. ✉ *Mongoose Junction Shopping Center, North Shore Rd.* ☎ *340/776–6638* ⊕ *www.big-planet.com.*

Bougainvillea Boutique. This store is your destination if you want to look as if you've stepped out of the pages of the resort-wear spread in an upscale travel magazine. Owner Susan Stair carries very chic men's and women's clothes, straw hats, leather handbags, and fine gifts. ✉ *Mongoose Junction Shopping Center, North Shore Rd.* ☎ *340/693–7190* ⊕ *www.shoppingstjohn.com.*

FOOD

If you're renting a villa, condo, or cottage and doing your own cooking, there are several good places to shop for food, particularly in Cruz Bay; just be aware that prices are much higher than those at home.

Dolphin Market. This small store in Cruz Bay is a good source for fresh produce, deli items, and all the basics. ✉ *Boulon Center, Rte. 10* ☎ *340/776–5322.*

St. John Market. This store has good prices (for St. John) and a nice selection of fruits, veggies, and the basics, plus items you don't find at other stores—like soy flour. ✉ *Rte. 104, near the Westin Resort and Villas* ☎ *340/773–8290.*

Starfish Market. The island's largest store usually has the best selection of meat, fish, and produce. ✉ *The Marketplace, Rte. 104* ☎ *340/779–4949* ⊕ *www.starfishmarket.com.*

GIFTS

Bamboula. This multicultural boutique carries unusual housewares, rugs, bedspreads, accessories, and men's and women's clothes and shoes that owner Jo Sterling has found on her world travels. ⊠ *Mongoose Junction Shopping Center, North Shore Rd.* ☎ *340/693–8699* ⊕ *www.bamboula stjohn.com.*

Best of Both Worlds. Pricey metal sculptures and attractive artworks hang from the walls of this gallery; the nicest are small glass decorations shaped like mermaids and sea horses. ⊠ *Mongoose Junction Shopping Center, North Shore Rd.* ☎ *340/693–7005* ⊕ *www.thebestofstjohn.com.*

Donald Schnell Studio. You'll find distinctive clay pieces, unusual hand-blown glass, wind chimes, kaleidoscopes, fanciful fountains, and pottery bowls here. Your purchases can be shipped worldwide. ⊠ *Amore Center, Rte. 104, near roundabout* ☎ *340/776–6420* ⊕ *donaldschnell. com/studio.*

Fabric Mill. There's a good selection of women's clothing in tropical brights, as well as lingerie, sandals, and batik wraps here. Or take home several yards of colorful batik fabric to make your own dress. ⊠ *Mongoose Junction Shopping Center, North Shore Rd.* ☎ *340/776–6194* ⊕ *www.fabricmillstj.com.*

Gallows Point Gift and Gourmet. The store at Gallows Point Resort has a bit of this and a bit of that. Shop for Caribbean books and CDs, picture frames decorated with shells, and T-shirts with tropical motifs. Residents and visitors also drop by for a cup of coffee. ⊠ *Gallows Point Resort, Bay St.* ☎ *340/693–7730* ⊕ *www.stjohnadventures.com.*

Nest and Company. This small shop carries perfect take-home gifts in colors that reflect the sea. Shop here for soaps in tropical scents, dinnerware, and much more. ⊠ *Mongoose Junction Shopping Center, North Shore Rd.* ☎ *340/715–2552* ⊕ *www.nestvi.com.*

Pink Papaya. Head to this shop and art gallery for the work of long-time Virgin Islands resident Lisa Etre. There's also a huge collection of one-of-a-kind gifts, including bright tableware, trays, and tropical jewelry. ⊠ *Lemon Tree Mall, King St.* ☎ *340/693–8535* ⊕ *www.pink papaya.com.*

JEWELRY

Free Bird Creations. This is your on-island destination for special hand-crafted jewelry—earrings, bracelets, pendants, chains—as well as a good selection of water-resistant watches. ⊠ *Dockside Mall, next to ferry dock* ☎ *340/693–8625* ⊕ *www.freebirdcreations.com.*

Little Switzerland. A branch of the St. Thomas store, Little Switzerland carries diamonds and other jewels in attractive yellow- and white-gold settings, as well as strings of creamy pearls, watches, and other designer jewelry. ⊠ *Mongoose Junction Shopping Center, North Shore Rd.* ☎ *340/776–6007* ⊕ *www.littleswitzerland.com.*

R&I Patton goldsmithing. This store is owned by Rudy and Irene Patton, who design most of the lovely silver and gold jewelry on display. The rest comes from various designer friends. Sea fans (those large, lacy plants that sway with the ocean's currents) in filigreed silver, starfish and hibiscus pendants in silver or gold, and gold sand-dollar-shape charms and earrings are choice selections. ⊠ *Mongoose Junction Shopping Center, North Shore Rd.* ☎ *340/776–6548* ⊕ *www.pattongold.com.*

Verace. This store is filled with jewelry from such well-known designers as Toby Pomeroy and Patrick Murphy. Murphy's stunning gold sailboats with gems for hulls will catch your eye. ⊠ *Wharfside Village, Strand St.* ☎ *340/693–7599* ⊕ *www.verace.com.*

CORAL BAY AND ENVIRONS

At the island's East End, there are a few stores—selling clothes, jewelry, and artwork—here and there from the village of **Coral Bay** to the small complex at **Shipwreck Landing**.

CLOTHING

Jolly Dog. Head here for the stuff you forgot to pack. Sarongs in cotton and rayon, beach towels with tropical motifs, and hats and T-shirts sporting the "Jolly Dog" logo fill the shelves. ⊠ *Skinny Legs Shopping Complex, Rte. 10, Coral Bay* ☎ *340/693–5900.*

Sloop Jones. This store's worth the trip all the way out to the island's East End to shop for made-on-the-premises clothing and pillows, in fabrics splashed with tropical colors. The clothes are made from cotton, gauze, and modal, and are supremely comfortable. Sloop also holds painting workshops. ⊠ *Off Rte. 10, East End* ☎ *340/779–4001* ⊕ *www. sloopjones.com.*

FOOD

Calabash Market. If you're renting a villa on the island's southeast end or headed to Salt Pond or Lameshur Bay for the day, provision at this minimarket. The selection is quite good, and villa renters will find enough choices for simple meals and snacking. The store has an ATM machine. ⊠ *Rte. 107, Calabash Boom* ☎ *340/775–7172.*

Love City Mini Mart. The store may not look like much from the road, but it's one of the very few places to shop in Coral Bay and has a surprising selection. ⊠ *Off Rte. 107, Coral Bay* ☎ *340/693–5790.*

GIFTS

Mumbo Jumbo. With what may be the best prices in St. John, Mumbo Jumbo carries tropical clothing, stuffed sea creatures, and other gifty items in a cozy little shop. ⊠ *Skinny Legs Shopping Complex, Rte. 10* ☎ *340/779–4277.*

JEWELRY

Steinworks. Tucked away on the basement level of a small shopping center, this tiny shop sells hand-crafted jewelry in gold, silver, and other metals. Owner Sandi Stein also conjures up jewelry using your ideas. ⊠ *Cocoloba shopping center, Rte. 107* ☎ *340/776–8355* ⊕ *www. sandisteinworks.com.*

DID YOU KNOW?

Virgin Islands National Park was created through a donation of more than 5,000 acres of land purchased by Laurance S. Rockefeller at the urging of businessman Frank Stick.

SPORTS AND THE OUTDOORS

BOATING AND SAILING

If you're staying at a hotel, your activities desk will usually be able to help you arrange a sailing excursion aboard a nearby boat. Most day sails leaving Cruz Bay head out along St. John's north coast. Those that depart from Coral Bay might drop anchor at some remote cay off the island's east end or even in the nearby British Virgin Islands. Your trip usually includes lunch, beverages, and at least one snorkeling stop. Keep in mind that inclement weather could interfere with your plans, though most boats will still go out if rain isn't too heavy.

Ocean Runner. For a speedier trip to the cays and remote beaches off St. John, you can rent a powerboat with a captain from Ocean Runner. The company rents two-engine boats for $580 to $710 per day. Gas and oil will run you $100 to $300 a day extra, depending on how far you're going. ⊠ *Wharfside Village, waterfront, Cruz Bay* ☎ *340/693–8809* ⊕ *www.oceanrunnerusvi.com.*

Sail Safaris. Even novice sailors can take off in a small sailboat from Cruz Bay Beach to one of the small islands off St. John with Sail Safaris. ⊠ *Bay St., Cruz Bay* ☎ *340/626–8181* ⊕ *www.sailsafaris.net* ⌁ *From $80.*

St. John Concierge Service. The capable staff can find a charter sail or power boat that fits your style and budget. The company also books fishing and scuba trips. ⊠ *Henry Samuel St., across from post office, Cruz Bay* ☎ *340/514–5262* ⊕ *www.stjohnconciergeservice.com.*

DIVING AND SNORKELING

Although just about every beach has nice snorkeling—Trunk Bay, Cinnamon Bay, and Waterlemon Cay at Leinster Bay get the most praise—you need a boat to head out to the more remote snorkeling locations and the best scuba spots. Sign on with any of the island's water-sports operators to get to spots farther from St. John. If you use the one at your hotel, just stroll down to the dock to hop aboard. Their boats will take you to hot spots between St. John and St. Thomas, including the tunnels at **Thatch Cay**, the ledges at **Congo Cay**, and the wreck of the *General Rogers*. Dive off St. John at **Stephens Cay**, a short boat ride out of Cruz Bay, where fish swim around the reefs as you float downward. At **Devers Bay**, on St. John's south shore, fish dart about in colorful schools. **Carval Rock**, shaped like an old-time ship, has gorgeous rock formations, coral gardens, and lots of fish. It can be too rough here in winter, though. Count on paying $90 for a one-tank dive and $120 for a two-tank dive. Rates include equipment and a tour. If you've never dived before, try an introductory course called a resort course. Or if certification is in your vacation plans, the island's dive shops can help you get your card.

Continued on page 118

BELOW THE WAVES
By Lynda Lohr

Colorful reefs and wrecks rife with corals and tropical fish make the islands as interesting underwater as above. Brilliantly colored reef fish vie for your attention with corals in wondrous shapes. Scuba diving gets you up close and personal with the world below the waves.

Bright blue tangs and darting blue-headed wrasses. Corals in wondrous shapes—some look like brains, others like elk antlers. Colorful, bulbous sponges. All these and more can be spotted along the myriad reefs of the U.S. and British Virgin Islands. You might see a pink conch making its way along the ocean bottom in areas with seagrass beds. If you're really lucky, a turtle may swim into view, or a lobster may poke its antennae out of a hole in the reef or rocks. If you do a night dive, you might run into an octopus. But you may be surprised at how much you can see by simply hovering just below the surface, with nothing more than a mask and snorkel. It's a bird's-eye view, but an excellent one. Whether scuba diving or snorkeling, take along an underwater camera to capture memories of your exciting adventure. You can buy disposable ones at most dive shops or bring one from home.

DIVE AND SNORKELING SITES IN BRITISH VIRGIN ISLANDS

TORTOLA

Although a major base for dive operations in the BVI (due to its proximity to so many exceptional dive sites), Tortola itself doesn't have as much to offer divers. However, there are still some noteworthy destinations. The massive **Brewer's Bay Pinnacles** grow 70 feet high to within 30 feet of the surface; the rock mazes are only for advanced divers because of strong currents and they are not always acces-sible. Abundant reefs close to shore make **Brewer's Bay** popular with snorkelers, as are **Frenchman's Cay** and **Long Bay Beef Island. Diamond Reef,** between Great Camanoe and Scrub Island, is a small wall about 200 yards long. **Shark Point,** off the northeast coast of Scrub Island, does have resident sharks. Though isolated in open ocean, the wreck of the **Chikuzen,** a Japanese refrigerator ship, is a popular site.

THE ISLANDS OF THE SIR FRANCIS DRAKE CHANNEL

Southeast of Tortola lie a string of islands with some of the BVI's finest dive sites, some world famous. The wreck of the royal mail ship **Rhone** is between Peter and Salt islands and is, perhaps, the most famous dive site in the BVI. **Wreck Alley,** consisting of three sunken modern ships, is between Salt and Cooper islands. At **Alice in Wonderland,** south of Ginger Island, giant, mushroom-shaped corals shelter reef fish, moray eels, and crustaceans. **Alice's Backside,** off the northwestern tip of Ginger Island, is usually smooth enough for snorkeling and shallow enough so that beginner divers can get a good look at the myriad sealife and sponges.

The Chikuzen

North Bay

Great Harbour

Green Cay

Little Harbour

White Bay

Great Harbour

JOST VAN DYKE

Brewer's Bay Pinnacles

Trunk Bay

Josiah's Bay

Brewer's Bay

East End

Cane Garden Bay

Todman Pk

Fort Shirley

Road Town

Road Town Harbour

Carrot Bay

Long Bay

Mt. Sage

Great Thatch Island

West End

TORTOLA

SIR FRANCIS DRAK

Frenchman's Cay

Great Harbour

ST. JOHN

Peter Island

The Indians

Norman Island

White Bay

Big Reef Bay

Peter Island

Peter Island Bluff

Privateer Bay

Caves Norman Island

Money Bay

KEY

Dive Sites
Snorkel
Ferry

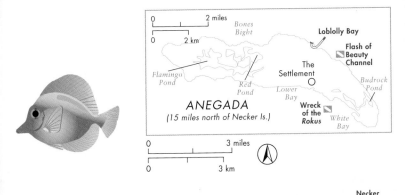

Bones
Bight

Loblolly Bay

**Flash of
Beauty
Channel**

The
Settlement

*Flamingo
Pond*

*Red
Pond*

*Lower
Bay*

*Budrock
Pond*

ANEGADA
(15 miles north of Necker Is.)

**Wreck
of the
*Rokus***

*White
Bay*

0   2 miles

0   2 km

0   3 miles

0   3 km

**Necker
Island**

**Eustatia
Island**

*Long
Bay*

*Berchers
Bay*

*North
Sound*

**Cockroach
Island**

North Bay **Shark
Point**

DOG ISLANDS

*Kitto
Ghut*

The Chimney

**Coral
Gardens**

*Virgin
Gorda
Peak*

*South
Sound*

**VIRGIN
GORDA**

*Scrub
Island*

*Great Dog
Island*

*Pond
Bay*

Anegada Passage

**Diamond
Reef**

*Handsome
Bay*

**Beef Island
International Airport**

The Aquarium

**Virgin Gorda
Airport**

**Spring
Bay**

**Spanish
Town**

*at Hogs
Bay*

*Long Bay Beef
Island*

The Baths

CHANNEL

**Alice's
Backside**

*Ginger
Island*

*Manchioneel
Bay*

**Cooper
Island**

**Ginger
Island**

**Alice in
Wonderland**

Rhone *Salt
Island*

**Wreck
Alley**

ANEGADA

Surrounded by the third-largest barrier reef in the world, Anegada has great snorkeling from virtually any beach on the island. But there are also some notable dive sites as well. The **Flash of**

Beauty Channel on the north shore is a great open-water dive, but only suitable for experienced divers. But even novices can enjoy diving at the **Wreck of the *Rokus***, a Greek cargo ship off the island's southern shore.

VIRGIN GORDA

The Baths, though busy, offers some of the best snorkeling in the Virgin Islands among giant boulders and the resulting grottoes. Nearby is **Spring Bay,** with fewer visitors and similar terrain. **The Aquarium,** close to Spanish Town and a good novice site, is so called because of the abundance of reef fish that swim around the submerged granite boulders that are similar to those of The Baths. Further west of Virgin Gorda, the Dog Islands have some in-

Virgin Gorda

teresting and popular sites, including **The Chimney,** a natural opening covered by sponges off Great Dog. South of Great Dog, **Coral Gardens** has a large coral reef with a submerged airplane wreck nearby. Fish are drawn to nearby **Cockroach Island.**

DIVE AND SNORKELING SITES IN U.S. VIRGIN ISLANDS

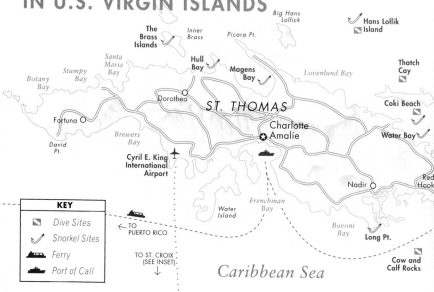

KEY

◣	*Dive Sites*
⌇	*Snorkel Sites*
⛴	*Ferry*
⛴	*Port of Call*

Big Hans Lollick

Hans Lollik Island

The Brass Islands

Inner Brass

Picara Pt.

Santa Maria Bay

Stumpy Bay

Botany Bay

Hull Bay

Magens Bay

Lovenlund Bay

Thatch Cay

Coki Beach

Dorothea

ST. THOMAS

Fortuna

Brewers Bay

Charlotte Amalie

Water Bay

David Pt.

Cyril E. King International Airport

Nadir

Red Hook

← TO PUERTO RICO

Water Island

Frenchman Bay

Bovoni Bay

Long Pt.

TO ST. CROIX (SEE INSET)

Caribbean Sea

Cow and Calf Rocks

ST. THOMAS

St. Thomas has at least 40 popular dive sites, most shallow. Favorite reef dives off St. Thomas include **Cow and Calf Rocks,** which barely break water off the southeast coast of St. Thomas; the coral-covered pinnacles of **Frenchcap** south of St. Thomas; and tunnels where you can explore undersea from the Caribbean to the Atlantic at **Thatch Cay** (where the Coast Guard cutter *General Rogers* rests at 65 feet). **Grass Cay** and **Mingo Cay** between St. Thomas

and St. John are also popular dive sites. **Coki Beach** offers the best off-the-beach snorkeling in St. Thomas. Nearby Coral World offers a dive-helmet walk for the untrained, and Snuba of St. Thomas has tethered shallow dives for non-certified divers. **Magens Bay,** the most popular beach on St. Thomas, provides lovely snorkeling if you head along the edges. You're likely to see some colorful sponges, darting fish, and maybe even a turtle if you're lucky. This is a stop on every island tour.

ST. JOHN

St. John is particularly known for its myriad good snorkeling spots—certainly more than for its diving opportunities, though there are many dive sites within easy reach of Cruz Bay. **Trunk Bay** often receives the most attention because of its underwater snorkeling trail created by the National Park Service; signs let you know what you're seeing in terms of coral and other underwater features. And the beach is easy to reach since taxis leave on demand from Cruz Bay.

A patchy reef just offshore means good snorkeling at **Hawksnest Beach.** Additionally, **Cinnamon Bay** and **Leinster Bay** also get their fair share of praise as snorkeling spots. That's not to say that you can't find good dive sites near St. John. **Deaver's Bay** is a short boat ride around the point from Cruz Bay, where you can see angelfish, southern stingrays, and triggerfish feeding at 30 to 50 feet. **The Leaf** is a large coral reef off St. John's southern shore.

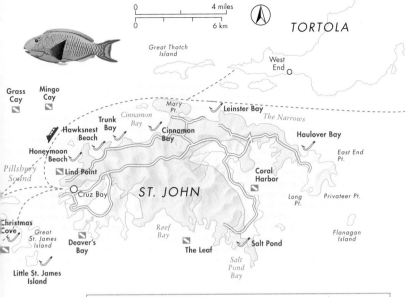

4 miles
6 km

TORTOLA

Great Thatch Island

West End

Grass Cay
Mingo Cay

Mary Pt.
Leinster Bay
The Narrows

Cinnamon Bay
Trunk Bay
Hawksnest Beach
Cinnamon Bay

Haulover Bay

East End Pt.

Honeymoon Beach

Pillsbury Sound

Lind Point

Coral Harbor

Cruz Bay

ST. JOHN

Long Pt.

Privateer Pt.

Christmas Cove

Great St. James Island

Reef Bay

Flanagan Island

Deaver's Bay

The Leaf

Salt Pond

Salt Pond Bay

Little St. James Island

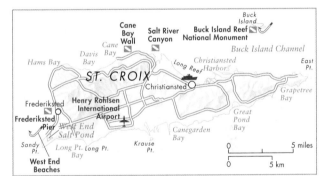

Cane Bay Wall

Salt River Canyon

Buck Island

Buck Island Reef National Monument

Cane Bay

Davis Bay

Buck Island Channel

Hams Bay

ST. CROIX

Long Reef

Christiansted Harbor

East Pt.

Christiansted

Grapetree Bay

Frederiksted

Henry Rohlsen International Airport

Frederiksted Pier

West End Salt Pond

Great Pond Bay

French Cap

Sandy Pt.

Long Pt. Long Pt. Bay

Krause Pt.

Canegarden Bay

5 miles
5 km

West End Beaches

Coral near St. Croix

ST. CROIX

The largest of the U.S. Virgin Islands is a favorite of both divers and snorkelers and offers something for everyone. Snorkelers are often fascinated by the marked snorkeling trail at **Buck Island Reef,** which is a short boat ride from the island's east end; it's a U.S. national monument. Divers are drawn to the north shore, especially the **Cane Bay Wall,** a spectacular drop-off that's reachable from the beach, though usually reached by boat. Another north-shore site is the **Salt River Canyon,** where you can float downward through a canyon filled with colorful fish and coral. On the island's west end, **Frederiksted Pier** is home to a colony of sea horses, creatures seldom seen in the waters of the Virgin Islands. Casual snorkelers would also enjoy snorkeling at the **West End Beaches.**

SCUBA DIVING

St.Croix

If you've never been diving, start with an introductory lesson—often called a "resort course"—run by any one of the Virgin Islands' dive shops. All meet stringent safety standards. If they didn't, they'd soon be out of business. If you're staying at a hotel, you can often find the dive shop on-site; otherwise, your hotel probably has an arrangement with one nearby. If you're on a cruise, cruise-ship companies offer shore excursions that include transportation to and from the ship as well as the resort course. Certification requires much more study and practice, but it is required to rent air tanks, get air refills, and join others on guided dives virtually anywhere in the world.

The number one rule of diving is safety. The basic rules for safe diving are simple, and fools ignore them at their own peril. Serious diving accidents are becoming increasingly rare these days, thanks to the high level of diver training. However, they do still occur occasionally. Surfacing too rapidly without exhaling—or going too deep for too long—can result in an air embolism or a case of the bends. Schneider Regional Medical Center in St. Thomas has a decompression chamber that serves all the Virgin Islands. If you get the bends, you'll be whisked to the hospital for this necessary treatment.

Fauna is another concern. Though sharks, barracuda, and moray eels are on the most-feared list, more often it's sea urchins and fire coral that cause pain when you accidentally bump them. Part of any scuba-training program is a

Divers learn how to jump in from a boat

St.Croix

review of sea life and the importance of respecting the new world you're exploring. Dive professionals recognize the value of protecting fragile reefs and ecosystems in tropical waters, and instructors emphasize look-don't-touch diving (the unofficial motto is: take only pictures, leave only bubbles). Government control and protection of dive sites is increasing, especially in such heavily used areas as the Virgin Islands.

While you can scuba dive off a beach—and you can find shops renting scuba equipment and providing airfills at the most popular beaches—a trip aboard a dive boat provides a more extensive glimpse into this wonderful undersea world. Since the dive shops can provide all equipment, there's no need to lug heavy weights and a bulky BC in your luggage. For the most comfort, you might want to bring your own regulator if you have one. The dive-boat captains and guides know the best dive locations, can find alternatives when the seas are rough, and will help you deal with heavy tanks and cumbersome equipment. Trips are easy to organize. Dive shops on all islands make frequent excursions to a wide variety of diving spots, and your hotel, villa manager, or cruise-ship staff will help you make arrangements.

If you fly too soon after diving, you're at risk for decompression sickness, which occurs when nitrogen trapped in your bloodstream doesn't escape. This creates a painful and sometimes fatal condition called the bends, not a sickness you want to develop while you're winging your way home after a fun-filled beach vacation. Opinions vary, but as a rule of thumb, wait at least 12 hours after a single dive to fly. However, if you've made multiple dives or dived several days in a row, you should wait at least 18 hours. If you've made dives that required decompression stops, you should also wait at least 24 hours before flying. To be safe, consult with your physician.

The Virgin Islands offer a plethora of dive sites, and you'll be taken to some of the best if you sign on to a dive trip run by one of the many dive operations scattered around the islands.

DIVER TRAINING

(top) Underwater shot of tropical reef, (bottom) Diver silhouette, Cane Bay, St Croix

Good to know: Divers can become certified through PADI *(www.padi.com)*, NAUI *(www.naui.org)*, or SSI *(www.divessi.com)*. The requirements for all three are similar, and if you do the classroom instruction and pool training with a dive shop associated with one organization, the referral for the open water dives will be honored by most dive shops. Note that you should not fly for at least 24 hours after a dive, because residual nitrogen in the body can pose health risks upon decompression. While there are no rigid rules on diving after flying, make sure you're well-hydrated before hitting the water.

NOT CERTIFIED?

Not sure if you want to commit the time and money to become certified? Not a problem. Most dive shops and many resorts will offer a discover scuba day-long course. In the morning, the instructor will teach you the basics of scuba diving: how to clear your mask, how to come to the surface in the unlikely event you lose your air supply, etc. In the afternoon, instructors will take you out for a dive in relatively shallow water— less than 30 feet. Be sure to ask where the dive will take place. Jumping into the water off a shallow beach may not be as fun as actually going out to the coral. If you decide that diving is something you want to pursue, the open dive may count toward your certification.

■ TIP➔ You can often book discover dives at the last minute. It may not be worth it to go out on a windy day when the currents are stronger. Also the underwater world looks a whole lot brighter on sunny days.

SNUBA

Beyond snorkeling or the requirements of scuba, you also have the option of "Snuba." The word is a trademarked portmanteau or combo of snorkel and scuba. Marketed as easy-to-learn family fun, Snuba lets you breathe underwater via tubes from an air-supplied vessel above, with no prior diving or snorkel experience required.

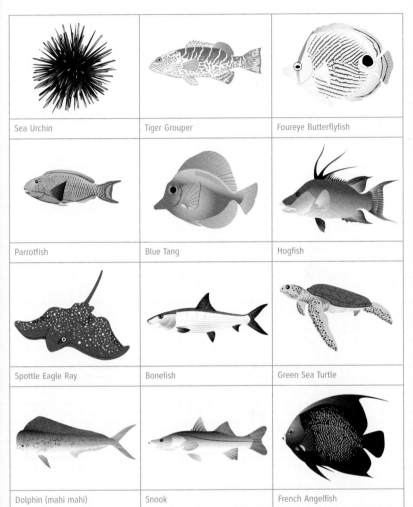

Sea Urchin	Tiger Grouper	Foureye Butterflyfish
Parrotfish	Blue Tang	Hogfish
Spottle Eagle Ray	Bonefish	Green Sea Turtle
Dolphin (mahi mahi)	Snook	French Angelfish

REEF CREATURES IN THE VIRGIN ISLANDS

From the striped sergeant majors to bright blue tangs, the reefs of the Virgin Islands are teeming with life, though not nearly as many as in eons past. Warming waters and pollution have taken their toll on both coral and fish species. But many reefs in the Virgin Islands still thrive; you'll also see sponges, crustaceans, perhaps a sea turtle or two, and bigger game fish like grouper and barracuda; sharks are seen but are rarely a problem for divers. Beware of fire corals, which are not really corals but rather a relative of the jellyfish and have a painful sting; if you brush up against a fire coral, spread vinegar on the wound as soon as possible to minimize the pain.

Cruz Bay Watersports. Cruz Bay Watersports offers regular reef, wreck, and night dives and USVI and BVI snorkel tours. The company holds both PADI Five Star and NAUI-Dream-Resort status. ✉ *Lumberyard Shopping Complex, Boulon Center Rd., Cruz Bay* ☎ *340/776–6234* ⊕ *www.cruzbaywatersports.com* ✉ *Westin St. John, Rte. 104, Great Cruz Bay* ☎ *340/776–6234.*

Low Key Watersports. Low Key Watersports offers two-tank dives and specialty courses. It's a PADI Five Star training facility. ✉ *1 Bay St., Cruz Bay* ☎ *340/693–8999, 800/835–7718* ⊕ *www.divelowkey.com.*

FISHING

Well-kept charter boats—approved by the U.S. Coast Guard—head out to the north and south drops or troll along the inshore reefs, depending on the season and what's biting. The captains usually provide bait, drinks, and lunch, but you need to bring your own hat and sunscreen. Fishing charters start at about $1,100 for a full-day trip.

FAMILY **Offshore Adventures.** An excellent choice for fishing charters, Captain Rob Richards is patient with beginners—especially kids—but also enjoys going out with more experienced anglers. He runs the 40-foot center console *Mixed Bag I* and 32-foot *Mixed Bag II*. Although he's based in St. John, he will pick up parties in St. Thomas. ✉ *Westin St. John, 3008 Chocolate Hole Rd., Great Cruz Bay, St. John* ☎ *340/513–0389* ⊕ *www.sportfishingstjohn.com.*

GUIDED TOURS

In St. John, taxi drivers provide tours of the island, making stops at various sites, including Trunk Bay and Annaberg Plantation. Prices run around $15 a person. The taxi drivers congregate near the ferry in Cruz Bay. The dispatcher will find you a driver for your tour. Along with providing trail maps and brochures about Virgin Islands National Park, the park service also gives several guided tours on- and offshore. Some are offered only during particular times of the year, and some require reservations.

V.I. National Park Visitors Center ✉ *North Shore Rd., near creek, Cruz Bay* ☎ *340/776–6201* ⊕ *www.nps.gov/viis.*

HIKING

Although it's fun to go hiking with a Virgin Islands National Park guide, don't be afraid to head out on your own. To find a hike that suits your ability, stop by the park's visitor center in Cruz Bay and pick up the free trail guide; it details points of interest, trail lengths, and estimated hiking times, as well as any dangers you might encounter. Although the park staff recommends long pants to protect against thorns and insects, most people hike in shorts because it can get very hot. Wear sturdy shoes or hiking boots even if you're hiking to the beach. Don't forget to bring water and insect repellent.

Fodor's Choice **Virgin Islands National Park.** Head to the park for more than 20 trails on
★ the north and south shores, with guided hikes along the most popular
routes. A full-day trip to Reef Bay is a must; it's an easy hike through
lush and dry forest, past the ruins of an old plantation, and to a sugar
factory adjacent to the beach. It can be a bit arduous for young kids,
however. The park runs a $30 guided tour to Reef Bay that includes
a safari bus ride to the trailhead and a boat ride back to the Visitors
Center. The schedule changes from season to season; call for times and
to make reservations, which are essential. ⊠ *North Shore Rd., near
creek, Cruz Bay* ☎ *340/776–6201* ⊕ *www.nps.gov/viis.*

HORSEBACK RIDING

Carolina Corral. Clip-clop along the island's byways for a slower-pace
tour of St. John. Carolina Corral offers horseback trips and wagon
rides down scenic roads with owner Dana Barlett. She has a way with
horses and calms even the most novice riders. ⊠ *Off Rte. 10, Coral Bay*
☎ *340/693–5778* ⊕ *www.carolinacorral.com* ⌖ *$75 for one-hour ride.*

SEA KAYAKING

Poke around crystal bays and explore undersea life from a sea kayak.
Rates run about $110 for a full day in a double kayak. Tours start at
$75 for a half day.

Arawak Expeditions. This company uses traditional and sit-on-top kayaks
for exploring the waters around St. John on guided tours. ⊠ *Mongoose
Junction Shopping Center, North Shore Rd., Cruz Bay* ☎ *340/693–
8312, 800/238–8687* ⊕ *www.arawakexp.com* ⌖ *From $75 per person.*

Crabby's Watersports. Explore Coral Bay Harbor and Hurricane Hole
on the eastern end of the island in a sea kayak or a stand-up paddleboard from Crabby's Watersports. Crabby's also rents snorkel
gear, beach chairs, umbrellas, coolers, and floats. ⊠ *Rte. 107, next
to Cocoloba shopping center, Coral Bay* ☎ *340/714–2415* ⊕ *www.
crabbyswatersports.com.*

Hidden Reef EcoTours. Coral reefs, mangroves, and lush sea-grass beds
filled with marine life are what you can see on Hidden Reef's two-
and three-hour, full-day and full-moon kayak tours through Coral
Reef National Monument and its environs. ⊠ *Rte. 10, Round Bay*
☎ *340/513–9613, 877/529–2575* ⊕ *www.kayaksj.com.*

WINDSURFING

Cinnamon Bay Campground. Steady breezes and expert instruction make
learning to windsurf a snap. Try Cinnamon Bay Campground, where
rentals are $40 to $100 per hour. Lessons are available right at the
waterfront; just look for the Windsurfers stacked up on the beach. The
cost for a one-hour lesson starts at $60, plus the cost of the board rental.
You can also rent kayaks, stand-up paddle boards, Boogie boards, small
sailboats, and surfboards. ⊠ *Rte. 20, Cinnamon Bay* ☎ *340/693–5902,
340/626–4769* ⊕ *www.windnsurfingadventures.com.*

ST. CROIX

WELCOME TO ST. CROIX

TOP REASONS TO GO

★ **Sailing to Buck Island:** The beach at the western end of the island is a great spot to relax after a snorkeling adventure or a hike up the hill to take in the stunning view.

★ **Diving the Wall:** Every dive boat in St. Croix makes a trip to the Wall, one of the Caribbean's best diving experiences, but you can also enjoy great shore diving from Cane Bay Beach.

★ **Exploring Fort Christiansvaern:** History buffs flock to Christiansted National Historic Site. Head to the upper ramparts of Fort Christiansvaern to ponder how life was for early settlers.

★ **Experiencing plantation life:** Whim Plantation showcases St. Croix's agrarian past. The estate has been lovingly restored.

★ **Strolling around Christiansted:** You can easily while away the better part of a day in Christiansted, St. Croix's main town. The shops carry everything from one-of-a-kind artworks to handcrafted jewelry to simple souvenirs.

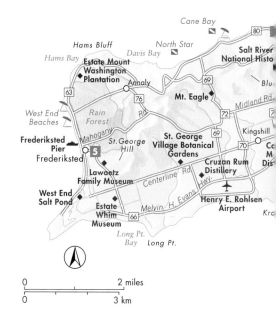

1 Christiansted. The island's main town has restaurants, shops, and a few places to stay.

2 West of Christiansted. This busy area includes a handful of condos and restaurants in Estates Golden Rock and Princesse.

3 East End. Most of the larger resorts are on the East End of St. Croix, but there are also some hidden treasures to explore.

4 Mid Island. This extensive area includes a small patch of rain forest, a handful of historic sites, the island's biggest shopping center at Sunny Isles, and a bed-and-breakfast.

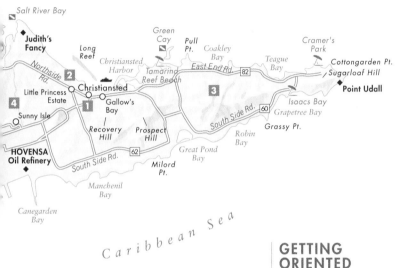

Buck Island

Buck Island Reef
National Monument

Salt River Bay

**Judith's
Fancy**

Long
Reef

Green
Cay

Pull
Pt.

Coakley
Bay

Cramer's
Park

Christiansted
Harbor

Tamarind
Reef Beach

East End Rd.

Teague
Bay

Cottongarden Pt.

Sugarloaf Hill

Northside
Rd.

2

Christiansted

3

Point Udall

Little Princess
Estate

1

Gallow's
Bay

4

Sunny Isle

Recovery
Hill

Prospect
Hill

South Side Rd.

Isaacs Bay

Grapetree Bay

Grassy Pt.

Robin
Bay

**HOVENSA
Oil Refinery**

South Side Rd.

Great Pond
Bay

Milord
Pt.

Manchenil
Bay

Canegarden
Bay

C a r i b b e a n   S e a

5 **Frederiksted.** The
island's westernmost settlement has a smattering of
stores, restaurants, activities,
and the island's cruise pier.

6 **North Shore.** Divers
head to Cane Bay, while
Salt River Bay has excel-
lent kayaking and diving
opportunities.

GETTING ORIENTED

Although there are things
to see and do in St. Croix's
two towns, Christiansted and
Frederiksted (both named
after Danish kings), there
are lots of interesting spots
in between them and to the
east of Christiansted. Just
be sure you have a map
in hand (pick one up at a
rental-car agency, or stop
by the tourist office for an
excellent one that's free).
Many secondary roads
remain unmarked; if you get
confused, ask for help. Locals
are always ready to point
you in the right direction.

Updated by Carol Buchanan

The largest of the USVI, St. Croix is 40 miles (64 km) south of St. Thomas. Plantation ruins, reminiscent of the days when St. Croix was a great producer of sugar, dot the island. Its northwest is covered by a lush rain forest, its drier East End spotted with cacti. The restored Danish port of Christiansted and the more Victorian-looking Frederiksted are its main towns; Buck Island, off the island's northeast shore, attracts many day visitors.

Until 1917 Denmark owned St. Croix and her sister Virgin Islands, an aspect of the island's past that is reflected in street names in the main towns of Christiansted and Frederiksted, as well as the surnames of many island residents. Those early settlers from Denmark and other European nations left behind slews of 18th- and 19th-century plantation ruins, all of them worked by slaves brought over on ships from Africa, their descendants, and white indentured servants lured to St. Croix to pay off their debt to society. Some of these ruins—such as the Christiansted National Historic site, Whim Plantation, the ruins at St. George Village Botanical Garden, and the ruins at Estate Mount Washington and Judith's Fancy—are open for easy exploration. Others are on private land, but a drive around the island passes the ruins of 100 plantations here and there on St. Croix's 84 square miles (218 square km). Their windmills, greathouses, and factories are all that's left of the 224 plantations that once grew sugarcane, tobacco, and other agricultural products at the height of the island's plantation glory.

The downturn began in 1801, when the British occupied the island. The demise of the slave trade in 1803, another British occupation from 1807 to 1815, droughts, the development of the sugar-beet industry in Europe, political upheaval, and a depression sent the island on a downward economic spiral.

St. Croix never recovered from these blows. The freeing of all of the slaves in the Virgin Islands in 1848, followed by labor riots, fires, hurricanes, and an earthquake during the last half of the 19th century, brought what was left of the island's economy to its knees. The start of Prohibition in 1922 called a halt to the island's rum industry, further crippling the economy. The situation remained dire—so bad that President Herbert Hoover called the territory an "effective poorhouse" during a 1931 visit—until the rise of tourism in the late 1950s and 1960s. With tourism came economic improvements coupled with an influx of residents from other Caribbean islands and the mainland. For years Hovensa Oil Refinery was an economic stimulus, until it shuttered its doors in 2012. Currently, the economy is struggling and a number of businesses have closed.

Today suburban subdivisions fill the fields where sugarcane once waved in the tropical breeze. Condominium complexes line the beaches along the north coast outside Christiansted. Homes that are more elaborate dot the rolling hillsides. Modern strip malls and shopping centers sit along major roads, and it's as easy to find a McDonald's as it is Caribbean fare.

Although St. Croix sits definitely in the 21st century, with only a little effort you can easily step back into the island's past.

GETTING HERE AND AROUND

AIR TRAVEL

While St. Croix is not as well served as St. Thomas when it comes to nonstop flights from the United States, you will still be able to fly nonstop from Atlanta (on Delta) or from Miami (on American Airlines). You can also get connecting service through San Juan or St. Thomas via Cape Air, which offers code-share arrangements with all major airlines, so your luggage can transfer seamlessly. Seaborne Airlines flies between St. Thomas, St. Croix, and San Juan.

Airports **Henry Rohlsen Airport** ✉ *Estate Mannings Bay, Christiansted* ☎ *340/778–1012* ⊕ *www.viport.com.*

BUS TRAVEL

Privately owned taxi vans crisscross St. Croix regularly, providing reliable service between Frederiksted and Christiansted along Route 70. This inexpensive ($2.50 one way) mode of transportation is favored by locals, and though the many stops on the 20-mile (32-km) drive between the two main towns make the ride slow, it's never dull. Vitran public buses aren't the quickest way to get around the island, but they're comfortable and affordable. The fare is $1 between Christiansted and Frederiksted or to places in between.

CAR TRAVEL

You can certainly get by without a car, particularly if your hotel is close to Christiansted and offers a shuttle into town, but more than on most of the other Virgin Islands, having a car is a big advantage on St. Croix. With a wide variety of good restaurants and no large concentration of accommodations around either Christiansted or Frederiksted, a car can be very helpful regardless of where you are staying. Accommodations along the north shore are even more isolated, making a car more of a necessity to travelers staying there. Even if you are staying in or near

Christiansted, you might want to rent a car for a day or two so you can explore the island.

Although roads are not well sign-posted, there's a highway from the airport to the East End of the island that makes travel fairly easy. Street parking can be hard to find in Christiansted, but there are some paid lots. Just remember that you drive on the *left* even though cars are U.S.–made with steering wheels on the left.

CAR RENTALS

Avis is at Henry Rohlsen Airport and at the seaplane ramp in Christiansted. Budget has branches at the airport and near the seaplane terminal in Christiansted. Hertz is at the airport. Judi of Croix delivers vehicles to your hotel. Olympic is outside Christiansted, but will pick up at hotels.

Contacts Avis ⊠ *Henry E. Rohlsen Airport* ☏ *340/778–9355, 800/354–2847* ⊕ *www.avis.com* ⊠ *Seaplane, Christiansted* ☏ *340/713–9355.* **Budget** ⊠ *Henry E. Rohlsen Airport* ☏ *340/778–9636, 888/264–8894* ⊕ *www.budgetstcroix. com* ⊠ *Prince St., across from Seaplane, Christiansted* ☏ *340/713–9289.* **Hertz** ⊠ *Henry E. Rohlsen Airport* ☏ *340/778–1402, 888/248–4261* ⊕ *www. rentacarstcroix.com.* **Judi of Croix** ☏ *340/773–2123, 877/903–2123* ⊕ *www. judiofcroix.com.* **Olympic** ⊠ *Rte. 70, Christiansted* ☏ *340/718–3000, 888/878– 4227* ⊕ *www.olympicstcroix.com.*

TAXI TRAVEL

Taxis are available in downtown Christiansted, at the Henry E. Rohlsen Airport, and at the Frederiksted pier during cruise-ship arrivals, or they can be called. In Frederiksted, all the shops are a short walk away, as is a great beach, so there's no need for a taxi if you are staying in town. Most cruise-ship passengers visit Christiansted on a tour since a taxi will cost $25 for one or two people (one way).

Contacts Antilles Taxi Service ⊠ *Christiansted* ☏ *340/773–5020.* **St. Croix Taxi Association** ⊠ *Henry E. Rohlsen Airport* ☏ *340/778–1088* ⊕ *www.stcroix taxi.com.*

ESSENTIALS

BANKS

St. Croix has branches of Banco Popular in the Orange Grove and Sunny Isle shopping centers. FirstBank is in Sunny Isle, Frederiksted, and Orange Grove. Scotia Bank has branches in Sunny Isle, Christiansted, and Sunshine Mall.

HOTELS

You can find everything from plush resorts to simple beachfront digs in St. Croix. If you sleep in either the Christiansted or Frederiksted area, you'll be closest to shopping, restaurants, and nightlife. Most of the island's other hotels will put you just steps from the beach. St. Croix has several small but special properties that offer personalized service. If you like all the comforts of home, you may prefer to stay in a condominium or villa. Whether you stay in a hotel, a condominium, or a villa, you'll enjoy up-to-date amenities.

Our hotel reviews have been shortened. For full information, go to Fodors.com.

RESTAURANTS

Seven flags have flown over St. Croix, and each has left its legacy in the island's cuisine. You can feast on Italian, French, and American dishes; there are even Chinese and Mexican restaurants in Christiansted. Fresh local seafood is plentiful and always good; wahoo, mahimahi, and conch are most popular. Island chefs often add Caribbean twists to familiar dishes. For a true island experience, stop at a local restaurant for goat stew, curried chicken, or ribs. Regardless of where you eat, your meal will be an informal affair. As is the case everywhere in the Caribbean, prices are higher than you'd pay on the mainland. Some restaurants may close for a week or two in September or October, so if you're traveling during these months it's best to call ahead.

WHAT IT COSTS IN U.S. DOLLARS				
	$	$$	$$$	$$$$
Restaurants	under $13	$13–$20	$21–$30	over $30
Hotels	under $276	$276–$375	$376–$475	over $475

Restaurant prices are the average cost of a main course at dinner or, if dinner is not served, at lunch. Hotel prices are the lowest cost of a standard double room in high season.

SAFETY

Don't wander the streets of Christiansted or Frederiksted alone at night. Don't leave valuables in your car, and keep it locked wherever you park. Don't leave cameras, purses, and other valuables lying on the beach while you snorkel for an hour (or even for a minute).

SCUBA DIVING EMERGENCIES

Roy L. Schneider Hospital on St. Thomas has the territory's only hyperbaric chamber.

Roy L. Schneider Hospital ⊠ *Sugar Estate, St. Thomas* ☎ *340/776–8311* ⊕ *www.rlshospital.org.*

TOUR OPTIONS

St. Croix Transit offers van tours of the island. Tours depart from Carambola Beach Resort, last about three hours, and cost from $65 per person. Sweeny's St. Croix Safari Tours offers van tours of St. Croix. Excursions depart from Christiansted and last about five hours starting at $70 per person. Walking tours of Christiansted's historic sites run $25.

Contacts St. Croix Transit ☎ 340/772–3333. **Sweeny's St. Croix Safari Tours** ⊠ Christiansted ☎ 340/773–6700 ⊕ www.gotostcroix.com.

VISITOR INFORMATION

If you want some friendly advice, stop by the St. Croix Visitor Center weekdays between 8 and 5 for maps and brochures.

Contacts **St. Croix Visitor Center** ⊠ *Frederiksted Pier, Strand St., Frederiksted* ☎ *340/773–0495* ⊕ *www.visitusvi.com.* **USVI Department of Tourism** ⊠ *321 King St., Frederiksted* ☎ *340/772–0357* ⊕ *www.visitusvi.com.*

EXPLORING ST. CROIX

CHRISTIANSTED

Christiansted is a historic Danish-style town that always served as St. Croix's commercial center. Your best bet is to see the historic sights in the morning, when it's still cool. Break for lunch at an open-air restaurant before spending as much time as you like shopping.

In the 1700s and 1800s Christiansted was a trading center for sugar, rum, and molasses. Today there are law offices, tourist shops, and restaurants, but many of the buildings, which start at the harbor and go up the gently sloped hillsides, still date from the 18th century. You can't get lost. All streets lead back downhill to the water.

TOP ATTRACTIONS

FAMILY

Fodor's Choice
★

Fort Christiansvaern. The large yellow fortress dominates the waterfront. Because it's so easy to spot, it makes a good place to begin a walking tour. In 1749 the Danish built the fort to protect the harbor, but the structure was repeatedly damaged by hurricane-force winds and had to be partially rebuilt in 1771. It's now a National Historic site, the best preserved of the few remaining Danish-built forts in the Virgin Islands. The park's visitor center is here. Rangers are on hand to answer questions. ■ TIP→ Your paid admission also includes the Steeple Building. ⊠ *Hospital St.* ☎ *340/773–1460* ⊕ *www.nps.gov/chri* ☞ *$3* ☉ *Weekdays 8:30–4:30, weekends 9–4:30.*

WORTH NOTING

Apothecary Hall. If you're strolling downtown Christiansted's streets, it's worth a peek into the Christiansted Apothecary Hall. Although the exhibits are behind Plexiglas, they give you a glimpse into a 19th-century pharmacy. This tiny museum is at the original location of a pharmacy that operated from 1816 to 1970. ⊠ *Company and Queen Sts.* ⊕ *www.stcroixlandmarks.com* ☞ *Free* ☉ *Mon.–Sat. 10–5.*

D. Hamilton Jackson Park. When you're tired of sightseeing, stop at this shady park on the street side of Fort Christiansvaern for a rest. It's named for a famed labor leader, judge, and journalist who started the first newspaper not under the thumb of the Danish crown (his birthday, November 1, is a territorial holiday celebrated with much fanfare in St. Croix). ⚠ There are no facilities. ⊠ *Between Fort Christiansvaern and Danish Customs House.*

Danish Customs House. Built in 1830 on foundations that date from a century earlier, the historic building, which is near Fort Christiansvaern, originally served as both a customshouse and a post office. In 1926 it became the Christiansted Library, and it's been a National Park facility since 1972. It's closed to the public, but the sweeping front steps make a nice place to take a break. ⊠ *King St.* ☎ *340/773–1460* ⊕ *www.nps. gov/chri.*

Government House. One of the town's most elegant structures was built as a home for a Danish merchant in 1747. Today it houses offices. If you're here weekdays from 8 to 4:30, slip into the peaceful inner courtyard to admire the still pools and gardens. A sweeping staircase leads you to a second-story ballroom, still used for official government functions. ⊠ *King St.* ☎ *340/773–1404.*

Post Office Building. Built in 1749, Christiansted's former post office was once the Danish West India & Guinea Company warehouse. It now serves as the National Park's administrative building. ⊠ *Church St.*

Scale House. Constructed in 1856, this was once the spot where goods passing through the port were weighed and inspected. The park staffers here have on offer a good selection of books about St. Croix history and its flora and fauna. ⊠ *King St.* ☎ *340/773–1460* ⊕ *www.nps.gov/chri.*

Steeple Building. The first Danish Lutheran church on the island when it was built in 1753, the Steeple Building is now used as a museum. It's worth the short walk to see the archaeological artifacts and exhibits on plantation life, the architectural development of Christiansted, the island's native inhabitants, and Alexander Hamilton, who grew up in St. Croix. Hours are irregular, so ask at the visitor center. ■TIP➔ Your paid admission includes Fort Christiansvaern, too. ⊠ *Church St.* ☎ *340/773– 1460* ⌧ *$3.*

WEST OF CHRISTIANSTED

Heading west from Christiansted there are few sights worth seeing, but it's a busy area with a handful of condos and Carringtons Inn, a standout bed-and-breakfast *(see review in Where to Stay)*, as well as a few restaurants in Estates Golden Rock and Princesse.

EAST END

An easy drive (roads are flat and well marked) to St. Croix's eastern end takes you through some choice real estate. Ruins of old sugar estates dot the landscape. You can make the entire loop on the road that circles the island in about an hour, a good way to end the day. If you want to spend a full day exploring, you can find some nice beaches and easy walks with places to stop for lunch.

WORTH NOTING

Buck Island Reef National Monument. Buck Island has pristine beaches that are just right for sunbathing, but there's also some shade for those who don't want to fry. The snorkeling trail set in the reef allows close-up study of coral formations and tropical fish. Overly warm seawater temperatures have led to a condition called coral bleaching that has killed some of the coral. The reefs are starting to recover, but how long it will take is anyone's guess. There's an easy hiking trail to the island's highest point, where you can be rewarded for your efforts by spectacular views of St. John. Charter-boat trips leave daily from the

DID YOU KNOW?

Some of St. Croix's best beaches are on the west end of the island north and south of Frederiksted. All sit right along the road.

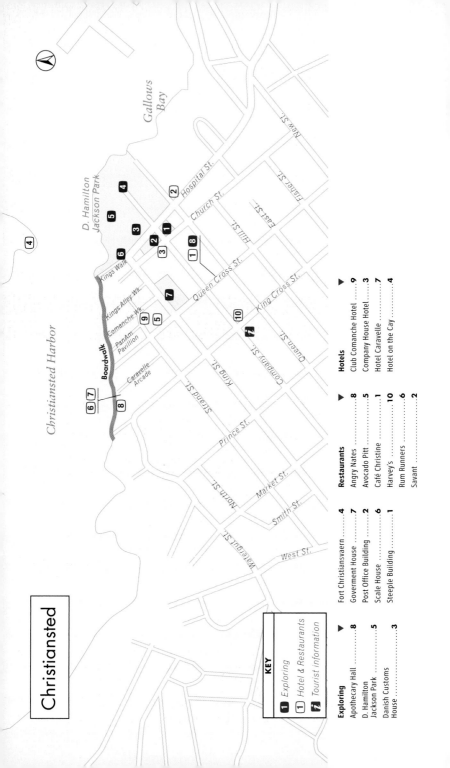

Christiansted

Christiansted Harbor

Gallows Bay

D. Hamilton Jackson Park

Kings Walk

Kings Alley Wk.

Comanche Wk.

PanAm Pavillion

Caravelle Arcade

Boardwalk

Hospital St.

Church St.

Queen Cross St.

King Cross St.

New St.

Fisher St.

East St.

Hill St.

Queen St.

Company St.

King St.

Strand St.

Prince St.

Market St.

Smith St.

West St.

North St.

Watergut St.

KEY

▶ Exploring

① Hotel & Restaurants

☛ Tourist Information

Exploring   ▶

Apothecary Hall **8**

D. Hamilton
Jackson Park **5**

Danish Customs
House **3**

Fort Christiansvaern **4**

Goverment House **7**

Post Office Building **2**

Scale House **6**

Steeple Building **1**

Restaurants   ▶

Angry Nates **8**

Avocado Pitt **5**

Café Christine **1**

Harvey's **10**

Rum Runners **6**

Savant **2**

Hotels   ▶

Club Comanche Hotel **9**

Company House Hotel **3**

Hotel Caravelle **7**

Hotel on the Cay **4**

Fort Christiansvaern, a National Historic site

Christiansted waterfront or from Green Cay Marina, about 2 miles (3 km) east of Christiansted. Check with your hotel for recommendations. ✉ *Off North Shore of St. Croix* ☎ *340/773–1460* ⊕ *www. nps.gov/buis.*

Point Udall. This rocky promontory, the easternmost point in the United States, is about a half-hour drive from Christiansted. A paved road

BIG EVENT

St. Croix celebrates Carnival in late December with the St. Croix Christmas Festival. If you don't book far ahead, it can be hard to find a room because of the influx of visitors from around the region and around the world.

takes you to an overlook with glorious views. More adventurous folks can hike down to the pristine beach below. On the way back, look for the Castle Aura, an enormous Moorish-style mansion. It was built by Nadia Farber, the former Contessa de Navarro, who's an extravagant local character. ⚠ Point Udall is sometimes a popular spot for thieves, so don't leave anything valuable in your car, and keep it locked. ✉ *Rte. 82, Et Stykkeland.*

MID ISLAND

A drive through the countryside between Christiansted and Frederiksted will take you past ruins of old plantations, many bearing whimsical names (Morningstar, Solitude, Upper Love) bestowed by early owners. The traffic moves quickly—by island standards—on the main roads, but you can pause and poke around if you head down some side lanes. It's easy to find your way west, but driving from north to south requires

Sea turtles nest in several places on St. Croix.

good navigation. Don't leave your hotel without a map. Allow an entire day for this trip, so you'll have enough time for a swim at a north-shore beach. Although you can find lots of casual eateries on the main roads, pick up a picnic lunch if you plan to head off the beaten path.

WORTH NOTING

Captain Morgan Distillery. The base for Captain Morgan brand rum is made from molasses at this distillery. The tour includes exhibits on island and rum history; a movie about the process; and a tram tour of the distillery. In keeping with the company's responsible-drinking policy, the drink samples at the end of the tour are limited to two. ✉ *Melvin Evans Hwy. and Rte. 663, Annaberg and Shannon Grove* ☎ *340/713–5654* ⊕ *www.captainmorgan.com* ✉ *$10* ⊗ *Weekdays 9–5.*

Cruzan Rum Distillery. A tour of the company's factory, which was established in 1760, culminates in a tasting of its products, all sold here at good prices. It's worth a stop to look at the distillery's charming old buildings even if you're not a rum connoisseur. ✉ *West Airport Rd., Estate Diamond* ☎ *340/692–2280* ⊕ *www.cruzanrum.com* ✉ *$8* ⊗ *Weekdays 9–4.*

FREDERIKSTED

St. Croix's second-largest town, Frederiksted was founded in 1751. While Christiansted is noted for its Danish buildings, Frederiksted is better known for its Victorian architecture. One long cruise-ship pier juts into the sparkling sea. It's the perfect place to start a tour of this quaint city. A stroll around its historic sights will take you no more

CLOSE UP

Turtles on St. Croix

Like creatures from the prehistoric past, green, leatherback, and hawksbill turtles crawl ashore during the annual April-to-November turtle nesting season to lay their eggs. They return from their life at sea every two to seven years to the beach where they were born. Since turtles can live for up to 100 years, they may return many times to nest in St. Croix.

The leatherbacks like Sandy Point National Wildlife Refuge and other spots on St. Croix's western end, but the hawksbills prefer Buck Island and the East End. Green turtles are also found primarily on the East End.

All are endangered species that face numerous predators, some natural, some the result of the human presence. Particularly in the Frederiksted area, dogs and cats prey on the nests and eat the hatchlings.

Occasionally a dog will attack a turtle about to lay its eggs, and cats train their kittens to hunt at turtle nests, creating successive generations of turtle-egg hunters. In addition, turtles have often been hit by fast-moving boats, leaving large gashes in their shells if not killing them outright.

The leatherbacks are the subject of a project by the international group Earthwatch. Each summer teams arrive at Sandy Point National Wildlife Refuge to ensure that poachers, both natural and human, don't attack the turtles as they crawl up the beach. The teams also relocate nests that are laid in areas prone to erosion. When the eggs hatch, teams stand by to make sure the turtles make it safely to the sea, and scientists tag them so they can monitor their return to St. Croix.

---

than an hour. Allow a little more time if you want to duck into the few small shops.

TOP ATTRACTIONS

FAMILY

Fodor'sChoice

★

Estate Whim Museum. The restored estate, with a windmill, cookhouse, and other buildings, gives a sense of what life was like on St. Croix's sugar plantations in the 1800s. The oval-shape greathouse has high ceilings and antique furniture and utensils. Notice its fresh, airy atmosphere—the waterless stone moat around the greathouse was used not for defense but for gathering cooling air. If you have kids, the grounds are the perfect place for them to run around, perhaps while you browse in the museum gift shop. It's just outside of Frederiksted. ⊠ *Rte. 70, Estate Whim* ☎ *340/772–0598* ⊕ *www.stcroixlandmarks.com* ⌑ *$10* ⊙ *Wed.–Sat. and cruise-ship days 10–4.*

Fodor'sChoice

★

St. George Village Botanical Garden. At this 17-acre estate, fragrant flora grows amid the ruins of a 19th-century sugarcane plantation. There are miniature versions of each ecosystem on St. Croix, from a semiarid cactus grove to a verdant rain forest. The small museum is also well worth a visit. ⊠ *Rte. 70, turn north at sign, St. George* ☎ *340/692–2874* ⊕ *www.sgvbg.org* ⌑ *$8* ⊙ *Daily 9–5.*

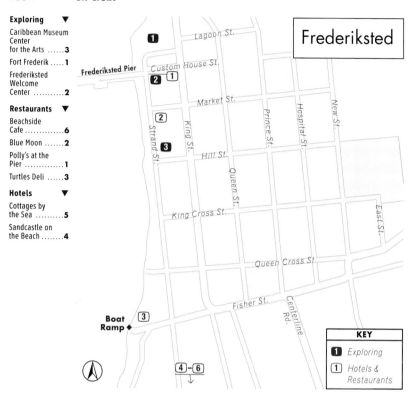

WORTH NOTING

Caribbean Museum Center for the Arts. Sitting across from the waterfront in a historic building, this small museum hosts an always-changing roster of exhibits. Many are cutting-edge multimedia efforts that you might be surprised to find in such an out-of-the-way location. The openings are popular events. ⊠ *10 Strand St.* ☎ *340/772–2622* ⊕ *www.cmcarts. org* ✉ *Free* ☉ *Thurs.–Sat. and cruise-ship days 10–5.*

Estate Mount Washington Plantation. Several years ago, while surveying the property, the owners discovered the ruins of a sugar plantation beneath the rain-forest brush. The grounds have since been cleared and opened to the public. You can take a self-guided walking tour of the mill, the rum factory, and other ruins. ⊠ *Rte. 63, Mount Washington* ☉ *Daily dawn–dusk.*

FAMILY **Fort Frederik.** On July 3, 1848, 8,000 slaves marched on this fort to demand their freedom. Danish governor Peter von Scholten, fearing they would burn the town to the ground, stood up in his carriage parked in front of the fort and granted their wish. The fort, completed in 1760, houses an art gallery and a number of interesting historical exhibits, including some focusing on the 1848 Emancipation and the 1917 transfer of the Virgin Islands from Denmark to the United States.

Marching on Frederiksted

On July 3, 1848, more than 8,000 slaves demanding their freedom marched half a mile from LaGrange to Frederiksted. Their actions forever changed the course of history. Governor General Peter von Scholten stood up in his carriage in front of Fort Frederick to declare: "You are now free. You are hereby emancipated. Go home peacefully."

Von Scholten was relieved of his position and charged with dereliction of duty by the Danish government. He departed from St. Croix on July 14, leaving behind his lover, a free black woman named Anna Heegaard. He never returned, and died in Denmark in 1852.

The revolt had its roots in the 1834 emancipation of slaves in Great Britain's Caribbean colonies, including what are now called the British Virgin Islands. The Danish government,

sensing what was coming, began to improve the working conditions for its slaves. These efforts, however, failed to satisfy the slaves who wanted full freedom.

On July 28, 1847, Danish King Christian VIII ruled that slavery would continue a dozen more years, but those born during those 12 years would be free. This further angered the island's slaves. On July 2, 1848, a conch shell sounded, signifying that the slaves should start gathering. The die was cast, and the rest, as they say, is history.

After emancipation, the former slaves were forced to sign yearly contracts with plantation owners. Those contracts could only be renegotiated on October 1, still called Contract Day. This angered the plantation workers and gave rise to other uprisings throughout the late 1800s.

It's within earshot of the Frederiksted Welcome Center. ⊠ *Waterfront* ☎ *340/772–2021* ✉ *$3* ⊘ *Weekdays (and any cruise-ship day) 9–4.*

Frederiksted Welcome Center. Located on the pier, Federiksted's welcome center has brochures from numerous St. Croix businesses, as well as a few exhibits about the island. ⊠ *Frederiksted Pier* ☎ *340/772–0495* ⊘ *Weekdays 8–5.*

West End Salt Pond. A bird-watcher's delight, this salt pond attracts a large number of winged creatures, including flamingos. ⊠ *Veteran's Shore Dr., Hesselberg.*

NORTH SHORE

WORTH NOTING

Judith's Fancy. In this upscale neighborhood are the ruins of an old greathouse and tower of the same name, both remnants of a circa-1750 Danish sugar plantation. The "Judith" comes from the first name of a woman buried on the property. From the guardhouse at the neighborhood entrance, follow Hamilton Drive past some of St. Croix's loveliest houses. At the end of Hamilton Drive the road overlooks Salt River Bay, where Christopher Columbus anchored in 1493. On the way back, make a detour left off Hamilton Drive onto Caribe Road for a close look at the ruins. The million-dollar villas are something to behold, too. ⊠ *Turn north onto Rte. 751, off Rte. 75, Judith's Fancy.*

Mount Eagle. At 1,165 feet, this is St. Croix's highest peak. Leaving Cane Bay and passing North Star Beach, follow the coastal road that dips briefly into a forest; then turn left on Route 69. Just after you make the turn, the pavement is marked with the words "The Beast" and a set of giant paw prints. The hill you're about to climb is the famous Beast of the St. Croix Half Ironman Triathlon, an annual event during which participants must cycle up this intimidating slope. ⊠ *Rte. 69, Davis Bay.*

Salt River Bay National Historical Park and Ecological Preserve. This joint national and local park commemorates the area where Christopher Columbus's men skirmished with the Carib Indians in 1493 on his second visit to the New World. The peninsula on the bay's east side is named for the event: Cabo de las Flechas (Cape of the Arrows). Although the park is still developing, it has several sights with cultural significance. A ball court, used by the Caribs in religious ceremonies, was discovered at the spot where the taxis park. Take a short hike up the dirt road to the ruins of an old earthen fort for great views of Salt River Bay. The area also encompasses a coastal estuary with the region's largest remaining mangrove forest, a submarine canyon, and several endangered species, including the hawksbill turtle and the roseate tern. A visitor center, open in winter only, sits just uphill to the west. The water at the beach can be on the rough side, but it's a nice place for sunning. ⊠ *Rte. 75 to Rte. 80, Salt River* ☎ *340/773–1460* ⊕ *www.nps. gov/sari* ☉ *Nov.–June, Tues.–Thurs. 9–4.*

BEACHES

EAST END

Buck Island. Part of Buck Island Reef National Monument, this is a must-see for anyone in St. Croix. The beach is beautiful, but its finest treasures are those you can see when you plop off the boat and adjust your mask, snorkel, and fins to swim over colorful coral and darting fish. Don't know how to snorkel? No problem—the boat crew will have you outfitted and in the water in no time. Take care not to step on those black-pointed spiny sea urchins or touch the mustard-color fire coral, which can cause a nasty burn. Most charter-boat trips start with a snorkel over the lovely reef before a stop at the island's beach. An easy 20-minute hike leads uphill to an overlook for a bird's-eye view of the reef below. You'll find restrooms at the beach. **Amenities:** toilets. **Best for:** snorkeling; swimming. ⊠ *5 miles (8 km) north of St. Croix* ☎ *340/773–1460* ⊕ *www.nps.gov/buis.*

FREDERIKSTED

West End beaches. There are several unnamed beaches along the coast road north of Frederiksted, but it's best if you don't stray too far from civilization. For safety's sake, most vacationers plop down their towel near one of the casual restaurants spread out along Route 63. The beach at the Rainbow Beach Club, a five-minute drive outside Frederiksted, has a bar, a casual restaurant, water sports, and volleyball. If you want to be close to the cruise-ship pier, just stroll on over to the adjacent sandy beach in front of Fort Frederik. On the way south out of Frederiksted, the stretch near Sandcastle on the Beach hotel is also lovely. **Amenities:** food and drink; water sports. **Best for:** snorkeling, swimming, walking. ✉ *Rte. 63, north and south of Frederiksted.*

NORTH SHORE

Cane Bay. On the island's breezy North Shore, Cane Bay does not always have gentle waters, but there are seldom many people around, and the scuba diving and snorkeling are wondrous. You can see elkhorn and brain corals, and less than 200 yards out is the drop-off called Cane Bay Wall. Cane Bay can be an all-day destination: you can rent kayaks and snorkeling and scuba gear at water-sports shops across the road, and a couple of casual restaurants beckon when the sun gets too hot. **Amenities:** food and drink; water sports. **Best for:** solitude; snorkeling; swimming. ✉ *Rte. 80, about 4 miles (6 km) west of Salt River, Cane Bay.*

4

WHERE TO EAT

St. Croix has restaurants scattered from one end to the other, so it's usually not hard to find a place to stop when you're exploring the island. Most travelers eat dinner near their hotel so as to avoid long drives on dark, unfamiliar roads. Christiansted has the island's widest selection of restaurants. Don't rule out Frederiksted, especially if you're out exploring the island. It has a handful of delightful restaurants.

CHRISTIANSTED

$$$ ECLECTIC 🍴 **Angry Nates.** Serving breakfast, lunch, and dinner, Angry Nates has something for everyone on its extensive menu. Dinner can be as fancy as tilapia and garlic shrimp with mushrooms, white wine, and garlic butter, or as basic as a burger or chicken sandwich. If your taste buds run to hot, try the shrimp pistolette—a hollowed-out baguette filled with shrimp and laced with really hot sauce. [$] *Average main: $22* ✉ *King Cross St., at the Boardwalk* ☎ *340/692–6283* 🌐 *www.angrynates.com.*

$ ECLECTIC 🍴 **Avocado Pitt.** Locals gather at this Christiansted waterfront spot for the breakfast and lunch specials, as well as for a bit of gossip. Breakfast runs to stick-to-the-ribs dishes like oatmeal and pancakes. Lunches include such basics as a crispy chicken-breast sandwich. The yellowfin tuna sandwich is made from fresh fish and gives a new taste to a standard lunchtime favorite. [$] *Average main: $12* ✉ *King Christian Hotel, 59 Kings Wharf* ☎ *340/773–9843* 🕒 *No dinner.*

$$ FRENCH 🍴 **Café Christine.** At this favorite with the professionals who work in downtown Christiansted, the presentations are as dazzling as the food. The small menu changes daily, but look for dishes such as shrimp-and-asparagus salad drizzled with a lovely vinaigrette or a vegetarian plate with quiche, salad, and lentils. Desserts are perfection. If the pear pie

St. Croix

↑
TO
ST. THOMAS

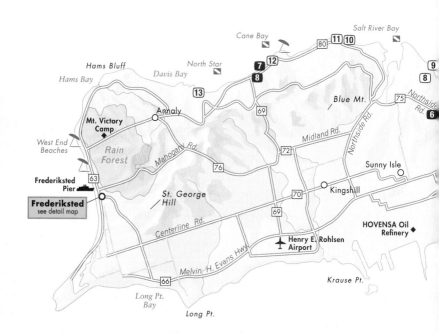

Salt River Bay

Cane Bay

80 11 10

North Star

7 12

8

Hams Bluff

Davis Bay

Hams Bay

9

8

13

Blue Mt.

75 Northside Rd.

6

Amaly

69

Mt. Victory Camp

West End Beaches

Rain Forest

Midland Rd.

Northside Rd.

Sunny Isle

Mahogany Rd.

72

Frederiksted Pier

63

76

Frederiksted
see detail map

St. George Hill

70 Kingshill

HOVENSA Oil Refinery

Centerline Rd.

69

Henry E. Rohlsen Airport

Melvin H. Evans Hwy

Krause Pt.

66

Long Pt. Bay

Long Pt.

KEY

⚲ Beaches
◣ Dive Sites
⛴ Cruise Ship Terminal
❶ Restaurants
1 Hotels
🌴 Rain Forest

0 — 2 miles
0 — 3 km

Buck Island

Buck Island Reef
National Monument

2 **3**

3

Christiansted
see detail map

Green
Cay

Pull
Pt.

Coakley
Bay

Cramer's
Park

Cottongarden Pt.

7 **5**

Tamarind
Reef
Beach

Teague
Bay

Sugarloaf Hill

Long
Reef

Christiansted
Harbor

2

4

82

4 East End Rd.

Little
Princess
Estate

5

Gallow's
Bay

1

Prospect
Hill

Isaacs Bay

1

South Side Rd.

60 **6** Grapetree
Bay

Recovery
Hill

Robin
Bay

Grassy Pt.

62

Great Pond
Bay

South Side Rd.

Milord
Pt.

Manchenil
Bay

Canegarden
Bay

Caribbean Sea

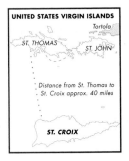

UNITED STATES VIRGIN ISLANDS

Tortola

ST. THOMAS

ST. JOHN

Distance from St. Thomas to
St. Croix approx. 40 miles

ST. CROIX

topped with chocolate is on the menu, don't hesitate. This tiny restaurant has tables in both the air-conditioned dining room and on the outside porch that overlooks historic buildings. [$] *Average main: $14* ✉ *Apothecary Hall Courtyard, 6 Company St.* ☎ *340/713–1500* ▭ *No credit cards* 🕒 *Closed weekends and July–mid-Nov. No dinner.*

$ CARIBBEAN 🍴 **Harvey's.** The dining room is plain, even dowdy, and plastic lace tablecloths constitute the sole attempt at decor. But who cares?—the food is delicious. Daily specials, such as mouthwatering goat stew and tender conch in butter, served with big helpings of rice and vegetables, are listed on the blackboard. Genial owner Sarah Harvey takes great pride in her kitchen, bustling out from behind the stove to chat and urge you to eat up. [$] *Average main: $11* ✉ *11B Company St.* ☎ *340/773–3433* 🕒 *No dinner. Closed Sun.*

$$$ ECLECTIC FAMILY Fodor's Choice ★ 🍴 **Rum Runners.** The view is as stellar as the food at this highly popular local standby. Sitting right on the Christiansted boardwalk, Rum Runners serves a little bit of everything, including a to-die-for salad of crispy romaine lettuce and tender grilled lobster drizzled with lemongrass vinaigrette. Heartier fare includes baby-back ribs cooked with the restaurant's special spice blend and Guinness stout. [$] *Average main: $25* ✉ *Hotel Caravelle, 44A Queen Cross St.* ☎ *340/773–6585* 🌐 *www.rumrunnersstcroix.com.*

$$$ ECLECTIC 🍴 **Savant.** Savant is one of those small but special spots that locals love. The cuisine is a fusion of Mexican, Thai, and Caribbean—an unusual combination that works surprisingly well. You can find anything from fresh fish to Thai curry with chicken to stuffed fillet with portobello mushrooms and goat cheese. With 20 tables crammed into the indoor dining room and small courtyard, this little place can get crowded. Call early for reservations. [$] *Average main: $27* ✉ *4C Hospital St.* ☎ *340/713–8666* 🌐 *www.savantstx.com* 🕒 *No lunch. Closed Sun.*

$$$ ITALIAN 🍴 **Tutto Bene.** With murals on the walls, brightly striped cushions, and painted trompe-l'oeil tables, Tutto Bene looks more like a sophisticated Mexican cantina than an Italian *cucina*. One bite of the food, however, will clear up any confusion. The menu includes such specialties as veal saltimbocca and medallions of veal with prosciutto and sage. Among the desserts is a decadent tiramisu. [$] *Average main: $24* ✉ *Hospital St., Gallows Bay* ☎ *340/773–5229* 🌐 *www.tuttobenerestaurant.com* 🕒 *Closed Mon. and Tues.*

WEST OF CHRISTIANSTED

$$$ ECLECTIC FAMILY 🍴 **Breezez.** This aptly named restaurant, *the* place on the island for Sunday brunch, is poolside at the Club St. Croix condominiums. Visitors and locals are drawn by its reasonable prices and good food. Locals also gather for lunch, when the menu includes everything from burgers to blackened prime rib with a horseradish sauce. For dessert, try the Amaretto cheesecake with either chocolate or fruit topping. [$] *Average main: $25* ✉ *Club St. Croix, 3280 Golden Rock, off Rte. 752, Golden Rock* ☎ *340/718–7077.*

$$$ ITALIAN 🍴 **Salud Bistro.** This eatery's imaginative menu takes its cue from the fresh flavors of the Mediterranean. Start with the savory cheese plate served with homemade bread and crostini before moving on to fresh

fish or grilled duck in a hibiscus confit. $ *Average main: $27* ✉ *Princess Plaza, Rte. 75, La Grande Princess* ☎ *340/718–7900* ⊕ *www.salud bistro.com* ⊘ *Closed Sun. No lunch.*

EAST END

$$ ✕ **Cheeseburgers in Paradise.** A perennial favorite with local and visiting
AMERICAN families, this open-air restaurant in the middle of a field serves up terrific
FAMILY New York strip steak, burgers with toppings that run from mushrooms to fried onions, and, of course, cheeseburgers. There's room for kids to run around before dinner. $ *Average main: $17* ✉ *Rte. 82, Green Cay* ☎ *340/773–1119.*

$$$ ✕ **The Deep End.** A favorite with locals and vacationers, this poolside
ECLECTIC restaurant serves up terrific burgers, steak, and seafood, as well as delicious pasta dishes and popular salads. To get here from Christiansted, take Route 82 and turn left at the sign for Green Cay Marina. $ *Average main: $23* ✉ *Tamarind Reef Hotel, Rte. 82, Annas Hope* ☎ *340/773–4455.*

$$$ ✕ **The Galleon.** This popular dockside restaurant is always busy. Start
ECLECTIC with the Caesar salad or perhaps a duck-liver pâté with cherry compote and arugula. The chef's signature dish is a beef tenderloin topped with fresh local lobster. Fish lovers should try the pan-seared sea scallops with roasted tomatoes and a kalamata olive risotto. Take Route 82 out of Christiansted, and then turn left at the sign for Green Cay Marina. The Galleon is open daily for dinner and serves Sunday brunch. $ *Average main: $30* ✉ *Green Cay Marina, off Rte. 82, Annas Hope* ☎ *340/718–9948* ⊘ *No lunch Mon.–Sat.*

FREDERIKSTED

$$$ ✕ **Beach Side Café.** Sunday brunch is big, but locals and visitors also flock
ECLECTIC to this oceanfront bistro at Sandcastle on the Beach resort for lunch and dinner. Both menus include burgers and salads, but at dinner the crispy half duck with berry sauce shines. For lunch, the hummus plate is a good bet. $ *Average main: $29* ✉ *Sandcastle on the Beach, 127 Smithfield* ☎ *340/772–1266* ⊕ *www.beachsidecafestx.com* ⊘ *Closed Tues. and Wed.*

$$$ ✕ **Blue Moon.** This terrific little bistro, which has a loyal local following,
AMERICAN offers a changing menu that draws on Cajun and Caribbean flavors.
Fodor's Choice Try the spicy gumbo with andouille sausage or crab cakes with a spicy
★ aioli for your appetizer. The pasta verde with vegetables makes a good entrée, and they serve delicious and decadent desserts. Sunday brunch is served and there's live jazz on Wednesday and Friday. $ *Average main: $23* ✉ *7 Strand St.* ☎ *340/772–2222* ⊕ *www.thebluemoonstcroix.com* ⊘ *Closed Mon.*

$$ ✕ **Polly's at the Pier.** With an emphasis on fresh ingredients, this very
ECLECTIC casual spot right on the waterfront serves delicious fare. The gourmet grilled-cheese sandwich comes with your choice of three cheeses as well as delicious additions like basil, fresh Bosc pears, and avocado. Salads are a specialty, and many are made with local Bibb lettuce and organic

mixed greens. $ *Average main: $13* ✉ *3 Strand St.* ☎ *340/719–9434* ⏷ *No dinner.*

$

DELI

FAMILY

× **Turtles Deli.** You can eat outside at this tiny spot just as you enter downtown Frederiksted. Lunches are as basic as a corned beef on rye or as imaginative as the Raven (turkey breast with bacon, tomato, and melted cheddar cheese on French bread). Also good is the Beast, named after the grueling hill that challenges bikers in the annual triathlon. It's piled high with hot roast beef, raw onion, and melted Swiss cheese with horseradish and mayonnaise. Early risers stop by for cinnamon buns and espresso. Turtles After Dark, upstairs, is open 5 to 10 pm. $ *Average main: $12* ✉ *38 Strand St., at Prince Passage* ☎ *340/772–3676* ⊕ *www.turtlesdeli.com* ▭ *No credit cards* ⏷ *Closed Sun.*

NORTH SHORE

$$

AMERICAN

Fodor's Choice

★

× **Eat @ Cane Bay.** The fabulous food matches the view of Cane Bay at this casual spot in the heart of Cane Bay. The lunch menu includes a build-your-own beef, veggie, or grilled chicken burger that gives you a choice of toppings, dressings, and cheese. If you opt for, say, a roasted turkey club sandwich, the onion rings that come with it are terrific. Dinner offerings include pasta, fish, steak, and sandwiches. $ *Average main: $18* ✉ *Rte. 80, Cane Bay* ☎ *340/718–0360* ⊕ *www.eatatcanebay. com* ⏷ *Closed Tues.*

$$

AMERICAN

× **Off the Wall.** Divers fresh from a plunge at the North Shore's popular Cane Bay Wall gather at this breezy spot on the beach. If you want to sit a spell before you order, a hammock beckons. Deli sandwiches, served with potato chips, make up most of the menu. Pizza and salads are also available. $ *Average main: $14* ✉ *Rte. 80, Cane Bay* ☎ *340/778–4771* ⊕ *www.otwstx.com.*

WHERE TO STAY

Although a stay right in historic Christiansted may mean putting up with a little urban noise, you probably won't have trouble sleeping. Christiansted rolls up the sidewalks fairly early, and humming air-conditioners drown out any noise. Solitude is guaranteed at hotels and inns outside Christiansted and on the outskirts of sleepy Frederiksted.

Families and groups may find more value in a condo that allows you to do a bit of cooking but still have access to a pool or a limited array of resort-style amenities. There are a lot of condos and apartment buildings on St. Croix, particularly along the North Shore and East End.

PRIVATE CONDOS AND VILLAS

St. Croix has more than 350 private villas scattered all over the island, from modest two-bedroom houses with just the basics to lavish and luxurious five-bedroom compounds with every imaginable amenity. But most are located in the center or in the East End. Renting a villa gives you all the convenience of home as well as top-notch amenities. Many have pools, hot tubs, and deluxe furnishings. Most companies meet you at the airport, arrange for a rental car, and provide helpful information about the island.

If you want to be close to the island's restaurants and shopping, look for a condominium or villa in the hills above Christiansted or on either side of the town. An East End location gets you out of Christiansted's hustle and bustle, but you're still only 15 minutes from town. North Shore locations are lovely, with gorgeous sea views and lots of peace and quiet.

RENTAL AGENTS
Vacation St. Croix ⊠ 4000 La Grande Princesse, Christiansted ☎ 340/718–0361, 877/788–0361 ⊕ www.vacationstcroix.com.

CHRISTIANSTED

$ 🏨 **Club Comanche Hotel St. Croix.** This historic townhouse built in 1756 is located in the center of town and has a rum and wine bar on the first floor. **Pros:** located near shopping and restaurants; friendly staff. **Cons:** no elevator; no close parking. $ Rooms from: $185 ⊠ 1 Strand St. ☎ 340/773–0210 ⊕ www.clubcomanche.com ➦ 23 rooms ⦿ No meals.

HOTEL

$ 🏨 **Company House Hotel.** With an elegant lobby, including a grand piano, and attractive rooms, this hotel provides comfortable and affordable accommodations in the heart of Christiansted. **Pros:** convenient location; attractive rooms. **Cons:** no parking; no beach; busy neighborhood. $ Rooms from: $115 ⊠ 2 Company St. ☎ 340/773–1377 ⊕ www.companyhousehotel.com ➦ 31 rooms, 2 suites ⦿ No meals.

HOTEL

$ 🏨 **Hotel Caravelle.** A stay at the Caravelle, which is near the harbor, puts you at the waterfront end of a pleasant shopping arcade and steps from shops and restaurants. **Pros:** good restaurant; convenient location; parking. **Cons:** no beach; busy neighborhood. $ Rooms from: $150 ⊠ 44A Queen Cross St. ☎ 340/773–0687, 800/524–0410 ⊕ www.hotelcaravelle.com ➦ 43 rooms, 1 suite ⦿ No meals.

HOTEL

$ 🏨 **Hotel on the Cay.** Hop on the free ferry to reach this peaceful lodging in the middle of Christiansted Harbor. **Pros:** quiet; convenient location; lovely beach. **Cons:** accessible only by ferry; no parking available. $ Rooms from: $149 ⊠ Protestant Cay ☎ 340/773–2035, 855/654–0301 ⊕ www.hotelonthecay.com ➦ 54 rooms ⦿ No meals.

RESORT

WEST OF CHRISTIANSTED

$ 🏨 **Carringtons Inn.** Local flavor, personalized service, and individual style make this intimate inn a welcome respite from the realm of cookie-cutter resorts, with its location in a former private home that offers a lovely pool and unbeatable ocean views. **Pros:** feels like a private home; welcoming host; tasteful rooms; great breakfasts. **Cons:** no beach; need car to get around. $ Rooms from: $150 ⊠ 4001 Estate Hermon Hill, Christiansted ☎ 340/713–0508, 877/658–0508 ⊕ www.carringtonsinn.com ➦ 5 rooms ⦿ Breakfast.

B&B/INN
Fodor's Choice
★

$ 🏨 **Club St. Croix.** Sitting beachfront just outside Christiansted, this modern condominium complex faces a lovely sandy beach. **Pros:** beachfront location; good restaurant; full kitchens. **Cons:** need car to get around; sketchy neighborhood. $ Rooms from: $195 ⊠ Rte. 752, Estate Golden Rock ☎ 340/718–9150, 800/524–2025 ⊕ www.antillesresorts.com ➦ 53 apartments ⦿ No meals.

RENTAL
FAMILY

4

The Buccaneer, St. Croix

$ RENTAL FAMILY

[H] **Colony Cove.** In a string of condominium complexes, Colony Cove lets you experience comfortable beachfront living. **Pros:** beachfront location; comfortable units; good views. **Cons:** sketchy neighborhood; need car to get around. [$] *Rooms from: $235* ✉ *Rte. 752, Estate Golden Rock* ☎ *340/718–1965, 800/524–2025* 🌐 *www.antillesresorts.com* 🛏 *62 apartments* 🍴 *No meals.*

$ RESORT

[H] **The Palms at Pelican Cove.** A 10-minute drive from Christiansted's interesting shopping and restaurants, this resort, with its mixed-bag of guests, has a gorgeous strand of white sand at its doorstep. **Pros:** nice beach; good dining options; friendly staff. **Cons:** need car to get out and about; neighborhood not the best. [$] *Rooms from: $254* ✉ *Off Rte. 752, La Grande Princesse* ☎ *340/718–8920, 800/548–4460* 🌐 *www.palmspelicancove.com* 🛏 *41 rooms* 🍴 *No meals.*

EAST END

$$ RESORT FAMILY

[H] **The Buccaneer.** Aimed at travelers who want everything at their fingertips, this resort has sandy beaches, swimming pools, and extensive sports facilities. **Pros:** beachfront location; numerous activities; nice golf course. **Cons:** pricey rates; insular environment; need car to get around. [$] *Rooms from: $360* ✉ *Rte. 82, Box 25200, Shoys* ☎ *340/712–2100, 800/255–3881* 🌐 *www.thebuccaneer.com* 🛏 *138 rooms, 1 villa* 🍴 *Breakfast.*

$ RESORT FAMILY

[H] **Chenay Bay Beach Resort.** The seaside setting and complimentary tennis and water-sports equipment make this resort a real find, particularly for families with active kids. **Pros:** beachfront location; pretty grounds; friendly staff. **Cons:** need car to get around; lacks pizzazz.

CAMPING IN ST. CROIX

Out on the west end, where few tourists stay, **Mount Victory Camp** (✉ *Creque Dam Rd., Frederiksted* ☎ *340/201–7983* ⊕ *www.mtvictorycamp.com*) offers a remarkable quietude that distinguishes this out-of-the-way spread on eight acres in the island's rain forest. If you really want to commune with nature, you'll be hard-pressed to find a better way to do it on St. Croix. Hosts Matt and Carmen are on hand to explain the environment. You sleep in a screened-in tent-cottage ($90–$110) perched on a raised platform and covered by a roof. Each has electricity and a rudimentary outdoor kitchen. There are also some bare tent sites for $25 per night. The shared, spotlessly clean bathhouse is an easy stroll away. The location feels remote, but a lovely sand beach is a 2-mile (3-km) drive down the hill. In another 10 minutes you're in Frederiksted. Reservations are preferred.

Ⓢ *Rooms from: $194* ✉ *Rte. 82, Green Cay* ☎ *340/773–2918* ⤴ *50 rooms* ⦿*No meals.*

$$$
ALL-INCLUSIVE
🛰 **Divi Carina Bay Resort.** An oceanfront location, the island's only casino, and plenty of activities make this resort a good bet. **Pros:** spacious beach; good restaurant; on-site casino. **Cons:** need car to get around; many stairs to climb; staff can seem chilly. Ⓢ *Rooms from: $418* ✉ *25 Rte. 60, Estate Turner Hole* ☎ *340/773–9700, 877/773–9700* ⊕ *www.divicarina.com* ⤴ *174 rooms, 2 suites, 20 villas* ⦿*All-inclusive.*

$
HOTEL
🛰 **Tamarind Reef Resort.** Spread out along a sandy beach, these low-slung buildings offer casual comfort. **Pros:** good snorkeling; tasty restaurant; rooms have kitchenettes. **Cons:** need car to get around; motel-style rooms. Ⓢ *Rooms from: $250* ✉ *5001 Tamarind Reef, off Rte. 82, Annas Hope* ☎ *340/718–4455, 800/619–0014* ⊕ *www.tamarindreefresort.com* ⤴ *46 rooms* ⦿*No meals.*

$$
RENTAL
🛰 **Villa Madeleine.** If you like privacy and your own private pool, you'll like Villa Madeleine. **Pros:** pleasant decor; full kitchens; private pools. **Cons:** lower units sometimes lack views; need car to get around; no beachfront. Ⓢ *Rooms from: $285* ✉ *Off Rte. 82, Teague Bay* ☎ *340/718–0361, 877/788–0361* ⊕ *www.vacationstcroix.com* ⤴ *43 villas* ⦿*No meals.*

FREDERIKSTED

$
RENTAL
🛰 **Cottages by the Sea.** Step out your door and onto a stunning stretch of white beach. **Pros:** beachfront location; delightful decor; friendly hosts. **Cons:** neighborhood sketchy at night; need car to get around; some rooms need freshening. Ⓢ *Rooms from: $120* ✉ *127A Smithfield* ☎ *340/772–0495, 800/323–7252* ⊕ *www.caribbeancottages.com* ⤴ *25 cottages* ⦿*No meals.*

$
RESORT
🛰 **Sandcastle on the Beach.** Right on a gorgeous stretch of white beach, Sandcastle has a tropical charm that harks back to a simpler time in the Caribbean; its nearness to Frederiksted's interesting dining scene is also a plus. **Pros:** lovely beach; close to restaurants; gay-friendly. **Cons:** neighborhood sketchy at night; need car to get around; no children's

activities. $ *Rooms from: $179* ⊠ *127 Smithfield* ☎ *340/772–1205, 800/524–2018* ⊕ *www.sandcastleonthebeach.com* ⇅ *9 rooms, 10 suites, 3 villas* ⦿ *No meals.*

NORTH SHORE

$

B&B/INN

⚄ **Arawak Bay: The Inn at Salt River.** With stellar views of St. Croix's North Shore and an affable host, this small inn allows you to settle into island life at a price that doesn't break the bank. **Pros:** 20 minutes from Christiansted; good prices. **Cons:** no beach nearby; can be some road noise. $ *Rooms from: $160* ⊠ *Rte. 80, Salt River* ☎ *340/772–1684* ⊕ *www. arawakbaysaltriver.co.vi* ⇅ *12 rooms* ⦿ *Breakfast.*

$$

RESORT

⚄ **Renaissance St. Croix Carambola Beach Resort and Spa.** This resort has a stellar beachfront setting and peaceful ambience as well as lovely rooms with attractive palm-theme accessories that match the resort's atmosphere. **Pros:** lovely beach; relaxing atmosphere; close to golf. **Cons:** remote location; need car to get around. $ *Rooms from: $349* ⊠ *Rte. 80, Davis Bay* ☎ *340/778–3800, 888/503–8760, 800/627–7468* ⊕ *www.carambolabeach.com* ⇅ *151 rooms* ⦿ *No meals.*

$

B&B/INN

⚄ **Villa Margarita.** This quiet retreat provides a particularly good base if you want to admire the dramatic views of the windswept coast. **Pros:** friendly host; great views; snorkeling nearby. **Cons:** isolated location; need car to get around; limited amenities. $ *Rooms from: $175* ⊠ *Off Rte. 80, Salt River* ☎ *340/713–1930* ⊕ *www.villamargarita.com* ⇅ *3 units* ⦿ *No meals.*

$

HOTEL

⚄ **Waves at Cane Bay.** St. Croix's famed Cane Bay Wall is just offshore from this hotel, giving it an enviable location. **Pros:** great diving; restaurants nearby; beaches nearby. **Cons:** need car to get around; on main road; bland decor. $ *Rooms from: $120* ⊠ *Rte. 80, Cane Bay* ☎ *340/718–1815* ⊕ *www.thewavescanebay.com* ⇅ *10 rooms* ⦿ *No meals.*

NIGHTLIFE AND PERFORMING ARTS

The island's nightlife is ever changing, and its arts scene is eclectic, ranging from Christmastime performances of *The Nutcracker* to locally organized shows. Folk-art traditions, such as quadrille dancers, are making a comeback. To find out what's happening, pick up the local newspapers—*V.I. Daily News* and *St. Croix Avis*—available at newsstands. Christiansted has a lively and eminently casual club scene near the waterfront. Frederiksted has a couple of restaurants and clubs offering weekend entertainment.

CHRISTIANSTED

NIGHTLIFE

Fort Christian Brew Pub. Locals and visitors come here to listen to live music several nights a week. ⊠ *Boardwalk at end of Kings Alley* ☎ *340/713–9820* ⊕ *www.fortchristianbrewpub.com.*

Hotel on the Cay. This off-shore resort hosts a West Indian buffet on Tuesday night in the winter season, when you can watch a broken-bottle dancer (a dancer who braves a carpet of shattered glass) and mocko jumbie (stilt-dancing) characters. ⊠ *Protestant Cay* ☎ *340/773–2035* ⊕ *www.hotelonthecay.com.*

EAST END

NIGHTLIFE

Divi Carina Bay Resort. Although you can gamble at the island's only casino, it's really the nightly music that draws big crowds to this resort. ⊠ *25 Rte. 60, Estate Turner Hole* ☎ *340/773–7529* ⊕ *www.divicarina. com.*

MID ISLAND

PERFORMING ARTS

Whim Plantation Museum. The museum outside Frederiksted hosts classical music concerts in winter. ⊠ *Rte. 70, Estate Whim* ☎ *340/772–0598* ⊕ *www.stcroixlandmarks.com.*

FREDERIKSTED

NIGHTLIFE

Fodor'sChoice ★ **Blue Moon.** Blue Moon is a popular waterfront restaurant in Frederiksted, and it's the place to be for live jazz on Wednesday and Friday. It's one of the few nightlife options at this end of the island. ⊠ *7 Strand St.* ☎ *340/772–2222* ⊕ *www.bluemoonstcroix.com.*

Fodor'sChoice ★ **Sunset Jazz.** This outdoor event is a hot ticket in Frederiksted, drawing crowds of visitors and locals at 5:30 pm on the third Friday of every month to watch the sun go down and listen to good music. ⊠ *Waterfront* ☎ *340/690–1741.*

SHOPPING

Although the shopping on St. Croix isn't as varied or extensive as that on St. Thomas, the island does have several small stores with unusual merchandise. St. Croix shop hours are usually Monday through Saturday 9 to 5, but there are some shops in Christiansted open in the evening. Stores are often closed on Sunday.

If you've rented a condominium or a villa, you'll appreciate St. Croix's excellent stateside-style supermarkets (albeit with prices that are at least 30% higher than on the U.S. mainland). Fresh vegetables, fruits, and meats arrive from the mainland frequently and are always available. Try the open-air stands strung out along Route 70 for island produce.

CHRISTIANSTED

AREAS AND MALLS

In Christiansted the best shopping areas are the **Pan Am Pavilion** and **Caravelle Arcade**, off Strand Street, and along **King** and **Company streets**. These streets give way to arcades filled with boutiques. **Gallows Bay** has a blossoming shopping area in a quiet neighborhood.

BOOKS

Undercover Books. This well-stocked independent bookseller sells Caribbean-themed books as well as the latest good reads. The store is in the Gallows Bay shopping area. ⊠ *5030 Anchor Way, across from post office, Gallows Bay* ☎ *340/719–1567* ⊕ *www.undercoverbooksvi.com.*

CLOTHING

From the Gecko. This store sells the hippest island-style clothes on St. Croix, as well as other items. ⊠ *55 Company St.* ☎ *340/778–9433* ⊕ *www.fromthegecko.com.*

Hot Heads. This small store sells hats, hats, and more hats, which are often perched on top of cotton shifts, comfortable shirts, and trendy tropical wear. If you forgot your bathing suit, this store has a good selection. ⊠ *1244 Queen Cross St.* ☎ *340/773–7888.*

Island Tribe. Colorful batik dresses, shirts, shifts, and scarves in soft rayon and cotton round out your tropical wardrobe. Sizes range from small to 4X. The clothing, and an interesting array of jewelry, comes from Bali. ⊠ *2100 Company St.* ☎ *340/719–0936.*

GIFTS

The Blue Mutt. Shop for a good cause at this small store that benefits the St. Croix Animal Welfare Center. The shelves are filled with local art, T-shirts, cards, soaps, candles, and much more. ⊠ *5 Company St.* ☎ *340/690–4624.*

Cache of the Day. This tiny store sells whatever its sea theme has tossed up. Mermaid dolls recline on shelves next to dishtowels printed with shapes of the sea. There are stuffed animals and jewelry that make perfect gifts. ⊠ *55 Company St.* ☎ *340/773–3648.*

Many Hands. This shop sells pottery in bright colors, paintings of St. Croix and the Caribbean, prints, and maps. They are all made by local artists, and they all make for perfect take-home gifts. ■ TIP→ The owners ship all over the world. ⊠ *21 Pan Am Pavilion, Strand St.* ☎ *340/773–1990.*

Mitchell-Larsen Studio. This glass gallery offers an interesting amalgam of carefully crafted glass plates, sun-catchers, and more. The pieces, all made on-site by a St. Croix glassmaker, are often whimsically adorned with tropical fish, flora, and fauna. ⊠ *58 Company St.* ☎ *340/719–1000* ⊕ *www.mitchelllarsenstudio.com.*

Fodor's Choice ★ **Royal Poinciana.** The attractive Royal Poinciana is filled with island seasonings and hot sauces, West Indian crafts, bath gels, and herbal teas. Shop here for tablecloths and paper goods in bright tropical colors. ⊠ *1113 Strand St.* ☎ *340/773–9892.*

Tesoro. Among the colorful and bold merchandise here are metal sculptures made from retired steel pans, mahogany bowls, and hand-painted place mats in bright tropical colors. ⊠ *3A Queen Cross St.* ☎ *340/773–1212* ⊕ *www.tesorostcroix.com.*

HOUSEWARES

Designworks. This store and gallery carries furniture as well as one of the largest selections of local art, along with Caribbean-inspired bric-a-brac and jewelry in all price ranges. If a mahogany armoire or four-poster bed catches your fancy, the staff can have it shipped to your home at no charge from its mainland warehouse. ⊠ *6 Company St.* ☎ *340/713–8102* ⊕ *www.islandlivingstore.com.*

JEWELRY

Crucian Gold. St. Croix native Brian Bishop's trademark piece is the Turk's Head ring (a knot of interwoven gold strands). His son, Nathan Bishop, is now creating contemporary sterling and gold pendants, rings, and earrings. ⊠ *1112 Strand St.* ☎ *340/773–5241* ⊕ *www.cruciangold.com.*

Gold Worker. This shop specializes in handcrafted jewelry in silver and gold that will remind you of the Caribbean. Hummingbirds dangle from silver chains and sand dollars adorn gold necklaces. The sugar mills in silver and gold speak of St. Croix's past. ⊠ *3 Company St.* ☎ *340/514–6042.*

ib designs. This small shop showcases the handcrafted jewelry of local craftsman Whealan Massicott. Whether in silver or gold, the designs are simply elegant. ⊠ *Company St. at Queen Cross St.* ☎ *340/773–4322* ⊕ *www.islandboydesigns.com.*

Nelthropp and Low. The jewelers at Nelthropp and Low can create one-of-a-kind pieces to your design. The shop specializes in gold jewelry but also carries diamonds, emeralds, rubies, and sapphires. ⊠ *1102 Strand St.* ☎ *340/773–0365* ⊕ *www.nelthropp-low.com.*

Sonya's. This store is owned and operated by Sonya Hough, who invented the popular hook bracelet. She has added an interesting decoration to these bracelets: the swirling symbol used in weather forecasts to indicate hurricanes. ⊠ *1 Company St.* ☎ *340/778–8605* ⊕ *www.sonyaltd.com.*

LIQUOR AND TOBACCO

Baci Duty Free. The walk-in humidor here has a good selection of Arturo Fuente, Partagas, and Macanudo cigars. Baci also carries high-end liquor, sleek Swiss-made watches, and fine jewelry. ⊠ *1235 Queen Cross St.* ☎ *340/773–5040* ⊕ *www.bacidutyfree.com.*

PERFUMES

Violette Boutique. Violette sells perfumes, cosmetics, and skin-care products. ⊠ *Caravelle Arcade, 38 Strand St.* ☎ *340/773–2148.*

WEST OF CHRISTIANSTED

FOOD

Pueblo. This market is similar to sister stores back on the mainland. ⊠ *Golden Rock Shopping Center, Rte. 75, Christiansted* ☎ *340/773–0118.*

EAST END

FOOD

Sea Side Market and Deli. Although it's on the smallish side, this market has good-quality deli items. ⊠ *Rte. 82, Mount Welcome* ☎ *340/719–9393.*

MID ISLAND

FOOD

Cost-U-Less. This warehouse-type store is great for visitors because it doesn't charge a membership fee. It's in the busy Sunny Isle area. ⊠ *Rte. 70, Peter's Rest* ☎ *340/719–4442* ⊕ *www.costuless.com.*

Plaza Extra. This supermarket chain has a good selection of Middle Eastern foods in addition to the usual grocery-store items. ⊠ *Queen Mary Hwy., Rte. 70, Mount Pleasant* ☎ *340/719–1870* ⊕ *www.plazaextra. com* ⊠ *Rte. 70, Sion Farm* ☎ *340/778–6240.*

Pueblo. This stateside-style market has another branch west of Christiansted. ⊠ *Villa La Reine Shopping Center, Rte. 75, La Reine* ☎ *340/778–1272.*

LIQUOR AND TOBACCO

Kmart. The U.S. discount chain has two branches on St. Croix, both of which carry a huge line of deep-discounted, duty-free liquor, among many other items. ⊠ *Sunshine Mall, Rte. 70, Frederiksted* ☎ *340/692–5848* ⊠ *Sunny Isle Shopping Center, Rte. 70, Sunny Isle* ☎ *340/719–9190.*

FREDERIKSTED

AREAS AND MALLS

The best shopping in Frederiksted is along **Strand Street** and in the side streets and alleyways that connect it with **King Street.** Most stores close on Sunday, except when a cruise ship is in port. One caveat: Frederiksted has a reputation for muggings, so for safety's sake stick to populated areas of Strand and King streets, where there are few—if any—problems.

SPORTS AND THE OUTDOORS

BOAT TOURS

Almost everyone takes a day trip to Buck Island aboard a charter boat. Most leave from the Christiansted waterfront or from Green Cay Marina and stop for a snorkel at the island's eastern end before

dropping anchor off a gorgeous sandy beach for a swim, a hike, and lunch. Sailboats can often stop right at the beach; a larger boat might have to anchor a bit farther offshore. A full-day sail runs about $100, with lunch included on most trips. A half-day sail costs about $70.

Big Beard's Adventure Tours. From catamarans that depart from the Christiansted waterfront you'll head to Buck Island for snorkeling before dropping anchor at a private beach for a barbecue lunch. ⊠ *Waterfront, Christiansted* ☎ *340/773–4482* ⊕ *www.bigbeards.com.*

Buck Island Charters. These charters are on two trimarans, *Teroro II* and *Dragonfly*, which leave Green Cay Marina for full- or half-day sails. Bring your own lunch. ⊠ *Green Cay Marina, Annas Hope* ☎ *340/773–3161* ⊕ *www.gotostcroix.com.*

Caribbean Sea Adventures. With their crafts leaving from the Christiansted waterfront, Caribbean Sea Adventures has both half- and full-day trips. ⊠ *Waterfront, Christiansted* ☎ *340/773–2628* ⊕ *www.caribbeanseaadventures.com.*

DIVING AND SNORKELING

Fodor's Choice
★
At **Buck Island,** a short boat ride from Christiansted or Green Cay Marina, the reef is so nice that it's been named a national monument. You can dive right off the beach at **Cane Bay,** which has a spectacular drop-off called the Cane Bay Wall. Dive operators also do boat trips along the Wall, usually leaving from Salt River or Christiansted. **Frederiksted Pier** is home to a colony of sea horses, creatures seldom seen in the waters of the Virgin Islands. At **Green Cay,** just outside Green Cay Marina in the East End, you can see colorful fish swimming around the reefs and rocks. Two exceptional North Shore sites are **North Star** and **Salt River,** which you can reach only by boat. At Salt River you can float downward through a canyon filled with colorful fish and coral.

The island's dive shops take you out for one- or two-tank dives. Plan to pay about $70 for a one-tank dive and $95 for a two-tank dive, including equipment and an underwater tour. All companies offer certification and introductory courses called resort dives.

Which dive outfit you pick usually depends on where you're staying. Your hotel may have one on-site. If so, you're just a short stroll away from the dock. If not, other companies are close by. Where the dive boat goes on a particular day depends on the weather, but in any case, all St. Croix's dive sites are special. All shops are affiliated with PADI, the Professional Association of Diving Instructors.

Cane Bay Dive Shop. This is the place to go if you want to do a beach dive or boat dive along the North Shore. The famed Cane Bay Wall is 200 yards from the PADI Five Star facility. This company also has shops at Pan Am Pavilion in Christiansted, on Strand Street in Frederiksted, and at the Divi Carina Bay Resort. ⊠ *Rte. 80, Cane Bay* ☎ *340/718–9913, 800/338–3843* ⊕ *www.canebayscuba.com.*

Dive Experience. Handy for those staying in Christiansted, Dive Experience runs trips to the North Shore walls and reefs, in addition to offering the usual certification and introductory classes. It's a PADI Five Star

Divers love the sponge-encrusted Rosa Maria, off the west end of St. Croix.

facility. ✉ *Boardwalk and Kings Alley, Christiansted* ☎ *340/773–3307, 800/235–9047* ⊕ *www.divexp.com.*

N2 the Blue. N2 takes divers right off the beach near the Frederiksted Pier, on night dives off the Frederiksted Pier, or on boat trips to the Salt River Wall. ✉ *Customs House St., Frederiksted* ☎ *340/772–3483* ⊕ *www.n2theblue.com.*

St. Croix Ultimate Bluewater Adventures. This company can take you to your choice of more than 75 sites; it also offers a variety of packages that include hotel stays. ✉ *Queen Cross St., Christiansted* ☎ *340/773–5994, 877/567–1367* ⊕ *www.stcroixscuba.com.*

FISHING

Since the early 1980s some 20 world records—many for blue marlin—have been set in these waters. Sailfish, skipjack, bonito, tuna (allison, blackfin, and yellowfin), and wahoo are abundant. A charter runs about $500 to $800 for a half day (for up to six people), with most boats going out for four-, six-, or eight-hour trips.

Captain Festus. Captain Festus takes you to spots all around St. Croix on his 55-foot boat *Sea Hunter* and 35-foot *Triton.* ✉ *Kings Wharf, Christiansted* ☎ *340/277–1751.*

Gone Ketchin'. Captain Grizz, a true old salt, heads these trips. ✉ *Salt River Marina, Rte. 80, Salt River* ☎ *340/713–1175* ⊕ *www.goneketchin. com.*

GOLF

St. Croix's three courses welcome you with spectacular vistas. Check with your hotel or the tourism department to determine when major celebrity tournaments will be held. There's often an opportunity to play with the pros.

Fodor's Choice
★
Buccaneer Golf Course. The Buccaneer Resort 18-hole course, near Christiansted, mixes fun with risk. Some of the par fours are within reach of a long drive, making birdies possible. However, miscues on holes that run near the ocean or have ponds can be costly for those keeping score. Most golfers' memories are of the beautiful views, not the sand traps. The signature third hole with the green sitting above a rocky coastline has some calling this course the Caribbean Pebble Beach. ⊠ *Rte. 82, Christiansted* ☎ *340/712–2144* ⊕ *www.thebuccaneer.com* ⊠ *$105* ⅓ *18 holes, 5169 yards, par 70.*

Carambola Golf Club. Golfers should enjoy the exotic beauty of this difficult course in the rain forest designed by Robert Trent Jones Sr., because they might not enjoy their score. An extra sleeve of balls might also be required. The long water holes never return splash balls and the jungle rough seldom does. Most fairways are forgiving with ample landing area, but the length of many holes makes it challenging. ⊠ *Rte. 69, River* ☎ *340/778–5638* ⊕ *www.golfcarambola.com* ⊠ *$125* ⅓ *18 holes, 5727 yards, par 72.*

The Links at Divi St. Croix. This attractive minigolf course is just across from the Divi Carina Bay Resort. ⊠ *Rte. 60, Turner Hole* ☎ *340/773–9700* ⊕ *www.divicarina.com* ⊠ *$8* ⊙ *Daily noon–8.*

Reef Golf Course. If you want to enjoy panoramic Caribbean views without paying high costs, the public nine-hole Reef Golf course on the island's East End is the place to go. The course design is basic, but the views from the hillside are spectacular. Trees on this course very seldom enter into play and sand traps are absent. The seventh hole with its highly elevated tee is the most interesting hole. ⊠ *Rte. 82, Teague Bay* ☎ *340/773–8844* ⊠ *$40* ⅓ *9 holes, 2395 yards, par 35.*

GUIDED TOURS

St. Croix Transit. Departing from Renaissance Carambola Beach Resort, St. Croix Transit's three-hour van tours start at $65 per person, which includes admission fees to all attractions. ⊠ *Renaissance Carambola Beach Resort, Rte. 80, Davis Bay* ☎ *340/772–3333.*

Sweeny's St. Croix Safari Tours. These van tours of St. Croix depart from Christiansted and last about five hours. Costs run from $70 per person, including admission fees to attractions. ⊠ *Christiansted* ☎ *340/773–6700* ⊕ *www.gotostcroix.com.*

HIKING

Although you can set off by yourself on a hike through a rain forest or along a shore, a guide will point out what's important and tell you why.

Scenic horseback riding on the beach on St. Croix

Ay-Ay Eco Hike and Tours. Ras Lumumba Corriette takes hikers up hill and down dale in some of St. Croix's most remote places, including the rain forest and Mount Victory. Some hikes include stops at old ruins. The cost is $60 per person for a three- or four-hour hike. There's a three-person minimum. ☎ 340/772–4079 ⊕ *www.chantvi.org.*

HORSEBACK RIDING

Paul and Jill's Equestrian Stables. From Sprat Hall, just north of Frederiksted, co-owner Jill Hurd will take you through the rain forest, across the pastures, along the beaches, and through valleys—explaining the flora, fauna, and ruins on the way. A 1½-hour ride costs $100. ⊠ *Rte. 58, Frederiksted* ☎ 340/772–2880, 340/772–2627 ⊕ *www.pauland jills.com.*

KAYAKING

Caribbean Adventure Tours. These kayak tours take you on trips through Salt River Bay National Historical Park and Ecological Preserve, one of the island's most pristine areas. All tours cost $50. ⊠ *Salt River Marina, Rte. 80, Salt River* ☎ 340/778–1522 ⊕ *www.stcroixkayak.com.*

Virgin Kayak Tours. Virgin runs guided kayak trips on the Salt River and rents kayaks so you can tour around the Cane Bay area by yourself. Tours start at $50, and kayak rentals are $40 for the entire day. ⊠ *Rte. 80, Cane Bay* ☎ 340/778–0071 ⊕ *www.virginkayaktours.com.*

TENNIS

The public courts in Frederiksted and Christiansted were refurbished in 2011 and are generally in good condition. One can also pay a fee and play at one of the hotel courts. Costs vary by resort, but count on paying about $10 an hour per person.

The Buccaneer. There are eight courts (two are lighted), plus a full tennis shop. ⊠ *The Buccaneer, Rte. 82, Shoys* ☎ *340/773–3036* ⊕ *www. thebuccaneer.com.*

Club St. Croix. There are two private tennis courts, one with lights. ⊠ *Club St. Croix, Rte 752, Estate Golden Rock* ☎ *340/718–4800* ⊕ *www.antillesresorts.com.*

Renaissance Carambola Beach Resort. Renaissance Carambola Beach Resort has one lighted court for guests only. ⊠ *Renaissance Carambola Beach Resort, Rte. 80, Davis Bay* ☎ *340/778–3800.*

WATER SPORTS

St. Croix Watersports. St. Croix Watersports rents WaveRunners, stand-up paddleboards, kayaks, windsurfers, and snorkel gear. The half-hour guided WaveRunner tour allows you to zip around Christiansted's harbor in style for $60. ⊠ *Hotel on Cay, Protestant Cay, Christiansted* ☎ *340/773–7060* ⊕ *www.stcroixwatersports.com.*

5

TORTOLA

Visit Fodors.com for advice, updates, and bookings

WELCOME TO TORTOLA

TOP REASONS TO GO

★ **Charter a boat:** Tortola is the charter-yacht capital of the Caribbean and a popular destination for boaters.

★ **Hit the road:** You'll get the real flavor of the island by heading out in whatever direction you choose. The views are dramatic, and the traffic is light enough to allow for easy driving.

★ **Shop in Road Town:** The island's largest community is also home to an eclectic collection of stores.

★ **Hit the trail:** Tortola is home to Sage Mountain National Park, a small but quite nice nature reserve.

★ **Get wet:** Dive trips to spectacular locations leave from Tortola. If you're not certified to dive, an introductory course can teach you the basics and whet your appetite for more adventures under the sea.

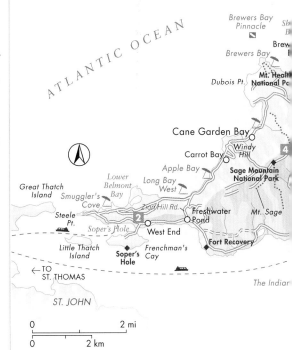

1 Road Town and Environs. In the middle of the island's south coast, the capital is a hub for shopping, dining, and ferries, which dock here.

2 West End. In addition to some resorts and private villas, the west end of Tortola has a major ferry pier, a few good beaches, and some shops and restaurants.

GETTING ORIENTED

The North Shore is where all the best beaches are found. Road Town, the island's tiny metropolis, has several restaurants and shops, as well as a smattering of historic sights and hotels. West End also has a concentration of establishments and a ferry pier. East End is isolated. Getting around is pretty easy, but the island's roads are extraordinarily steep and twisting, making driving demanding. It's best to explore the island a bit at a time.

3 North Shore. The best beaches and some good resorts (mostly concentrated in Cane Garden Bay and Brewer's Bay) can be found on the North Shore.

4 Mid Island. Tortola's steep midsection is home to several restaurants, national parks, and slews of villas.

5 East End. Both the airport (on Beef Island) and several resorts are on the more isolated east end of Tortola. There are also a few good beaches here.

Updated by
Susan Zaluski

A day might not be enough to tour this island—all 21 square miles (56 square km) of it—not because there's so much to see and do but because you're meant to relax while you're here. Time stands still even in Road Town, the island's biggest community (though not as still as it did even in the early 1990s), where the hands of the central square's clock occasionally move but never tell the right time. The harbor, however, is busy with sailboats—this is the charter-boat capital of the Caribbean. Tortola's roads dip and curve around the island and lead to lovely, secluded accommodations.

Tortola is definitely busy these days, particularly when several cruise ships tie up at the Road Town dock. Passengers crowd the streets and shops, and open-air jitneys filled with them create bottlenecks on the island's byways. That said, most folks visit Tortola to relax on its deserted sands or linger over lunch at one of its many delightful restaurants. Beaches are never more than a few miles away, and the steep green hills that form Tortola's spine are fanned by gentle trade winds. The neighboring islands glimmer like emeralds in a sea of sapphire. It can be a world far removed from the hustle of modern life, but it simply doesn't compare to Virgin Gorda in terms of beautiful beaches—or even luxury resorts, for that matter.

Still a British colonial outpost, the island's economy depends on tourism and its offshore financial-services businesses. With a population of around 24,000, most people work in those industries or for the local government. You'll hear lots of crisp British accents thanks to a large number of expats who call the island home, but the melodic West Indian accent still predominates.

Initially settled by Taíno Indians, Tortola saw a string of visitors over the years. Christopher Columbus sailed by in 1493 on his second voyage to the New World, and Spain, Holland, and France made periodic visits about a century later. Sir Francis Drake arrived in 1595, leaving his name on the passage between Tortola and St. John. Pirates and buccaneers followed, the British finally laying claim to the island in the late 1600s. In 1741 John Pickering became the first lieutenant governor of Tortola, and the seat of the British government moved from Virgin Gorda to Tortola. As the agrarian economy continued to grow, slaves were imported from Africa. The slave trade was abolished in 1807, but slaves in Tortola and the rest of the BVI did not gain their freedom until August 1, 1834, when the Emancipation Proclamation was read at Sunday Morning Well in Road Town. That date is celebrated every year with the island's annual Carnival.

Visitors have a choice of accommodations, but most fall into the small and smaller still category. Only Long Bay on Tortola's North Shore qualifies as a resort, but even some of the smaller properties add amenities occasionally. A couple of new hotel projects are in the works, so look for more growth in the island's hotel industry over the next decade.

GETTING HERE AND AROUND

AIR TRAVEL

There's no nonstop air service from the continental United States to Tortola; connections are usually made through San Juan, Puerto Rico, or St. Thomas.

CAR TRAVEL

You might get by with taxis, especially if you are staying in Road Town, but if you are in a villa or an isolated resort, a car is a necessity here. Remember that driving is on the *left* even though cars are generally American-made. Tortola's main roads are well paved for the most part, but there are exceptionally steep hills and sharp curves; driving demands your complete attention. A main road circles the island, and several roads cross it, mostly through mountainous terrain.

Road Town's traffic and parking can be horrific, so avoid driving along Waterfront Drive during morning and afternoon rush hours. ■ TIP➜ It's longer—but often quicker—to drive through the hills above Road Town. (And the views are great as well.) Parking can also be very difficult in Road Town, particularly during high season. There's parking along the waterfront and on the inland side on the eastern end of downtown, but if you're planning a day of shopping, go early to make sure you snag a space.

CAR RENTALS

Only Hertz and National have offices at the airport, but most companies will pick you up. It's usually best to reserve a car in advance.

Contacts Avis ⊠ Opposite police station, Road Town ☎ 284/494-2193 ⊕ www. avis.com. **D&D** ⊠ West End Rd., West End ☎ 284/495-4765. **Itgo Car Rental** ⊠ Wickham's Cay I, Road Town ☎ 284/494-2639 ⊕ www.itgobvi.com. **National** ⊠ Airport, Beef Island ☎ 284/495-2626 ⊕ www.nationalcar.com ⊠ West End ☎ 284/495-4877 ⊠ Waterfront Dr., Duff's Bottom, Road Town ☎ 284/494-3197.

FERRY TRAVEL

Frequent daily ferries connect Tortola with St. Thomas, which many vacationers decide to use as their main air gateway. Ferries go to and from both Charlotte Amalie and Red Hook. There's huge competition between the Tortola-based ferry companies on the St. Thomas–Tortola runs, with boats leaving close together. As you enter the ferry terminal to buy your ticket, crews may try to convince you to take their ferry. Ferries also link Tortola to St. John, where all Red Hook–bound ferries stop in Cruz Bay to clear customs and immigration. Ferries also link Tortola with Jost Van Dyke, Peter Island, and Virgin Gorda. Tortola has two ferry terminals—one at West End and one in Road Town—and a jetty at Beef Island where ferries depart for Virgin Gorda, so make sure you hop a ferry that disembarks closest to where you want to go. Ferry schedules vary, and not all companies make daily trips. Departures can be suddenly canceled, particularly in the summer. The BVI Tourist Board website (⊕ *www.bvitourism.com*) has links to all the ferry companies.

TAXI TRAVEL

Taxi rates are set on Tortola, but you should still check with your driver before you start your trip. Fares are per destination, not per person here, so it's cheaper to travel in groups, because the fare will be the same whether you have one, two, or three passengers. On Tortola the BVI Taxi Association has stands in Road Town near Wickham's Cay I. The Waterfront Taxi Association picks up passengers from the Road Town ferry dock. The Airport Taxi Association operates at the Terrance B. Lettsome Airport on Beef Island. You can also usually find a West End Taxi Association taxi at the West End ferry dock.

Contacts Airport Taxi Association ☎ *284/495–1982, 284/495–7162.*
Waterfront Taxi Association ☎ *284/494–6362.* **West End Taxi Association**
☎ *284/495–4934.*

ESSENTIALS

BANKS

On Tortola banks are near the waterfront at Wickham's Cay I. All have ATM machines. Look for Banco Popular, First Caribbean International Bank, First Bank, and Scotia Bank, among others.

HOTELS

Tortola resorts are intimate—only a handful has more than 50 rooms. Guests are treated as more than just room numbers, and many return year after year. This can make booking a room at popular resorts difficult, even off-season, despite the fact that more than half the island's visitors stay aboard their own or chartered boats. Hotels in Road Town don't have beaches, but they do have pools and are within walking distance of restaurants, bars, and shops. Accommodations outside Road Town are relatively isolated, but most face the ocean. Some places close during the peak of hurricane season—August through October—to give their owners a much-needed break.

Hotel reviews have been shortened. For full information, visit Fodors. com.

RESTAURANTS

Local seafood is plentiful on Tortola, and although other fresh ingredients are scarce, the island's chefs are a creative lot who apply their skills to whatever the boat delivers. Contemporary American dishes with Caribbean influences are very popular, but you can find French and Italian fare as well. The more expensive restaurants have dress codes: long pants and collared shirts for men and elegant but casual resort wear for women. Prices are often a bit higher than you'd expect to pay back home, and the service can sometimes be a tad on the slow side, but enjoy the chance to linger over the view.

WHAT IT COSTS IN U.S. DOLLARS			
$	$$	$$$	$$$$
Restaurants	under $13	$13–$20	$21–$30	over $30
Hotels	under $276	$276–$375	$376–$475	over $475

Restaurant prices are the average cost of a main course at dinner or, if dinner is not served, at lunch. Hotel prices are the lowest cost of a standard double room in high season.

SAFETY

Although crime is rare, use common sense: don't leave your camera on the beach while you take a dip or your wallet on a hotel dresser when you go for a walk.

TOUR OPTIONS

Romney Associates/Travel Plan Tours can arrange island tours, boat tours, snorkeling and scuba-diving trips, dolphin swims, and yacht charters from its Tortola base.

Contacts **Romney Associates/Travel Plan Tours** ☎ *284/494–4000.*

VISITOR INFORMATION

Contacts **BVI Tourist Board** ☎ *212/563–3117, 800/835–8530 in the U.S.*
⊕ *www.bvitourism.com.*

EXPLORING TORTOLA

Tortola doesn't have many historic sights, but it does have lots of spectacular natural scenery and beautiful beaches. Although you could explore the island's 21 square miles (56 square km) in a few hours, opting for such a whirlwind tour would be a mistake. There's no need to live in the fast lane when you're surrounded by some of the Caribbean's most breathtaking panoramas. In any event, you come to Tortola to relax, read in the hammock, and spend hours at dinner, not to dash madly around the island ticking yet another sight off your list. Except for the Dolphin Discovery, where advance booking is recommended, the other island sights are best seen when you stumble upon them on your round-the-island drive.

ROAD TOWN AND ENVIRONS

The bustling capital of the BVI looks out over Road Harbour. It takes only an hour or so to stroll down Main Street and along the waterfront, checking out the traditional West Indian buildings painted in pastel colors and with corrugated-tin roofs, bright shutters, and delicate fretwork trim. For sightseeing brochures and the latest information on everything from taxi rates to ferry schedules, stop in the BVI Tourist Board office. Or just choose a seat on one of the benches in Sir Olva Georges Square, on Waterfront Drive, and watch the people come and go from the ferry dock and customs office across the street.

TOP ATTRACTIONS

J.R. O'Neal Botanic Gardens. Take a walk through this 4-acre showcase of lush plant life. There are sections devoted to prickly cacti and succulents, hothouses for ferns and orchids, gardens of medicinal herbs, and plants and trees indigenous to the seashore. From the tourist office, cross Waterfront Drive and walk one block over to Main Street and turn right. Keep walking until you see the high school. The gardens are on your left. ⊠ *Botanic Station* ☎ *284/494–3650* ⊕ *www. bvinationalparkstrust.org* ✉ *$3* ⊘ *Mon.–Sat. 8:30–4:30.*

Fodor's Choice **Old Government House Museum.** The official government residence until
 ★ 1997, this gracious building now displays a nice collection of artifacts from Tortola's past. The rooms are filled with period furniture, hand-painted china, books signed by Queen Elizabeth II on her 1966 and 1977 visits, and numerous items reflecting Tortola's seafaring legacy. ⊠ *Waterfront Dr.* ☎ *284/494–4091* ⊕ *www.oghm.org* ✉ *$5* ⊘ *Weekdays 9–3.*

WORTH NOTING

Dolphin Discovery. Get up close and personal with dolphins as they swim in a spacious seaside pen. There are three different programs. In the Royal Swim, dolphins tow participants around the pen. The less expensive Adventure and Discovery programs allow you to touch the dolphins. ⊠ *Waterfront Dr.* ☎ *284/494–7675, 888/393–5158* ⊕ *www. dolphindiscovery.com* ✉ *Royal Swim $149, Adventure $99, Discovery $79* ⊘ *Royal Swim daily at 10, noon, 2, and 4. Adventure and Discovery daily at 11 and 1.*

Fort Burt. The most intact historic ruin on Tortola was built by the Dutch in the early 17th century to safeguard Road Harbour. It sits on a hill at the western edge of Road Town and is now the site of a small hotel and restaurant. The foundations and magazine remain, and the structure offers a commanding view of the harbor. ⊠ *Waterfront Dr.* ✉ *Free* ⊘ *Daily dawn–dusk.*

WEST END

WORTH NOTING

Fort Recovery. The unrestored ruins of a 17th-century Dutch fort sit amid a profusion of tropical greenery on the grounds of Fort Recovery Beachfront Villas and Suites. There's not much to see here, and there are no guided tours, but you're welcome to stop by and poke around. ⊠ *Waterfront Dr., Pockwood Pond* ☎ *284/495–4467* ✉ *Free.*

Soper's Hole. On this little island connected by a causeway to Tortola's western end, you can find a marina and a captivating complex of pastel West Indian–style buildings with shady balconies, shuttered windows, and gingerbread trim that house art galleries, boutiques, and restaurants. Pusser's Landing is a lively place to stop for a cold drink (many are made with Pusser's famous rum) and a sandwich, and to watch the boats in the harbor. ⊠ *Soper's Hole.*

NORTH SHORE

TOP ATTRACTIONS

Fodor'sChoice
★
Cane Garden Bay. Once a sleepy village, Cane Garden Bay has become one of Tortola's most important destinations. Stay at a small hotel or guesthouse here, or stop by for lunch, dinner, or drinks at a seaside restaurant. You can find a few small stores selling clothing and basics such as suntan lotion, and one of Tortola's most popular beaches is at your feet. Myett's offers hotel rooms almost directly on the beach. The roads in and out of this area are dauntingly steep, so use caution when driving. ⊠ *Cane Garden Bay.*

MID ISLAND

WORTH NOTING

Mount Healthy National Park. The remains of an 18th-century sugar plantation can be seen here. The windmill structure has been restored, and you can see the ruins of a mill, a factory with boiling houses, storage areas, stables, a hospital, and many dwellings. It's a nice place to picnic. ⊠ *Ridge Rd., Todman Peak* ⊕ *www.bvinpt.org* ✉ *Free* ☉ *Daily dawn–dusk.*

Sage Mountain National Park. At 1,716 feet, Sage Mountain is the highest peak in the BVI. From the parking area, a trail leads you in a loop not only to the peak itself (and extraordinary views) but also to a small rain forest that is sometimes shrouded in mist. Most of the forest was cut down over the centuries for timber, to create pastureland, or for growing sugarcane, cotton, and other crops. In 1964 this park was established to preserve what remained. Up here you can see mahogany trees, white cedars, mountain guavas, elephant-ear vines, mamey trees, and giant bullet woods, to say nothing of such birds as mountain doves and thrushes. Take a taxi from Road Town or drive up Joe's Hill Road and make a left onto Ridge Road toward Chalwell and Doty villages. The road dead-ends at the park. ⊠ *Ridge Rd., Sage Mountain* ☎ *284/852–3650* ⊕ *www.bvinpt.org* ✉ *$3* ☉ *Daily dawn–dusk.*

BEACHES

Beaches in the BVI are less developed than those on St. Thomas or St. Croix, but they are also less inviting. The best BVI beaches are on deserted islands reachable only by boat, so take a snorkeling or sailing

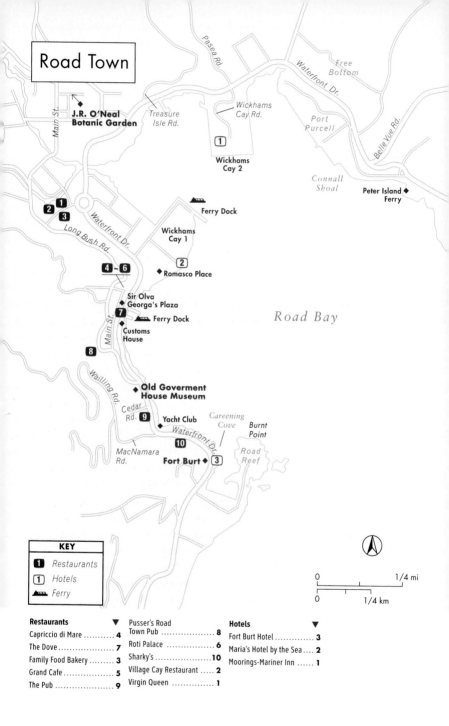

Road Town

J.R. O'Neal Botanic Garden

Treasure Isle Rd.

Pasea Rd.

Waterfront Dr.

Free Bottom

Wickhams Cay Rd.

Port Purcell

Belle Vue Rd.

Main St.

1 Wickhams Cay 2

Connall Shoal

Peter Island Ferry

2 1
3

Long Bush Rd.

Waterfront Dr.

Ferry Dock

Wickhams Cay 1

4 – 6

2 Romasco Place

Road Bay

Sir Olva Georga's Plaza

7 Ferry Dock

Customs House

8

Main St.

Wailling Rd.

Old Goverment House Museum

Cedar Rd.

9 Yacht Club

Careening Cove

Burnt Point

Waterfront Dr.

10

MacNamara Rd.

Fort Burt 3

Road Reef

KEY

1 *Restaurants*
1 *Hotels*
Ferry

0 ——— 1/4 mi
0 ——— 1/4 km

Old Government House Museum, Road Town

trip at least once. Tortola's north side has several palm-fringed, white-sand beaches that curl around turquoise bays and coves, but none really achieves greatness. Nearly all are accessible by car (preferably a four-wheel-drive vehicle), albeit down bumpy roads that corkscrew precipitously. Some of these beaches are lined with bars and restaurants as well as water-sports-equipment stalls; others have absolutely nothing.

WEST END

Long Bay Beach West. This beach is a stunning, mile-long stretch of white sand; have your camera ready to snap the breathtaking approach. Although Long Bay Resort sprawls along part of it, the entire beach is open to the public. The water isn't as calm here as at Cane Garden or Brewers Bay, but it's still swimmable. Rent water-sports equipment and enjoy the beachfront restaurant at the resort. Turn left at Zion Hill Road; then travel about half a mile. **Amenities:** food and drink; toilets; water sports. **Best for:** swimming. ⊠ *Long Bay Rd., Long Bay.*

Smuggler's Cove Beach. A beautiful, palm-fringed beach, Smuggler's Cove is down a pothole-filled dirt road. After bouncing your way down, you'll feel as if you've found a hidden piece of the island. You probably won't be alone on weekends, though, when the beach fills with snorkelers and sunbathers. There's a fine view of Jost Van Dyke from the shore. The beach is popular with Long Bay Resort guests who want a change of scenery. Follow Long Bay Road past Long Bay Resort, keeping to the roads nearest the water until you reach the beach. It's about a mile past the resort. **Amenities:** parking. **Best for:** snorkeling; swimming. ⊠ *Long Bay Rd., Long Bay.*

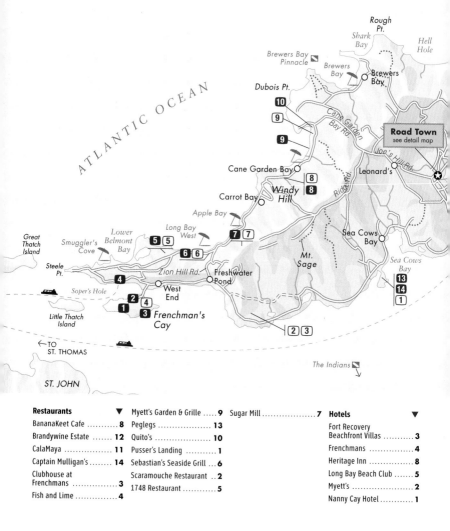

The Chikuzen

Rough Pt.

Shark Bay

Hell Hole

Brewers Bay Pinnacle

Brewers Bay

Brewers Bay

Dubois Pt.

Road Town
see detail map

Joe's Hill Rd.

10

9

9

Cane Garden Bay Rd.

Cane Garden Bay

Leonard's

8
8

Carrot Bay

Windy Hill

Ridg Rd.

Sea Cows Bay

Apple Bay

Long Bay West

Lower Belmont Bay

5 **5**

7 **7**

6 **6**

Mt. Sage

Sea Cows Bay

13

14

①

Great Thatch Island

Smuggler's Cove

Steele Pt.

4

Zion Hill Rd.

West End

Freshwater Pond

Soper's Hole

2

4

1

3 *Frenchman's Cay*

2 3

Little Thatch Island

←TO
ST. THOMAS

The Indians

ST. JOHN

ATLANTIC OCEAN

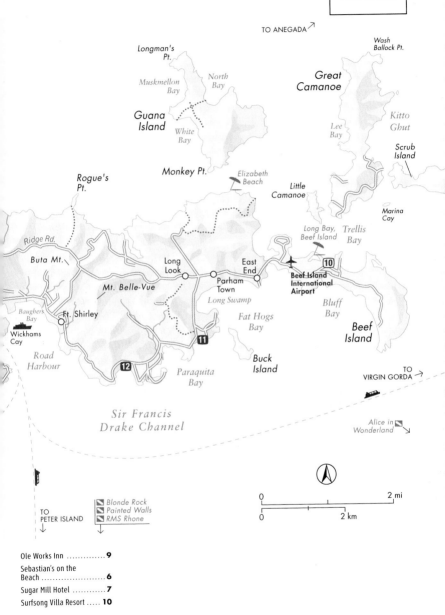

Tortola

TO ANEGADA ↗

Wash
Ballock Pt.

Longman's
Pt.

North
Bay

Great
Camanoe

Muskmellon
Bay

Guana
Island

White
Bay

Kitto
Ghut

Lee
Bay

Scrub
Island

Monkey Pt.

Elizabeth
Beach

Little
Camanoe

Rogue's
Pt.

Marina
Cay

Long Bay,
Beef Island

Trellis
Bay

Ridge Rd.

Buta Mt.

Long
Look

East
End

10

Mt. Belle-Vue

Parham
Town

Beef Island
International
Airport

Bluff
Bay

Long Swamp

Baughers
Bay

Ft. Shirley

Fat Hogs
Bay

Beef
Island

Wickhams
Cay

11

Road
Harbour

12

Paraquita
Bay

Buck
Island

TO
VIRGIN GORDA →

Sir Francis
Drake Channel

Alice in
Wonderland

Blonde Rock
Painted Walls
RMS Rhone

TO
PETER ISLAND

0   2 mi

0   2 km

NORTH SHORE

Apple Bay Beach. Along with nearby Little Apple Bay and Capoon's Bay, this is your spot if you want to surf—although the white, sandy beach itself is narrow. Sebastian's, a casual hotel, caters to those in search of the perfect wave. The legendary Bomba's Surfside Shack—a landmark festooned with all manner of flotsam and jetsam—serves drinks and casual food. Otherwise, there's nothing else in the way of amenities. Good waves are never a sure thing, but you're more apt to find them in January and February. If you're swimming and the waves are up, take care not to get dashed on the rocks. **Amenities:** food and drink; toilets. **Best for:** surfing; swimming. ⊠ *North Shore Rd. at Zion Hill Rd., Apple Bay.*

Brewers Bay Beach. This beach is easy to find, but the steep, twisting paved roads leading down the hill to it can be a bit daunting. An old sugar mill and ruins of a rum distillery are off the beach along the road. You can actually reach the beach from either Brewers Bay Road East or Brewers Bay Road West. **Amenities:** none. **Best for:** snorkeling; swimming. ⊠ *Brewers Bay Rd. E, off Cane Garden Bay Rd., Brewers Bay.*

Cane Garden Bay Beach. A silky stretch of sand, Cane Garden Bay has exceptionally calm, crystalline waters—except when storms at sea turn the water murky. Snorkeling is good along the edges. Casual guesthouses, restaurants, bars, and shops are steps from the beach in the growing village of the same name. The beach is a laid-back, even somewhat funky place to put down your towel. It's the closest beach to Road Town—one steep uphill and downhill drive—and one of the BVI's best-known anchorages (unfortunately, it can be very crowded). Watersports shops rent equipment. **Amenities:** food and drink; toilets; water sports. **Best for:** snorkeling; swimming. ⊠ *Cane Garden Bay Rd., off Ridge Rd., Cane Garden Bay.*

EAST END

Elizabeth Beach. Home to a small resort, Elizabeth Beach is a palm-lined, wide, and sandy beach with parking along its steep downhill access road. Other than at the hotel and its restaurant, which welcomes nonguests, there are no amenities aside from peace and quiet. Turn at the sign for Lambert Beach Resort. If you miss it, you wind up at Her Majesty's Prison. **Amenities:** food and drink; parking; toilets. **Best for:** solitude; swimming. ⊠ *Lambert Rd., off Ridge Rd., on eastern end of island, Lambert Bay.*

Long Bay Beach, Beef Island. Long Bay on Beef Island has superlative scenery: the beach stretches seemingly forever, and you can catch a glimpse of Little Camanoe and Great Camanoe islands. If you walk around the bend to the right, you can see little Marina Cay and Scrub Island. Long Bay is also a good place to search for seashells. Swim out to wherever you see a dark patch for some nice snorkeling. There are no amenities, so come prepared with your own drinks and snacks. Turn left shortly after crossing the bridge to Beef Island. **Amenities:** none. **Best for:** snorkeling; swimming; bird-watching. ⊠ *Beef Island Rd., Beef Island.*

WHERE TO EAT

Restaurants are scattered from one end of the island to the other, so you're never far from a good meal. Cane Garden Bay, with a handful of restaurants along the beach, is a popular dining destination. Eateries in Road Town are a short stroll from each other, making it easy to find a place that pleases everyone. Most hotels have restaurants that welcome nonguests.

ROAD TOWN AND ENVIRONS

$$$$
MEDITERRANEAN
Fodor's Choice
★

✕ **Brandywine Estate.** At this Brandywine Bay restaurant, candlelit outdoor tables have sweeping views of nearby islands. With a Mediterranean flair, the menu changes often, but you might find a three-cheese tortellini with garlic-and-truffle sauce or scallops in a saffron sauce. Finish your meal with a delightful cheese platter. $ *Average main: $41* ☒ *Sir Francis Drake Hwy., east of Road Town, Brandywine Bay* ☎ *284/495–2301* ⊕ *www.brandywinerestaurant.com* ⊘ *Closed Tues.*

$$
ITALIAN
Fodor's Choice
★

✕ **Capriccio di Mare.** Stop by this casual, authentic Italian outdoor café for an espresso, a fresh pastry, a bowl of perfectly cooked penne, or a crispy tomato-and-mozzarella pizza. Drink specialties include a mango Bellini, an adaptation of the famous cocktail served at Harry's Bar in Venice. $ *Average main: $19* ☒ *Waterfront Dr.* ☎ *284/494–5369* ⚘ *Reservations not accepted* ⊘ *Closed Sun.*

$$
AMERICAN
FAMILY

✕ **Captain Mulligan's.** Located at the entrance to Nanny Cay, this sports bar attracts expats, locals, and sailors with its promise to have "the second-best burger on the island," underlining the eatery's irreverent tone (we never found out who has the best!). Hot wings, pizza, ribs, and burgers are on the menu, and most people come to watch the game on the big screen. A mini-golf course has also been established and provides an activity for children of all ages, along with a children's recreation area. $ *Average main: $15* ☒ *Nanny Cay* ☎ *284/494–0602* ⊕ *www.captainmulligans.com.*

$$$
ECLECTIC

✕ **The Dove.** The food matches the romantic feeling at this Road Town restaurant. Start with jumbo prawns sautéed with vanilla bean and almonds before moving on to the mushroom-and-parmesan-crusted ribeye steak. Desserts are often new twists on old standards, as with the soursop (the fruit of a Caribbean evergreen tree) crème brûlée. Lunch offerings were added in 2014. $ *Average main: $29* ☒ *Waterfront Dr.* ☎ *284/494–0313* ⊕ *www.thedovebvi.com* ⊘ *Closed Sun. and Mon. No lunch Sat.*

$$
BAKERY

✕ **Family Food Bakery.** Fresh coffee, artisanal breads, and other delicious baked goods lure visitors into this breezy, casual eatery for a quick meal or to pick up prepared meals on the go. $ *Average main: $14* ☒ *Main St.* ☎ *284/340–0077* ⊘ *Closed Sun.*

$$$
FRENCH

✕ **Grand Cafe.** Birds and bougainvillea brighten the patio of this breezy French restaurant and bar, a popular gathering spot for locals and visitors alike. French onion soup and smoked salmon salad are good appetizer choices. From there, move on to the grilled tuna with wasabi sauce, sole in a brown butter sauce, or beef tenderloin with green peppercorn sauce. Save room for such tasty desserts as chocolate cake and crème brûlée, or opt for a platter of French cheeses. $ *Average main: $23* ✉ *Waterfront Dr.* ☎ *284/494–8660* ⊗ *Closed Sun.*

$$$ ✕**Peglegs.** At Peglegs, views of Sir Francis Drake Channel complement
AMERICAN the modern nautical decor of the dining room, and yachties swap sea
stories at the outside beach bar. Menu offerings range from burgers and
pizzas to daily fresh seafood offerings. Nanny Cay is the home for the
annual BVI Spring Regatta and things really get swinging at the event's
afterparties, which are held here. $ *Average main: $29* ✉ *Nanny Cay*
☎ *284/494–0028.*

$$$ ✕**The Pub.** At this lively waterfront spot, tables are arranged along a
ECLECTIC terrace facing a small marina and the harbor in Road Town. Ham-
burgers, salads, and sandwiches are typical lunch offerings, along with
classic British fare such as shepherd's pie and liver and onions. In the
evening you can also choose grilled fish, sautéed conch, sizzling steaks,
or barbecued ribs. There's live entertainment Thursday and Friday, and
locals gather here nightly for spirited games at the pool table. $ *Aver-
age main: $26* ✉ *Waterfront Dr.* ☎ *284/494–2608* ⌲ *Reservations not
accepted* ⊗ *No lunch Sun.*

$$ ✕**Pusser's Road Town Pub.** Almost everyone who visits Tortola stops
ECLECTIC here at least once to have a bite to eat and to sample the famous Puss-
FAMILY er's Rum Painkiller (fruit juice and rum). The nonthreatening menu
includes cheesy pizza, shepherd's pie, fish-and-chips, and hamburgers.
Dine inside in air-conditioned comfort or outside on the verandah,
which looks out on the harbor. $ *Average main: $15* ✉ *Waterfront Dr.*
☎ *284/494–3897* ⊕ *www.pussers.com.*

$$ ✕**Roti Palace.** You might be tempted to pass this tiny spot on Road
CARIBBEAN Town's Main Street when you see the plastic tablecloths and fake flow-
ers, but the restaurant's reputation for dishing up fantastic roti is known
far and wide. Flatbread is filled with curried potatoes, onions, and either
chicken, beef, conch, goat, or vegetables. Ask for the bones out if you
order the chicken, to save yourself the trouble of fishing them out of
your mouth. $ *Average main: $15* ✉ *Main St.* ☎ *284/494–4196* ▬ *No
credit cards* ⊗ *Closed Sun. No dinner.*

$$$ ✕**Sharky's Cantina.** Enjoy Mexican fare, pizza, or American sandwich
PIZZA classics at this breezy outdoor patio overlooking Sir Francis Drake
Channel. The restaurant is adjacent to the Royal British Virgin Islands
Yacht Club, lending a casual "island yachtie" feel. $ *Average main: $22*
✉ *Waterfront Dr.* ☎ *284/494–8140* ⊕ *www.sharkysbvi.com* ⊗ *Closed
Mon. and Tues.*

$$$$ ✕**Village Cay Restaurant.** Docked sailboats stretch nearly as far as the
ECLECTIC eye can see at this busy Road Town restaurant. Its alfresco dining and
convivial atmosphere make it popular with both locals and visitors. For
lunch, try the grouper club sandwich with an ancho chili mayonnaise,
or their extensive lunch buffet which is popular with local professionals
and yachties alike. Dinner offerings run to fish served a variety of ways,
including West Indian–style with okra, onions, and peppers, as well as
a seafood jambalaya with lobster, crayfish, shrimp, mussels, crab, and
fish in a mango–passion fruit sauce. $ *Average main: $32* ✉ *Wickhams
Cay I* ☎ *284/494–2771.*

$$
ECLECTIC
✕**Virgin Queen.** The sailing and rugby crowds head here to play darts, drink beer, and eat Queen's Pizza—a crusty, cheesy pie topped with sausage, onions, green peppers, and mushrooms. Also on the menu is excellent West Indian and English fare: barbecued ribs with beans and rice, bangers and mash, shepherd's pie, and grilled sirloin steak. Ⓢ *Average main: $17* ✉ *Flemming St.* ☎ *284/494–2310* ⊕ *www.virginqueenbvi. com* ⊘ *Closed Sun. No lunch Sat.*

WEST END

$$$
FRENCH FUSION
✕**The Clubhouse at Frenchman's Cay.** This idyllic, off-the-beaten-path restaurant nestled within the well-manicured grounds of Frenchman's Hotel offers exceptional food. Chef Paul Mason works diligently to incorporate fresh, local Caribbean ingredients and spices into traditional French meals. On Sundays, the restaurant offers a three-course fixed-price brunch that is one of the best values on the island and includes eggs Benedict, rum-and-coconut–battered French toast, yellowfin tuna, and sirloin steaks. Brunch guests dine leisurely both indoors and by the small pool. Dinner items include piña colada–drunken duckling, conch pasta carbonara, Bajan seasoned filet mignon, and fresh seafood selections. Ⓢ *Average main: $29* ✉ *Frenchman's Cay* ☎ *284/494–8811* ⊕ *www.frenchmansbvi.com* ⊘ *Closed Mon.*

$$$
SEAFOOD
✕**Fish and Lime Inn.** In walking distance of the West End Ferry terminal, this pleasantly breezy, waterside restaurant delights daytime visitors with burger, salad, and sandwich offerings that are accompanied by hand-cut french fries. After sunset, candles illuminate the picnic tables on the waterside deck and visiting yachties arrive by dinghy to enjoy menu items that include grilled lobster, cornish game hen, Asian-marinated barbecue ribs, and a savory hot spinach-and-avocado cheesecake that will delight vegetarians. Occasional live music and happy hour specials also keep the bar lively—it fills with local expats on weekends. Ⓢ *Average main: $26* ✉ *West End* ☎ *284/495–4276* ⊕ *www.fishnlime.com.*

$$$
AMERICAN
✕**Pusser's Landing.** Yachters navigate their way to this waterfront restaurant. Downstairs, from late morning to well into the evening, you can belly up to the outdoor mahogany bar or sit inside for sandwiches, fish-and-chips, and pizzas. At dinnertime head upstairs for a harbor view and a quiet alfresco meal of grilled steak or fresh fish. Ⓢ *Average main: $26* ✉ *Soper's Hole* ☎ *284/495–4554* ⊕ *www.pussers.com.*

$$$
ITALIAN
✕**Scaramouche Restaurant.** Eclectic up-cycled furniture, world music, and an idyllic waterside Caribbean setting give this Italian-owned eatery a unique global flair. Stop in for coffee or a cocktail or linger over authentic Italian brunch, lunch, or dinner offerings. Ⓢ *Average main: $27* ✉ *West End* ☎ *284/343–1602* ⊕ *www.scaramouchebvi.com.*

NORTH SHORE

$$$
ECLECTIC
Fodor's Choice
★
✕**Bananakeet Cafe.** The sunset sea-and-mountain views are stunning, so arrive early for the predinner happy hour. "Caribbean fusion" best describes the fare, with an emphasis on seafood, including local Anegada conch swimming in an herb-butter broth. Those without a taste

for seafood won't go hungry—the menu also includes lamb, beef, and chicken dishes. Locals and tourists alike come to enjoy the spectacular sunset, and enjoy a complimentary "sundowner" shot. $ *Average main: $24* ✉ *North Coast Rd., Great Carrot Bay* ☎ *284/494–5842* ⊘ *No lunch.*

$$$$ ✕ **Myett's Garden and Grille.** Partly because it's right on the beach, this
ECLECTIC   bilevel restaurant and bar is hopping day and night for breakfast, lunch, and dinner. Chowder made with fresh conch is the specialty here, and the menu includes vegetarian dishes as well as grilled shrimp, steak, and tuna. There's live entertainment every night in winter. $ *Average main: $32* ✉ *Cane Garden Bay* ☎ *284/495–9649* ⊕ *www.myetts.com.*

$$$ ✕ **Quito's Bar and Restaurant.** This rustic beachside bar and restaurant
CARIBBEAN   is owned and operated by island native Quito Rymer, a multitalented recording star who plays and sings solo on Tuesday and Thursday and performs with his reggae band on Friday. The menu is Caribbean, with an emphasis on fresh fish, but you should try the conch fritters or the barbecue chicken. $ *Average main: $22* ✉ *Cane Garden Bay* ☎ *284/495–4837* ⊘ *No lunch.*

$$$ ✕ **Sebastian's Seaside Grill.** The waves practically lap at your feet at this
ECLECTIC   beachfront restaurant on Tortola's North Shore. The menu emphasizes seafood—especially lobster, conch, and local fish—but you can also find dishes such as ginger chicken and filet mignon. It's a perfect spot to stop for lunch on your around-the-island tour. Try the grilled dolphinfish (mahimahi) sandwich, served on a soft roll with an onion tartar sauce. Finish off with a cup of Sebastian's coffee, spiked with home-brewed rum. $ *Average main: $29* ✉ *Sebastian's on the Beach, North Coast Rd., Apple Bay* ☎ *284/495–4212* ⊕ *www.sebastiansbvi.com.*

$$$ ✕ **1748 Restaurant.** Relax over dinner in this open-air eatery at Long
INTERNATIONAL   Bay Beach Club. Tables are well spaced, offering enough privacy for intimate conversations. The menu changes daily, but several dishes show up regularly. Start your meal with a seafood cocktail, creamy carrot soup, or a mixed green salad. Entrées include grilled London broil served with a rosemary-mushroom sauce, roasted potatoes and vegetables, grilled tuna steak in a spicy cilantro-coconut sauce, and a pesto-marinated grilled vegetable plate. There are always at least five desserts, and they might include Belgian chocolate mousse, strawberry cheesecake, or a fluffy lemon-and-coconut cake. $ *Average main: $28* ✉ *Long Bay Beach Club, Long Bay Rd., Long Bay* ☎ *284/495–4252* ⊕ *www.longbay.com.*

$$$$ ✕ **Sugar Mill Restaurant.** Candles gleam and the background music is
ECLECTIC   peaceful in this romantic restaurant inside a 17th-century sugar mill.
Fodor's Choice   Well-prepared selections on the à la carte menu, which changes nightly,
★   include some pasta and vegetarian entrées. Lobster bisque with basil croutons and a creamy conch chowder are good starters. Favorite entrées include fresh fish with soba noodles, shiitake mushrooms, and a scallion broth; filet mignon topped with an herb-cream sauce; grilled shrimp and scallops with mango salsa; and pumpkin-and–black bean lasagna. $ *Average main: $32* ✉ *Sugar Mill Hotel, North Coast Rd., Apple Bay* ☎ *284/495–4355* ⊕ *www.sugarmillhotel.com* ⊘ *No lunch.*

EAST END

$$
ECLECTIC
✕ **CalaMaya.** Casual fare is what you can find at this waterfront restaurant. You can always order a burger or Caesar salad; the chicken wrap with sweet-and-sour sauce is a tasty alternative. For dinner, try the mahimahi with sautéed vegetables and rice. $ *Average main: $17* ✉ *Hodge's Creek Marina, Blackburn Hwy., Hodge's Creek* ☎ *284/495–2126.*

WHERE TO STAY

Luxury on Tortola is more about a certain state of mind—serenity, seclusion, gentility, and a bit of Britain in the Caribbean—than about state-of-the-art amenities and fabulous facilities. Some properties, especially the vacation villas, are catching up with current trends, but others seem stuck in the 1980s. But don't let a bit of rust on the screen door or a chip in the paint on the balcony railing mar your appreciation of the ambience. You will likely spend most of your time outside, so the location, size, or price of a hotel should be more of a deciding factor than the decor.

TORTOLA'S CARNIVAL

Tortola celebrates Carnival on and around August 1 to mark the anniversary of the end of slavery in 1834. A slew of activities culminating with a parade through the streets take place in Road Town. Hotels fill up fast, so make sure to reserve your room and rental car well in advance.

A stay at any one of the hotels and guesthouses on Tortola's north side will put you closer to the beach, but not to worry: it doesn't take that long to get from one side of the island to the other. Visitors who want to be closer to Road Town's restaurants and shops can find a handful of places in and around the island's main town.

PRIVATE VILLAS

Renting a villa is growing in popularity. Vacationers like the privacy, the space to spread out, and the opportunity to cook meals. As is true everywhere, the most important thing is location. If you want to be close to the beach, opt for a villa on the North Shore. If you want to dine out in Road Town every night, a villa closer to town may be a better bet. Prices per week during the winter season run from around $2,000 for a one- or two-bedroom villa up to $10,000 for a five-room beachfront villa. Rates in summer are substantially less. Most, but not all, villas accept credit cards.

RENTAL AGENCIES

Areana Villas. Areana Villas represents top-of-the-line properties. Pastel-color villas with one to five bedrooms can accommodate up to 10 guests. Many have pools, whirlpool tubs, and tiled courtyards. ☎ *284/494–5864* ⊕ *www.areanavillas.com.*

McLaughlin-Anderson Luxury Villas. The St. Thomas–based McLaughlin-Anderson Luxury Villas manages nearly two dozen properties around Tortola. Villas range from one to six bedrooms and come with full

Cay Marina

kitchens and stellar views. Most have pools. The company can hire a chef and stock your kitchen with groceries. ☎ *340/776–0635, 800/537–6246* 🌐 *www.mclaughlinanderson.com.*

Smiths Gore. Although Smiths Gore has properties all over the island, many are in the Smuggler's Cove area. They range from two to five bedrooms: all have stellar views, lovely furnishings, and lush landscaping. ☎ *284/494–2446* 🌐 *www.smithsgore.com.*

ROAD TOWN AND ENVIRONS

$ HOTEL 🏨 **Fort Burt Hotel.** The Fort Burt Hotel surrounds the ruins of an old Dutch fort, giving you a sense of history along with a night's sleep. **Pros:** nice views; historic site; walk to shops and restaurants. **Cons:** little parking; long walk to Road Town; need car to get around; Wi-Fi only in public areas. [$] *Rooms from: $115* ✉ *Waterfront Dr.* ☎ *284/494–2587* 🌐 *www.fortburt.com* 🛏 *10 rooms, 8 suites* 🍴 *No meals.*

$ HOTEL 🏨 **Maria's Hotel by the Sea.** Sitting near the water in busy Road Town, Maria's Hotel by the Sea is perfect for budget travelers who want to be near shops and restaurants but who don't need many frills. **Pros:** good location; spacious rooms; walk to shops and restaurants. **Cons:** busy street; little parking; need car to get around. [$] *Rooms from: $170* ✉ *Waterfront Dr.* ☎ *284/494–2595* 🌐 *www.mariasbythesea.com* 🛏 *40 rooms* 🍴 *No meals.*

$ HOTEL 🏨 **Moorings-Mariner Inn.** If you enjoy the camaraderie of a busy marina, this inn on the edge of Road Town may appeal to you. **Pros:** good dining options; friendly guests; excellent spot to charter boats. **Cons:** busy location; long walk to Road Town; need car to get around. [$] *Rooms*

CLOSE UP

American or British?

Yes, the Union Jack flutters overhead in the tropical breeze, schools operate on the British system, place names have British spellings, Queen Elizabeth II appoints the governor—and the queen's picture hangs on many walls. Indeed, residents celebrate the queen's birthday every June with a public ceremony. You can overhear that charming English accent from a good handful of expats when you're lunching at Road Town restaurants, and you can buy British biscuits—which Americans call cookies—in the supermarkets.

But you can pay for your lunch and the biscuits with American money because the U.S. dollar is legal tender here. The unusual circumstance is a matter of geography. The practice started in the mid-20th century, when BVI residents went to work in the nearby USVI. On trips home, they brought their U.S. dollars with them. Soon they abandoned the exchange system, and in 1959 the U.S. dollar became the official currency. Interestingly, the government sells stamps for use only in the BVI that often carry pictures of Queen Elizabeth II and other royalty with the monetary value in U.S. dollars and cents.

The American influence continued to grow when Americans began to open businesses in the BVI because they preferred its quieter ambience to the hustle and bustle of St. Thomas. Inevitably, cable and satellite TV's U.S.-based programming, along with Hollywood-made movies, further influenced life in the BVI. And most goods are shipped from St. Thomas in the USVI, meaning you can find more American-made Oreos than British-produced Peak Freans on the supermarket shelves.

from: $220 ✉ *Waterfront Dr.* ☎ *284/494–2333, 800/535–7289* 🌐 *www.bvimarinerinnhotel.com* 🛏 *32 rooms, 7 suites* 🍴 *No meals.*

$ HOTEL 🏨 **Nanny Cay Hotel.** This quiet oasis is far enough from Road Town to give it a secluded feel but close enough to make shops and restaurants convenient. **Pros:** nearby shops and restaurants; pleasant rooms; marina atmosphere. **Cons:** busy location; need car to get around. [$] *Rooms from: $150* ✉ *Waterfront Dr., Nanny Cay* ☎ *284/494–2512* 🌐 *www.nannycay.com* 🛏 *38 rooms* 🍴 *No meals.*

WEST END

$$ RESORT FAMILY 🏨 **Fort Recovery Beachfront Villas.** This is one of those small but special properties that stands out because of its friendly service and the chance to get to know your fellow guests rather than the poshness of the rooms and the upscale amenities. **Pros:** beautiful beach; spacious units; historic site. **Cons:** need car to get around; isolated location. [$] *Rooms from: $345* ✉ *Waterfront Dr.* ☎ *284/495–4354, 855/349–3355* 🌐 *www.fortrecoverytortola.com* 🛏 *30 suites* 🍴 *No meals.*

$$$$ RESORT Fodor's Choice ★ 🏨 **Frenchmans.** Relaxation is the main event at this comfortable resort on Tortola's West End. **Pros:** beautiful, modern decor; easy walk to Soper's Hole. **Cons:** need a car to get around; lots of steps. [$] *Rooms from: $535*

✉ *Off Sir Francis Drake Hwy.* ☎ *284/494–8811* 🌐 *www.frenchmansbvi.com* 🛏 *8 rooms, 3 villas* 🍴 *Multiple meal plans.*

NORTH SHORE

$ B&B/INN 🏨 **Heritage Inn.** The gorgeous sea and mountain views are the stars at this small hotel perched on the edge of a cliff. **Pros:** stunning views; fun vibe; room has kitchenette. **Cons:** need car to get around; close to road. [$] *Rooms from: $225* ✉ *North Coast Rd., Great Carrot Bay* ☎ *284/494–5842* 🌐 *heritageinnbvi.com* 🛏 *6 rooms* 🍴 *No meals.*

$$$ RESORT 🏨 **Long Bay Beach Club.** If you want all the resort amenities, including a beach, pool, spa, and tennis courts, in an intimate setting, then this is your only choice for Tortola. **Pros:** beach-club atmosphere; good restaurant on-site; many activities. **Cons:** need car to get around; sometimes curt staff; uphill hike to some rooms. [$] *Rooms from: $395* ✉ *Long Bay Rd., Long Bay* ☎ *284/495–4252, 800/858–4618* 🌐 *www.longbay.com* 🛏 *20 villas, 10 suites, 10 cabanas* 🍴 *Multiple meal plans.*

$ HOTEL 🏨 **Myett's.** Tucked away in a beachfront garden, this tiny hotel puts you right in the middle of Cane Garden Bay's busy hustle and bustle. **Pros:** beautiful beach; good restaurant; shops nearby. **Cons:** busy location. [$] *Rooms from: $200* ✉ *Cane Garden Bay* ☎ *284/495–9649* 🌐 *www.myetts.com* 🛏 *6 rooms, 4 cottages, 1 villa* 🍴 *No meals.*

$ HOTEL 🏨 **Ole Works Inn.** The small hotel's location on busy Cane Garden Bay and the fact that it's owned by Quito Rymer, one of the island's most popular musicians, guarantees that it's not a quiet retreat. **Pros:** near bars and restaurants; near beach; good restaurant. **Cons:** busy location; loud music; need car to get around; Wi-Fi only in public areas. [$] *Rooms from: $95* ✉ *Cane Garden Bay* ☎ *284/495–4837* 🌐 *www.quitorymer.com* 🛏 *17 rooms, 3 suites* 🍴 *No meals.*

$ RESORT 🏨 **Sebastian's on the Beach.** Sitting on the island's north coast, Sebastian's definitely has a beachy feel, and that's its primary charm. **Pros:** nice beach; good restaurants; beachfront rooms. **Cons:** on busy road; some rooms nicer than others; need car to get around. [$] *Rooms from: $135* ✉ *North Coast Rd., Apple Bay* ☎ *284/495–4212, 800/336–4870* 🌐 *www.sebastiansbvi.com* 🛏 *26 rooms, 9 villas* 🍴 *No meals.*

$$ RESORT Fodor's Choice ★ 🏨 **Sugar Mill Hotel.** Though it's not a sprawling resort, the Sugar Mill Hotel has a Caribbean cachet that's hard to beat, and it's a favorite place to stay on Tortola. **Pros:** lovely rooms; excellent restaurants on-site; nice views. **Cons:** on busy road; small beach; need car to get around. [$] *Rooms from: $350* ✉ *North Coast Rd., Apple Bay* ☎ *284/495–4355, 800/462–8834* 🌐 *www.sugarmillhotel.com* 🛏 *19 rooms, 2 suites, 1 villa, 1 cottage* 🍴 *No meals.*

EAST END

$$$$ RESORT Fodor's Choice ★ 🏨 **Surfsong Villa Resort.** Nestled in lush foliage right at the water's edge, this small resort on Beef Island provides a pleasant respite for vacationers who want a villa atmosphere with some hotel amenities. **Pros:** lovely rooms; beautiful beach; chef on call. **Cons:** need car to get around; no restaurants nearby. [$] *Rooms from: $465* ✉ *Off Beef Island Rd.,*

5

Beef Island ☎ *284/495–1864* ⊕ *www.surfsong.net* ⤴ *1 suite, 7 villas*
⊘ *Multiple meal plans.*

NIGHTLIFE AND PERFORMING ARTS

Like any other good sailing destination, Tortola has watering holes that
are popular with salty and not-so-salty dogs. Many offer entertainment;
check the weekly *Limin' Times* for schedules and up-to-date information. The local beverage is the Painkiller, an innocent-tasting mixture of
fruit juices and rums. It goes down smoothly but packs quite a punch,
so give yourself time to recover before you order another.

ROAD TOWN AND ENVIRONS

PERFORMING ARTS
Performing Arts Series. Musicians from around the world take to the
stage during the island's Performing Arts Series, held annually October
through May. Past artists have included Latin jazz artist Tito Puente
Jr., gospel singer Kim Burrell, and pianist Richard Ormond. ⊠ *H.
Lavity Stoutt Community College, Blackburn Hwy., Paraquita Bay*
☎ *284/494–4994* ⊕ *www.hlscc.edu.vg.*

NIGHTLIFE
The Pub. At this popular watering hole, there's a happy hour from 5 to
7 every day and live music on Thursday and Friday. ⊠ *Waterfront St.*
☎ *284/494–2608.*

Pusser's Road Town Pub. Courage is what people are seeking here—
John Courage beer by the pint. Or try Pusser's famous mixed drink,
called the Painkiller, and snack on the excellent pizza. ⊠ *Waterfront St.*
☎ *284/494–3897* ⊕ *www.pussers.com.*

NORTH SHORE

NIGHTLIFE
Bomba's Surfside Shack. By day, you can see that Bomba's, which is covered with everything from crepe-paper leis to ancient license plates to
spicy graffiti, looks like a pile of junk; by night it's one of Tortola's
liveliest spots. There's a fish fry and a live band every Wednesday and
Sunday. People flock here from all over on the full moon, when bands
play all night long. ⊠ *North Coast Rd., Apple Bay* ☎ *284/495–4148.*

Fodor's Choice **Myett's.** Local bands play at this popular spot, which has live music dur-
★ ing happy hour. There's usually a lively dance crowd. ⊠ *Cane Garden
Bay* ☎ *284/495–9649* ⊕ *www.myetts.com.*

Quito's Bar and Restaurant. BVI recording star Quito Rymer sings island
ballads and love songs at his rustic beachside bar–restaurant. Solo shows
are on Tuesday and Thursday at 8:30; on Friday at 9:30 Quito performs
with his band. ⊠ *North Coast Rd., Cane Garden Bay* ☎ *284/495–4837.*

Sebastian's. There's often live music at Sebastian's on Sunday evenings
in season, and you can dance under the stars (but call ahead for the

schedule). ⊠ *North Coast Rd., Apple Bay* ☎ *284/495–4212* ⊕ *www. sebastiansbvi.com.*

SHOPPING

The BVI aren't really a shopper's delight, but there are many shops showcasing original wares—from jams and spices to resort wear and excellent artwork.

ROAD TOWN AND ENVIRONS

Many shops and boutiques are clustered along and just off Road Town's **Main Street.** You can shop in Road Town's **Wickham's Cay I** adjacent to the marina. The **Crafts Alive Market** on the Road Town waterfront is a collection of colorful West Indian–style buildings with shops that carry items made in the BVI. You might find pretty baskets or interesting pottery or perhaps a bottle of home-brewed hot sauce.

ART

Allamanda Gallery. Photography by the gallery's owner, Amanda Baker, as well as books, gifts, and cards are on display and available to purchase. ⊠ *124 Main St.* ☎ *284/494–6680* ⊕ *www.virginportraits.com.*

Sunny Caribbee. This gallery has many paintings, prints, and watercolors by artists from around the Caribbean, and is also known for its collection of spices, hot sauces, and other food products. ⊠ *119 Main St.* ☎ *284/494–2178* ⊕ *www.sunnycaribbee.com.*

CLOTHES AND TEXTILES

Arawak. This boutique carries batik sundresses, sportswear, and resort wear for men and women. There's also a selection of children's clothing. ⊠ *Nanny Cay Marina, Nanny Cay* ☎ *284/494–3983.*

Latitude 18°. This store sells Maui Jim, Ray-Ban, and Oakley sunglasses; Freestyle watches; and a fine collection of beach towels, sandals, Crocs, sundresses, and sarongs. ⊠ *Waterfront Drive* ☎ *284/494–6196* ⊕ *www. latitude18.com.*

Pusser's Company Store. The Road Town Pusser's sells nautical memorabilia, ship models, and marine paintings. There's also an entire line of clothing for both men and women, handsome decorator bottles of Pusser's rum, and gift items bearing the Pusser's logo. ⊠ *Main St. at Waterfront Rd.* ☎ *284/494–2467* ⊕ *www.pussers.com.*

FOODSTUFFS

Ample Hamper. This grocer has an outstanding collection of cheeses, wines, fresh fruits, and canned goods from the United Kingdom and the United States. The staff will stock your yacht or rental villa. ⊠ *Inner Harbour Marina* ☎ *284/494–2494* ⊕ *www.amplehamper.com.*

Best of British. This boutique has lots of nifty British food you won't find elsewhere. Shop here for Marmite, Vegemite, shortbread, frozen meat pies, and delightful Christmas "crackers" filled with surprises. ⊠ *Wickham's Cay I* ☎ *284/494–3462.*

Most of Tortola's shops are in Road Town.

RiteWay. This market carries a good (but not massive) selection of the usual supplies. RiteWay will stock villas and yachts. ⊠ *Waterfront Dr. at Pasea Estate* ☎ *284/494–2263* ⊕ *www.rtwbvi.com* ⊠ *Flemming St.* ☎ *284/347–1230.*

GIFTS

Crafts Alive Village. The collection of colorful West Indian cottages offering handicrafts, fabrics, and souvenirs at the Crafts Alive Village makes for excellent one-stop souvenir shopping. ⊠ *Waterfront Dr.* ☎ *284/494–3134.*

Sunny Caribbee. In a brightly painted West Indian house, this store packages its own herbs, teas, coffees, vinegars, hot sauces, soaps, skin and suntan lotions, and exotic concoctions—Arawak Love Potion and Island Hangover Cure, for example. ⊠ *119 Main St.* ☎ *284/494–2178* ⊕ *www.sunnycaribbee.com.*

JEWELRY

Samarkand. The charming jewelry sold here includes gold-and-silver pendants, earrings, bracelets, and pins, many with island themes such as seashells, lizards, pelicans, and palm trees. There are also reproduction Spanish pieces of eight (old Spanish coins) similar to those found on sunken galleons and jewelry made with local Virgin Islands green jasper. ⊠ *Main St.* ☎ *284/494–6415* ⊙ *Closed Sun.*

WEST END

There's an ever-growing number of art and clothing stores at **Soper's Hole** in West End.

Rocking the Bay

Cane Garden Bay is the place to go for live music, with Quito Rymer frequently delighting the crowds at his Quito's Bar and Restaurant. Myett's is also a happening place some nights. The entire village really jams come May, when the BVI Music Fest gets going. Thousands of people arrive from around the Caribbean and around the world to listen to the best of the Caribbean's reggae, blues, and soca musicians.

Cane Garden Bay is a small but growing community on Tortola's North Shore. There are no chain hotels or sprawling resorts here—all the places to stay are small and locally owned. In addition to the handful of properties on the beach, there are plenty of others up on the hillsides that have eye-popping views. The area has plenty of places to eat, with lobster the specialty on many a menu.

The area fairly bustles on cruise-ship days as busload after busload of round-the-island tour groups disembark to snap a few pictures. Once they're gone, however, a modicum of peace returns to the village.

CLOTHES AND TEXTILES

Pusser's Company Store. Pusser's West End store sells nautical memorabilia, ship models, and marine paintings. There's also an entire line of clothing for both men and women, handsome decorator bottles of Pusser's rum, and gift items bearing the Pusser's logo. ⊠ *Soper's Hole Marina, Soper's Hole* ☎ *284/495–4599.*

Zenaida's of West End. Vivian Jenik Helm travels through South America, Africa, and India in search of batiks, hand-painted and hand-blocked fabrics, and interesting weaves that can be made into *pareus* (women's wraps) or wall hangings. The shop also sells unusual bags, belts, sarongs, scarves, and ethnic jewelry. ⊠ *Soper's Hole Marina* ☎ *284/495–4867.*

FOODSTUFFS

Ample Hamper. The West End branch of this market has an outstanding collection of cheeses, wines, fresh fruits, and canned goods from the United Kingdom and the United States. The staff will stock your yacht or rental villa. ⊠ *Frenchman's Cay Marina* ☎ *284/494–2494* ⊕ *www.amplehamper.com.*

SPORTS AND THE OUTDOORS

BOATING

Big Sexy Day Charters. The private half-day and day tours aboard a 36-foot powerboat start at $400. ⊠ *West End* ☎ *284/544–9141* ⊕ *www.bigsexyboatrentals.com.*

CRICKET

Fans of this sport are fiercely loyal and exuberant. Matches are held at the New Recreation Grounds, next to the J.R. O'Neal Botanic Gardens, on weekends from February to April. Check local newspapers or ask at your hotel front desk for information on times and teams.

DIVING AND SNORKELING

Fodor's Choice
★

Clear waters and numerous reefs afford some wonderful opportunities for underwater exploration. In some spots visibility reaches 100 feet, but colorful reefs teeming with fish are often just a few feet below the sea surface. The BVI's system of marine parks means the underwater life visible through your mask will stay protected.

There are several popular dive spots around the islands. **Alice in Wonderland** is a deep dive south of Ginger Island, with a wall that slopes gently from 15 feet to 100 feet. It's an area overrun with huge mushroom-shape coral, hence its name. Crabs, lobsters, and shimmering fan corals make their homes in the tunnels, ledges, and overhangs of **Blonde Rock,** a pinnacle that goes from 15 feet below the surface to 60 feet deep. It's between Dead Chest and Salt Island. When the currents aren't too strong, **Brewers Bay Pinnacle** (20 to 90 feet down) teems with sea life. At the **Indians,** near Pelican Island, colorful corals decorate canyons and grottoes created by four large, jagged pinnacles that rise 50 feet from the ocean floor. The **Painted Walls** is a shallow dive site where corals and sponges create a kaleidoscope of colors on the walls of four long gullies. It's northeast of Dead Chest.

The **Chikuzen,** sunk northwest of Brewers Bay in 1981, is a 246-foot vessel in 75 feet of water; it's home to thousands of fish, colorful corals, and big rays. In 1867 the **RMS Rhone,** a 310-foot royal mail steamer, split in two when it sank in a devastating hurricane. It's so well preserved that it was used as an underwater prop in the movie *The Deep.* You can see the crow's nest and bowsprit, the cargo hold in the bow, and the engine and enormous propeller shaft in the stern. Its four parts are at various depths from 30 to 80 feet. Get yourself some snorkeling gear and hop aboard a dive boat to this wreck near Salt Island (across the channel from Road Town). Every dive outfit in the BVI runs scuba and snorkel tours to this part of the BVI National Parks Trust; if you only have time for one trip, make it this one. Rates start at around $70 for a one-tank dive and $100 for a two-tank dive.

Your hotel probably has a dive company right on the premises. If not, the staff can recommend one nearby. Using your hotel's dive company makes a trip to the offshore dive and snorkel sites a breeze. Just stroll down to the dock and hop aboard. All dive companies are certified by PADI, the Professional Association of Diving Instructors, which ensures that your instructors are qualified to safely take vacationers diving. The boats are also inspected to make sure they're seaworthy. If you've never dived, try a short introductory dive, often called a resort course, which teaches you enough to get you underwater. In the unlikely event you get a case of the bends, a condition that can happen when you rise to the

Continued on page 196

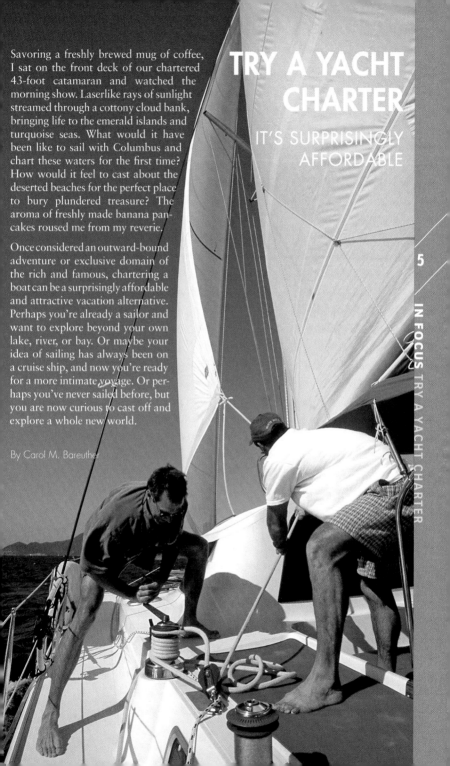

TRY A YACHT CHARTER

IT'S SURPRISINGLY AFFORDABLE

Savoring a freshly brewed mug of coffee, I sat on the front deck of our chartered 43-foot catamaran and watched the morning show. Laserlike rays of sunlight streamed through a cottony cloud bank, bringing life to the emerald islands and turquoise seas. What would it have been like to sail with Columbus and chart these waters for the first time? How would it feel to cast about the deserted beaches for the perfect place to bury plundered treasure? The aroma of freshly made banana pancakes roused me from my reverie.

Once considered an outward-bound adventure or exclusive domain of the rich and famous, chartering a boat can be a surprisingly affordable and attractive vacation alternative. Perhaps you're already a sailor and want to explore beyond your own lake, river, or bay. Or maybe your idea of sailing has always been on a cruise ship, and now you're ready for a more intimate voyage. Or perhaps you've never sailed before, but you are now curious to cast off and explore a whole new world.

By Carol M. Bareuther

CREWED CHARTER

On a crewed charter, you sit back and relax while the crew provides for your every want and need. Captains are licensed by the U.S. Coast Guard or the equivalent in the British maritime system. Cooks—preferring to be called chefs—have skills that go far beyond peanut butter and jelly sandwiches. There are four meals a day, and many chefs boast certificates from culinary schools ranging from the Culinary Institute of America in New York to the Cordon Bleu in Paris.

The advantage of a crewed yacht charter, with captain and cook, is that it takes every bit of stress out of the vacation. With a captain who knows the local waters, you get to see some of the coves and anchorages that are not necessarily in the guidebooks. Your meals are prepared, cabins cleaned, beds made up every day—and turned down at night, too. Plus, you can sail and take the helm as often as you like. But at the end of the day, the captain is the one who will take responsibility for anchoring safely for the night while the chef goes below and whips up a gourmet meal.

APPROXIMATE COSTS	PROS	CONS
From $4,300 for 2 people for 5 days	▪ Passengers just have to lay back and relax (unless they want to help sail)	▪ More expensive than a bareboat, especially if you get a catamaran
From $5,500 for 2 people for 7 days	▪ Most are catamarans, offering more space than monohulls	▪ Less privacy for your group than on a bareboat
From $8,600 for 6 people for 5 days	▪ You have an experienced, local hand on board if something goes wrong	▪ Captain makes ultimate decisions about the course
From $10,500 for 6 people for 7 days	▪ Water toys and other extras are often included	▪ Chance for personality conflicts: you have to get along with the captain and chef. This is where a charter yacht broker is helpful in determining what yachts and crews might be a good fit.
Prices are all-inclusive for a 50- to 55-foot yacht in high season except for 15%–20% gratuity.	▪ Competively priced within an all-inclusive resort	

(top) Family sailing in the British Virgin Islands

BAREBOAT

If you'd like to bareboat, don't be intimidated. It's a myth that you must be a graduate of a sailing school in order to pilot your own charter boat. A bareboat company will ask you to fill out a resume. The company checks for prior boat-handling experience, the type of craft you've sailed (whether powerboat or sailboat), and in what type of waters. Real-life experience, meaning all those day and weekend trips close to home, count as valuable know-how. If you've done a bit of boating, you may be more qualified than you think to take out a bareboat.

Costs can be very similar for a bareboat and crewed charter, depending on the time of year and size of the boat. You'll pay the highest rates between Christmas and New Year's, when you may not be allowed to do a charter of less than a week. But there are more than 800 bareboats between the USVI and BVI, so regardless of your budget, you should be able to find something in your price range. Plus, you might save a bit by chartering an older boat from a smaller company instead of the most state-of-the-art yacht from a larger company.

APPROXIMATE COSTS	PROS	CONS
From $3,200 for a small monohull (2–3 cabins)	■ The ultimate freedom to set the yacht's course	■ Must be able to pass a sailing test
From $5,200 for a large monohull (4–5 cabins)	■ A chance to test your sailing skills	■ Those unfamiliar with the region may not find the best anchorages
From $5,500 for a small catamaran (2 cabins)	■ Usually a broader range of boats and prices to choose from	■ You have to cook for and clean up after yourself
From $7,500 for a large catamaran (4 cabins)	■ More flexibility for meals (you can always go ashore if you don't feel like cooking)	■ You have to do your own provisioning and planning for meals
Prices exclude food, beverages, fuel, and other supplies. Most bareboat rates do not include water toys, taxes, insurance, and permits.	■ You can always hire a captain for a few days	■ If something goes wrong, there isn't an experienced hand onboard

Three women rigging the sails.

WHAT TO CONSIDER

Whether bareboat or a crewed yacht, there are a few points to ponder when selecting your boat.

HOW BIG IS YOUR GROUP?

As a general rule, count on one cabin for every two people. Most people also prefer to have one head (bathroom) per cabin. A multihull, also called a catamaran, offers more space and more equal-size cabins than a monohull sailboat.

WHAT TYPE OF BOAT?

If you want to do some good old traditional sailing, where you're heeling over with the seas at your rails, monohulls are a good option. On the other hand, multihulls are more stable, easier to board, and have a big salon for families. They're also ideal if some people get seasick or aren't as gung-ho for the more traditional sailing experience. If you'd like to cover more ground, choose a motor yacht.

DO YOU HAVE A SPECIAL INTEREST?

Some crewed charter boats specialize in certain types of charters. Among these are learn-to-sail excursions, honeymoon cruises, scuba-diving adventures, and family-friendly trips. Your broker can steer you to the boats that fit your specific needs.

WHAT KIND OF EQUIPMENT DO YOU WANT ONBOARD?

Most charter boats have satellite navigation systems and autopilots, as well as regulation safety gear, dinghies with motors, and even stereos and entertainment systems. But do you want a generator or battery-drive refrigeration system? How about a/c? Do you want a satellite phone? Do you want water toys like kayaks, boogie boards, and Windsurfers?

Now that you've decided on bareboat versus crewed charter and selected your craft, all you need to do is confirm the availability of the date with the company or broker and pay a nonrefundable deposit equal to 50% of the charter price.

TO SAIL OR NOT TO SAIL?

If you're not sure whether a charter yacht vacation is right for you, consider this: would you enjoy a floating hotel room where the scenery outside your window changed according to your desires? A "yes" may entice wary companions to try chartering. A single one-week trip will have them hooked.

Two catamaran sailboats seen from behind.

CATAMARANS
Multihulls are more stable, easier to board and have a big salon for families. Seasickness is less of an issue.

MOTOR YACHT
Best if you want to cover more ground, but costs a lot more than a sailboat.

MONOHULLS
Good for more traditional and active sailing, but the movement may not appeal to non-sailors.

CHOOSING A CHARTER

Information on charters is much easier to find now than even a decade ago. Websites for bareboat companies show photos of different types of boats—both interiors and exteriors—as well as layout schematics, lists of equipment and amenities, and sample itineraries. Many sites will allow you to book a charter directly, while others give you the option of calling a toll-free number to speak with an agent first.

There are two types of websites for crewed charters. If you just want some information, the **Virgin Islands Charteryacht League** (⊕ www.vicl.org) and the **Charter Yacht Society of the British Virgin Islands** (⊕ www.bvicrewedyachts.com) both help you understand what to look for in a crewed charter, from the size of the boat to the amenities. You can't reserve on these sites, but they link to the sites of brokers, who are the sales force for the charter yacht industry. Most brokers, whether they're based in the Caribbean, the United States, or Europe, attend annual charter yacht shows in St. Thomas, Tortola, and Antigua. At these shows, brokers visit the boats and meet the crews. This is what gives brokers their depth of knowledge for "matchmaking," or linking you with a boat that will meet your personality and preferences.

The charter companies also maintain websites. About 30% of the crewed charter yachts based out of the U.S. and British Virgin Islands can be booked directly. This saves the commission an owner has to pay to the broker. But while "going direct" might seem advantageous, there is usually little difference in pricing, and if you use a broker, he or she can help troubleshoot if something goes wrong or find a replacement boat if the boat owner has to cancel.

Timing also matters. Companies may offer last-minute specials that are available only online. These special rates—usually for specific dates, destinations, and boats—are updated weekly or even daily.

PREPARING FOR YOUR CHARTER

British Virgin Islands—anchorage in a tropical sea with breakfast on board.

PROVISIONING

Bareboaters must do their own provisioning. It's a good idea to arrange provisioning at least a week in advance.

Provisioning packages from the charter company are usually a bit more expensive, at $30 to $35 per person per day, but they save you the hassle of planning the details. You can also shop on arrival. Both St. Thomas and Tortola have markets, though larger grocery stores may require a taxi ride. If you shop carefully, this route can still save you money. Just be sure to allow yourself a few hours after arrival to get everything done.

PLANNING

For a crewed charter, your broker will send a preference sheet for both food and your wishes for the trip. Perhaps you'd like lazy days of sleeping late, sunning, and swimming. Or you might prefer active days of sailing with stops for snorkeling and exploring ashore. If there's a special spot you'd like to visit, list it so your captain can plan the itinerary accordingly.

PACKING TIPS

Pack light for any type of charter. Bring soft-sided luggage (preferably a duffle bag) since space is limited and storage spots are usually odd shapes. Shorts, T-shirts, and swimsuits are sufficient. Bring something a bit nicer if you plan to dine ashore. Shoes are seldom required except ashore, but you might want beach shoes to protect your feet in the water. Most boats provide snorkel equipment, but always ask. Bring sunscreen, but a type that will not stain cockpit cushions and decks.

WHAT YOU'LL SEE IN THE USBVI

Cruz Bay in St. John

MAIN CHARTER BASES

The U.S. and British Virgin Islands boast more than 100 stepping-stone islands and cays within a 50-nautical-mile radius. This means easy line-of-sight navigation and island-hopping in protected waters, and it's rare that you'll spend more than a few hours moving between islands.

Tortola, in the British Virgin Islands, is the crewed charter and bareboat mecca of the Caribbean. This fact is plainly apparent from the forest of masts rising out from any marina.

The U.S. Virgin Islands fleet is based in **St. Thomas**. Direct flights from the mainland, luxurious accommodations, and duty-free shopping are drawing cards for departures from the U.S. Virgin Islands, whereas the British Virgins are closer to the prime cruising grounds.

POPULAR ANCHORAGES

On a typical weeklong charter you could set sail from Red Hook, St. Thomas, then cross Pillsbury Sound to St. John, which offers popular north-shore anchorages in Honeymoon, Trunk, or Francis bays.

But the best sailing and snorkeling always includes the British Virgin Islands (which require a valid passport or passport card). After clearing customs in West End, Tortola, many yachts hop along a series of smaller islands that run along the south side of the Sir Francis Drake Channel. But some yachts will also visit Guana Island, Great Camanoe, or Marina Cay off Tortola's more isolated east end.

The islands south of Tortola include **Norman Island**, the rumored site of Robert Lewis Stevenson's *Treasure Island*. The next island over is **Peter Island**, famous for it's posh resort and a popular anchorage for yachters. Farther east, off Salt Island, is the wreck of the **RMS *Rhone***—the most magnificent dive site in the eastern Caribbean. Giant boulders form caves and grottos called The Baths at the southern end of **Virgin Gorda**.

A downwind run along Tortola's north shore ends at **Jost Van Dyke**, where that famous guitar-strumming calypsonian Foxy Callwood sings personalized ditties that make for a memorable finale.

surface too fast, your dive team will whisk you to the decompression chamber at Schneider Regional Medical Center in nearby St. Thomas.

RECOMMENDED DIVE OPERATORS

Blue Waters Divers. If you're chartering a sailboat, Blue Waters Divers will meet yours at Peter, Salt, Norman, or Cooper Island for a rendezvous dive. The company teaches resort, open-water, rescue, and advanced diving courses, and also makes daily dive trips. Rates include all equipment as well as instruction. Reserve two days in advance. ⊠ *Nanny Cay Marina, Nanny Cay* ☎ *284/494–2847* ⊕ *www.bluewaterdiversbvi. com* ⊠ *Soper's Hole Marina, Soper's Hole, Tortola* ☎ *284/495–1200* ⊕ *www.bluewaterdiversbvi.com.*

FISHING

Most of the boats that take you deep-sea fishing for bluefish, wahoo, swordfish, and shark leave from nearby St. Thomas, but local anglers like to fish the shallower water for bonefish. A three-quarter-day trip runs about $650, a full day around $850. Wading trips are $325.

Caribbean Fly Fishing ⊠ *Nanny Cay Marina, Nanny Cay* ☎ *284/494–4797, 284/499–1590* ⊕ *www.caribflyfishing.com.*

HIKING

FAMILY Sage Mountain National Park attracts hikers who enjoy the quiet trails that crisscross the island's loftiest peak. There are some lovely views and the chance to see rare plant species that grow only at higher elevations.

SAILING

FAMILY
Fodor'sChoice
★

The BVI are among the world's most popular sailing destinations. They're clustered together and surrounded by calm waters, so it's fairly easy to sail from one anchorage to the next. Most of the Caribbean's biggest sailboat charter companies have operations in Tortola. If you know how to sail, you can charter a bareboat (perhaps for your entire vacation); if you're unschooled, you can hire a boat with a captain. Prices vary depending on the type and size of the boat you wish to charter. In season, a weekly charter runs from $1,500 to $35,000. Book early to make sure you get the boat that fits you best. Most of Tortola's marinas have hotels, which give you a convenient place to spend the nights before and after your charter.

If a day sail to some secluded anchorage is more your spot of tea, the BVI have numerous boats of various sizes and styles that leave from many points around Tortola. Prices start at around $80 per person for a full-day sail, including lunch and snorkeling equipment.

Aristocat Charters. This company's 48-foot catamaran sets sail daily to Jost Van Dyke, Norman Island, and other small islands. ⊠ *West End* ☎ *284/499–1249* ⊕ *www.aristocatcharters.com.*

BVI Yacht Charters. The 31- to 52-foot sailboats for charter here come with or without a captain and crew. ⊠ *Port Purcell, Road Town* ☎ *284/494–4289, 888/615–4006* ⊕ *www.bviyachtcharters.com.*

DID YOU KNOW?

The wreck of the RMS *Rhone*, which sank in 75 feet of water near Salt Island in 1867, is one of the most famous wreck dives in the Caribbean.

The Catamaran Company. The catamarans here come with or without a captain. ✉ *Maya Cove Marina, Fat Hog's Bay* ☎ *284/494–6661, 800/262–0308* ⊕ *www.catamarans.com.*

Horizon Yacht Charters BVI. Horizon rents monohull and catamaran sailing vessels with bareboat, captain only, or full-crew options. ✉ *Nanny Cay* ☎ *877/494–8787, 284/494–8787* ⊕ *www.horizonyachtcharters.com.*

The Moorings. One of the world's best bareboat operations, The Moorings has a large fleet of both monohulls and catamarans. Hire a captain or sail the boat yourself. ✉ *Wickham's Cay II, Road Town* ☎ *800/535–7289* ⊕ *www.moorings.com.*

Regency Yacht Vacations. If you prefer a powerboat, call Regency Yacht Vacations. It handles captain and full-crew sail and powerboat charters. ✉ *Wickham's Cay I, Road Town* ☎ *284/495–1970, 800/524–7676* ⊕ *www.regencyvacations.com.*

Sunsail. A full fleet of boats to charter with or without a captain is available here. ✉ *Wickham's Cay II, Road Town* ☎ *888/350–3568, 800/327–2276* ⊕ *www.sunsail.com.*

Voyage Charters. Voyage has a variety of sailboats for charter, with or without a captain and crew. ✉ *Soper's Hole Marina, West End* ☎ *284/494–0740, 888/869–2436* ⊕ *www.voyagecharters.com.*

White Squall II. This 80-foot schooner has regularly scheduled day sails to The Baths at Virgin Gorda, Cooper, the Indians, and the Caves at Norman Island. ✉ *Village Cay Marina, Road Town* ☎ *284/541–2222* ⊕ *www.whitesquall2.com.*

SURFING

Surfing is big on Tortola's North Shore, particularly when the winter swells come in to Josiah's and Apple bays. Rent surfboards starting at $65 for a full day.

HIHO. Lots of good surfboards and stand-up paddleboards are available for rent as well as for sale. The staff will give you advice on the best spots to put in your board. ✉ *Trellis Bay, Trellis Bay* ☎ *284/494–7694* ⊕ *www.go-hiho.com.*

6

VIRGIN GORDA

WELCOME TO VIRGIN GORDA

TOP REASONS TO GO

★ **Beautiful beaches:** Virgin Gorda's stunning, white, sandy beaches are the number one reason to visit. The Baths are the most crowded, but other beaches are usually quiet.

★ **The Baths:** The ever-popular Baths, an area strewn with giant boulders—many as big as houses—draw hordes of visitors during peak hours. Go early or late to enjoy the solitude.

★ **Vacation villas:** Virgin Gorda villas come in all sizes and price ranges. Some are so spectacular that they grace the pages of glossy magazines, but there are plenty of more modest choices.

★ **North Sound:** Even if you aren't a guest at one of North Sound's handful of resorts, you still should visit. Ferries depart frequently. Stay for lunch, or just enjoy an afternoon drink.

★ **Solitude:** You don't go to Virgin Gorda for the nightlife (although there is some here and there) or endless activities (but you might want to rent a kayak). This is a spot for relaxation.

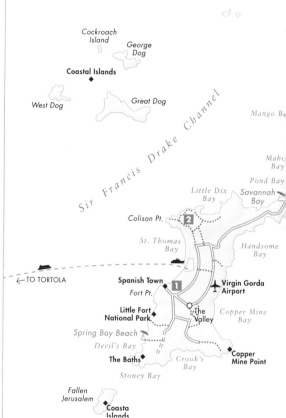

1 The Valley. Virgin Gorda's main settlement, Spanish Town, has almost all the island's independent businesses and restaurants. There are several resorts in or around the main hub, with others near The Baths and Spring Bay to the southwest. The main ferry terminal is here as well.

2 Northwest Shore. Except for those resorts and villas in The Valley, most of the island's other resorts and prime villa rental areas are along the northwest shoreline.

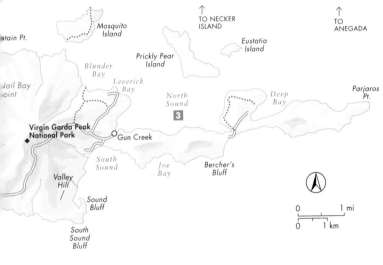

TO NECKER ISLAND

TO ANEGADA

Mosquito Island

tain Pt.

Eustatia Island

Prickly Pear Island

Blunder Bay

Leverick Bay

North Sound

3

Deep Bay

Parjaros Pt.

Jail Bay oint

Virgin Gorda Peak National Park

Gun Creek

South Sound

Joe Bay

Bercher's Bluff

Valley Hill

Sound Bluff

South Sound Bluff

0   1 mi

0   1 km

6

Caribbean Sea

GETTING ORIENTED

Beautiful beaches are scattered all over the island and are worth exploring. If you rent a car, you can easily hit all the sights in one day. The best plan is to explore the area near your hotel (either The Valley or North Sound) first, then take a day to drive to the other end. Stop to climb Gorda Peak, which is in the island's center.

3 **North Sound.** With no road access, this quiet and isolated part of the island is home to several resorts and frequent ferry service. The beautiful beaches and solitude keep visitors coming back. Be sure to spend at least one day here.

Updated by
Susan Zaluski

Progressing from laid-back to more laid-back, mountainous and arid Virgin Gorda fits right in. Its main road sticks to the center of the island, connecting its odd-shaped north and south appendages; sailing is the preferred mode of transportation. Spanish Town, the most noteworthy settlement, is on the southern wing, as are The Baths. Here smooth, giant boulders are scattered about the beach and form delightful sea grottoes just offshore.

Lovely Virgin Gorda sits at the end of the chain that stretches eastward from St. Thomas. Virgin Gorda, or "Fat Virgin," received its name from Christopher Columbus. The explorer envisioned the island as a reclining pregnant woman, with Virgin Gorda Peak being her belly and the boulders of The Baths her toes.

Virgin Gorda runs at a slow pace. Goats still wander across the roads in places like North Sound. But that's changing. Virgin Gorda Yacht Harbour, the center of commerce and activity in Spanish Town, is expanding. More hotels and condominium developments are in the works, and pricey villas are going up all over the island. That said, budget travelers can still find modest villas and guesthouses all over the island to while away a few days or more.

Virgin Gorda isn't all that easy to get to, but once you're here you can find enough diversions to make getting out of your chaise lounge worthwhile. You can drive from one end of the island to the other in about 20 minutes, but make sure to take time to visit Copper Mine Point to learn about the island's history or to hike up Virgin Gorda Peak to survey the surroundings. At numerous spots with stellar views, the local government has thoughtfully built viewing platforms with adjacent parking. It's worth a stop to snap some photos.

The scenery on the northeastern side of the island is the most dramatic, with a steep road ending at Leverick Bay and Gun Creek in North Sound. For lunch you can hop aboard a ferry to Biras Creek Resort, the Bitter End Yacht Club, or Saba Rock Resort. Head to the other end of the island for views of the huge boulders that spill over from The Baths into the southwest section of Virgin Gorda. You can find several restaurants dotted around this end of the island.

In truth, though, it's the beaches that make Virgin Gorda special. Stretches of talcum-powder sand fringe aquamarine waters. Popular places like The Baths see hordes of people, but just a quick walk down the road brings you to quieter beaches like Spring Bay. On the other side of Spanish Town you may be the only person at such sandy spots as Savannah Bay.

If shopping's on your agenda, you can find stores in Virgin Gorda Yacht Harbour selling items perfect for rounding out your tropical wardrobe or tucking into your suitcase to enjoy when you get home.

Virgin Gorda has very little crime and hardly any frosty attitudes among its more than 3,100 permanent residents. In short, the island provides a welcome respite in a region that's changing rapidly.

GETTING HERE AND AROUND

6

AIR TRAVEL

There's no nonstop service from the continental United States to Virgin Gorda. Air Sunshine flies between Virgin Gorda and St. Thomas and San Juan, Puerto Rico. If you have seven or more people in your party, it probably pays to hire a charter plane from St. Thomas or San Juan. Fly BVI is one of the local charter services. If you're coming from San Juan Airport in Puerto Rico, Seaborne flies to Virgin Gorda's airport.

CAR TRAVEL

Virgin Gorda has a small road system, and a single, very steep road links the north and south ends of the island. You will probably need a car to get around for at least a few days of your stay unless you plan on staying put at your resort. If your resort is reachable only by boat, you should rent only for those days when you want to explore the island. Remember that driving is on the *left*, British-style, even though almost all cars are American-made.

The main route sticks resolutely to the center of the island, linking The Baths on the southern tip with Gun Creek and Leverick Bay at North Sound. Signage is erratic, so come prepared with a map.

CAR RENTAL

None of the major companies have outlets on Virgin Gorda, but you can rent a car from several local companies.

Contacts L&S Jeep Rental ⊠ *The Valley, Virgin Gorda* ☎ *284/495–5297* ⊕ *www.landsjeeprental.com.* **Mahogany Rentals & Taxi Service** ⊠ *Spanish Town, Virgin Gorda* ☎ *284/495–5469* ⊕ *www.mahoganycarrentalsbvi.com.* **Speedy's Car Rentals** ⊠ *The Valley, Virgin Gorda* ☎ *284/495–5240, 284/495–5235* ⊕ *www.speedyscarrentals.com.*

FERRY TRAVEL

Ferries connect St. Thomas with Virgin Gorda; they leave from both Charlotte Amalie and Red Hook, but not daily. Ferries also link St. John and Tortola with Virgin Gorda. Ferries to Virgin Gorda land in Spanish Town. All ferries to Red Hook, St. Thomas stop in St. John first to clear U.S. customs. Ferry schedules vary by day, and not all companies make daily trips. The BVI Tourist Board website (⊕ *www.bvitourism.com*) has links for all the ferry companies, and their individual websites are the best up-to-date sources of information for specific routes and schedules.

■TIP➔ The ferry service from the public dock in Spanish Town can be a tad erratic. Get there early to be sure it hasn't changed, and ask at the dock whether you're getting on the right boat. The Thursday and Sunday service between Virgin Gorda and St. John is particularly prone to problems.

TAXI TRAVEL

Taxi rates aren't set on Virgin Gorda, so you should firm up the fare with your driver before you set out. It's cheaper to travel in groups; fares are per trip, not per person. The taxi number is also the license plate number. Andy's Taxi & Jeep Rental offers service from one end of Virgin Gorda to the other. Mahogany Rentals & Taxi Service provides taxi service all over Virgin Gorda.

Contacts Andy's Taxi and Jeep Rental ⊠ *The Valley, Virgin Gorda* ☏ *284/495–5252* ⊕ *www.virgingordatours.com.*

ESSENTIALS

BANKS

First Caribbean International is in Virgin Gorda Yacht Harbour. First Bank is across the street from Virgin Gorda Yacht Harbour.

HOTELS

Virgin Gorda's charming hostelries appeal to a select, appreciative clientele; repeat business is extremely high. Those who prefer Sheratons, Marriotts, and the like may feel they get more for their money on other islands, but the peace and pampering offered on Virgin Gorda are priceless to the discriminating traveler. Villas are plentiful on the island and are widely distributed, but most of the resorts are concentrated in three places: The Valley (a catch-all geographic name that encompasses the southwestern part of the island), the Northwest Shore, and the North Sound, which is reachable only by ferry.

Hotel reviews have been shortened. For full information, visit Fodors. com.

RESTAURANTS

Restaurants range from simple to elegant. Hotels that are accessible only by boat will arrange transport in advance upon request from non-guests who wish to dine at their restaurants. Most other independent restaurants are in The Valley or the vicinity. It's wise to make dinner reservations almost everywhere except at really casual spots.

WHAT IT COSTS IN U.S. DOLLARS				
	$	$$	$$$	$$$$
Restaurants	under $13	$13–$20	$21–$30	over $30
Hotels	under $276	$276–$375	$376–$475	over $475

Restaurant prices are the average cost of a main course at dinner or, if dinner is not served, at lunch. Hotel prices are the lowest cost of a standard double room in high season.

SAFETY

Although crime is rare, use common sense: don't leave your camera on the beach while you take a dip or your wallet on a hotel dresser when you go for a walk.

TOUR OPTIONS

Romney Associates/Travel Plan Tours can arrange island tours, boat tours, snorkeling and scuba-diving trips, dolphin swims, and yacht charters from its Virgin Gorda base.

Contacts Romney Associates/Travel Plan Tours ☎ 284/494–4000.

VISITOR INFORMATION

Contacts Virgin Gorda BVI Tourist Board ✉ Virgin Gorda Yacht Harbour, Spanish Town ☎ 284/495–5181 ⊕ www.bvitourism.com.

EXPLORING VIRGIN GORDA

Virgin Gorda's most popular attractions are those provided by Mother Nature. Beautiful beaches, crystal-clear water, and stellar views are around nearly every bend in the road. That said, remember to get a taste of the island's past at Copper Mine Point.

THE VALLEY

TOP ATTRACTIONS

FAMILY
Fodor's Choice
★

The Baths National Park. At Virgin Gorda's most celebrated sight, giant boulders are scattered about the beach and in the water. Some are almost as large as houses and form remarkable grottoes. Climb between these rocks to swim in the many placid pools. Early morning and late afternoon are the best times to visit if you want to avoid crowds. If it's privacy you crave, follow the shore northward to quieter bays—Spring Bay, the Crawl, Little Trunk, and Valley Trunk—or head south to Devil's Bay. ✉ Off Tower Rd. ☎ 284/852–3650 ⊕ www.bvinationalparkstrust. org 🖾 $3 ☉ Daily dawn–dusk.

WORTH NOTING

Copper Mine Point. A tall stone shaft silhouetted against the sky and a small stone structure that overlooks the sea are part of what was once a copper mine, now in ruins. Established 400 years ago, it was worked first by the Spanish, then by the English, until the early 20th century. The route is not well marked, so turn inland near LSL Restaurant and

The Baths are filled with grottoes and hidden pools.

look for the hard-to-see sign pointing the way. ⊠ *Copper Mine Rd.* ⊕ *www.bvinpt.org* ✉ *Free.*

Spanish Town. Virgin Gorda's peaceful main settlement, on the island's southern wing, is so tiny that it barely qualifies as a town at all. Also known as The Valley, Spanish Town has a marina, some shops, and a couple of car-rental agencies. Just north of town is the ferry slip. At the Virgin Gorda Yacht Harbour you can stroll along the dock and do a little shopping. ⊠ *Spanish Town.*

NORTHWEST SHORE

WORTH NOTING

Fallen Jerusalem Island and Dog Islands. You can easily reach these quaintly named islands by boat, which you can rent in either Tortola or Virgin Gorda. They're all part of the National Parks Trust of the Virgins Islands, and their seductive beaches and unparalleled snorkeling display the BVI at their beachcombing, hedonistic best. ⊕ *www.bvinpt. org* ✉ *Free.*

Virgin Gorda Peak National Park. There are two trails at this 265-acre park, which contains the island's highest point, at 1,359 feet. Signs on North Sound Road mark both entrances. It's about a 15-minute hike from either entrance up to a small clearing, where you can climb a ladder to the platform of a wooden observation tower to see a spectacular 360-degree view. ⊠ *North Sound Rd., Gorda Peak* ⊕ *www.bvinpt.org* ✉ *Free.*

BEACHES

Although some of the best beaches are reachable only by boat, don't worry if you're a landlubber, because you can find plenty of places to sun and swim. Anybody going to Virgin Gorda must experience swimming or snorkeling among its unique boulder formations, which can be visited at several sites along Lee Road. The most popular is The Baths, but there are several other similar places nearby that are easily reached.

THE VALLEY

The Baths Beach. This stunning maze of huge granite boulders extending into the sea is usually crowded midday with day-trippers. The snorkeling is good, and you're likely to see a wide variety of fish, but watch out for dinghies coming ashore from the numerous sailboats anchored offshore. Public bathrooms and a handful of bars and shops are close to the water and at the start of the path that leads to the beach. Lockers are available to keep belongings safe. **Amenities:** food and drink; parking; toilets. **Best for:** snorkeling; swimming. ⊠ *Tower Rd., about 1 mile (1½ km) west of Spanish Town ferry dock* ☎ *284/852–3650* ⊕ *www. bvinpt.org* 🖾 *$3* ☉ *Daily dawn–dusk.*

Spring Bay Beach. This National Park beach gets much less traffic than the nearby Baths, and has the similarly large, imposing boulders that create interesting grottoes for swimming. It also has no admission fee, unlike the more popular Baths. The snorkeling is excellent, and the grounds include swings and picnic tables. Guavaberry Spring Bay Vacation has villas and cottages right near the beach. **Amenities:** none. **Best for:** snorkeling; swimming. ⊠ *The Valley* ☎ *284/852–3650* ⊕ *www. bvinpt.org* 🖾 *Free* ☉ *Daily dawn–dusk.*

NORTHWEST SHORE

Nail Bay Beach. At the island's north tip, the three beaches at Nail Bay Resort are ideal for snorkeling. Mountain Trunk Bay is perfect for beginners, and Nail Bay and Long Bay beaches have coral caverns just offshore. The resort has a restaurant, which is an uphill walk but perfect for beach breaks. **Amenities:** food and drink; toilets. **Best for:** snorkeling; swimming. ⊠ *Nail Bay Resort, off Plum Tree Bay Rd., Nail Bay* 🖾 *Free* ☉ *Daily dawn–dusk.*

Savannah Bay Beach. This is a wonderfully private beach close to Spanish Town. It may not always be completely deserted, but you can find a spot to yourself on this long stretch of soft, white sand. Bring your own mask, fins, and snorkel, as there are no facilities. Villas are available through rental property agencies. The view from above is a photographer's delight. **Amenities:** none. **Best for:** solitude; snorkeling; swimming. ⊠ *Off N. Sound Rd., ¾ mile (1¼ km) east of Spanish Town ferry dock, Savannah Bay* 🖾 *Free* ☉ *Daily dawn–dusk.*

6

Spring Bay has boulders similar to those at The Baths.

WHERE TO EAT

Dining out on Virgin Gorda is a mixed bag, with everything from hamburgers to lobster available. Most folks opt to have dinner at or near their hotel to avoid driving on Virgin Gorda's twisting roads at night. The Valley does have a fair number of restaurants if you're sleeping close to town.

THE VALLEY

$$ ECLECTIC 🍴 **Bath and Turtle.** You can sit back and relax at this informal tavern with a friendly staff (or enjoy the outdoor Rendezvous Bar on the waterfront), although the noise from the television can sometimes be a bit much. Well-stuffed sandwiches, homemade pizzas, pasta dishes, and daily specials such as conch soup round out the casual menu. Local musicians perform many Wednesday and Sunday nights. [$] *Average main: $19* ✉ *Virgin Gorda Yacht Harbour, Lee Rd., Spanish Town* ☎ *284/495–5239* 🌐 *www.bathandturtle.com.*

$$$ ECLECTIC 🍴 **Chez Bamboo.** This pleasant little hideaway isn't difficult to find; look for the building with bamboo fencing. Candles in the dining room and on the patio help make this a mellow place where you can enjoy a bowl of lobster bisque, something from the tapas menu, or one of the specialties such as lobster curry. For dessert, try the chocolate cake or crème brûlée. Stop by Friday night for live music. [$] *Average main: $29* ✉ *Lee Rd., Spanish Town* ☎ *284/495–5752* 🌐 *www.chezbamboo.com.*

$$$$ ECLECTIC 🍴 **Fischer's Cove Restaurant.** Dine seaside at this alfresco restaurant that's open to the breezes. If pumpkin soup is on the menu, give it a try for a

true taste of the Caribbean. Although you can get burgers and salads at lunch, local fish (whatever is available) and *fungi* (a cornmeal-based side dish) are tasty alternatives. For dinner, try the Caribbean lobster or grilled mahimahi with lemon and garlic. $ *Average main: $36* ⊠ *Lee Rd.* ☎ *284/495–5252* ⊕ *www.fischerscove.com.*

$$$$ ✕ **Little Dix Bay Pavilion.** For an elegant evening, you can't do better
INTERNATIONAL than this—the candlelight in the open-air pavilion is enchanting, the always-changing menu sophisticated, the service attentive. Superbly prepared seafood, meat, and vegetarian entrées draw locals and visitors alike. Favorites include a Cajun pork loin with mango salsa and scallion potatoes, and mahimahi with warm chorizo and chickpea salad served with a zucchini-and-tomato chutney. The Monday evening buffet shines. $ *Average main: $33* ⊠ *Little Dix Bay Resort, Off Little Rd., Spanish Town* ☎ *284/495–5555* ⊕ *www.littledixbay.com* ⌨ *Reservations essential.*

$$ ✕ **LSL Bake Shop & Restaurant.** Along the road to The Baths, this small
ECLECTIC restaurant with pedestrian decor is a local favorite. You can always find fresh fish on the menu, but folks with a taste for other dishes won't be disappointed. Try the pork tenderloin pesto with herb potatoes and a peppercorn sauce, or the banana curry shrimp with a coconut-milk sauce. $ *Average main: $15* ⊠ *Tower Rd.* ☎ *284/495–5151.*

$$ ✕ **Mine Shaft Café.** Perched on a hilltop that offers a view of spectacular
ECLECTIC sunsets, this restaurant near Copper Mine Point serves simple, well-prepared food, including grilled fish, steaks, and baby back ribs. Tuesday night features an all-you-can-eat Caribbean-style barbecue. The monthly full-moon parties draw a big local crowd. $ *Average main: $20* ⊠ *Near Copper Mine Point* ☎ *284/495–5260.*

$$$$ ✕ **The Rock Café.** Good Italian cuisine and seafood is served among the
ITALIAN waterfalls and giant boulders that form the famous Baths. For dinner at this open-air eatery, feast on saffron lobster pasta or fresh red snapper with a creamy risotto. For dessert, don't miss the chocolate mousse. $ *Average main: $39* ⊠ *Tower Rd.* ☎ *284/495–5482* ⊕ *www.bvidining.com* ⊗ *No lunch.*

$$$ ✕ **Top of the Baths.** At the entrance to The Baths, this popular restaurant
ECLECTIC has tables on an outdoor terrace or in an open-air pavilion; all have
FAMILY stunning views of the Sir Francis Drake Channel. The restaurant starts serving at 8 am; for lunch, hamburgers, coconut chicken sandwiches, and fish-and-chips are among the offerings. Sushi was recently added to the menu. For dessert, the key lime pie is excellent. The Sunday barbecue, served from noon until 3 pm, is an island event. $ *Average main: $23* ⊠ *The Valley* ☎ *284/495–5497* ⊕ *www.topofthebaths.com.*

$$$ ✕ **The Village Cafe and Restaurant.** Meals are served poolside under the
ECLECTIC shade of umbrellas at this casual eatery. The lunch menu includes salads, wraps, and burgers, but the lobster-and-crab salad (yes, it contains both!) is a must-have. A new dinner menu includes fish, chicken, and pork offerings with island spices. $ *Average main: $27* ⊠ *Virgin Gorda Village, North Sound Rd.* ☎ *284/495–5350* ⊗ *Closed Mon.*

6

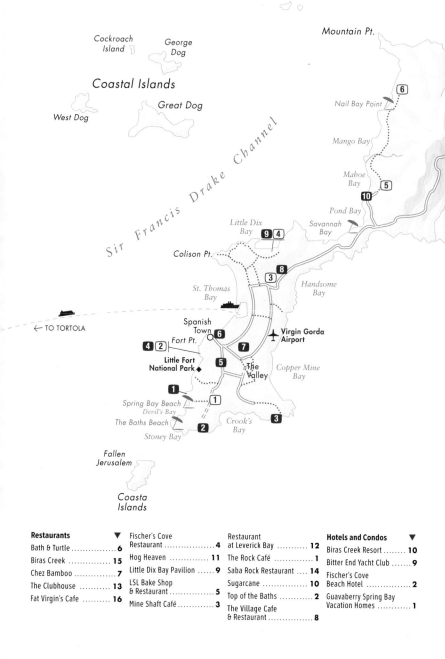

Virgin Gorda

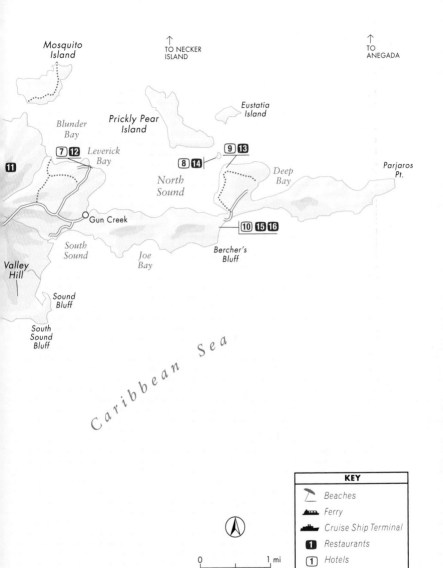

NORTHWEST SHORE

$$$
AMERICAN

✕ **Sugarcane.** The conch fritters are the stars on the menu of this Nail Bay Resort restaurant, a popular gathering place for vacationers staying in nearby villas. They're light, fluffy, nicely seasoned, and stuffed with conch, just the way conch fritters should be. For lunch, try the jerk chicken. The best choices on the dinner menu tend to be the fresh local fish prepared in a variety of ways. $ *Average main: $26* ✉ *Nail Bay Resort, Bay Rd., off Plum Tree Bay Rd., Nail Bay* ☎ *284/494–8000* ⊕ *www.nailbay.com.*

> ### EASTER ON VIRGIN GORDA
>
> Easter is also Carnival on Virgin Gorda. The celebration is smaller than those you'll find on more heavily touristed islands, but people visiting family and friends do come from around the Caribbean. If you're heading to Virgin Gorda during the three-day annual event, make sure you've booked your room well in advance.

NORTH SOUND

$$$$
INTERNATIONAL

✕ **Biras Creek Restaurant.** This hilltop restaurant at the Biras Creek Hotel has eye-popping views of North Sound. For starters, there may be an artichoke, green bean, and wild-mushroom salad topped with balsamic vinaigrette, or cream of sweet-potato soup accompanied by potato straws. Entrées may include pan-seared snapper over horseradish pearl pasta. The desserts, including a lemon-ricotta cheesecake with a spicy passion-fruit sauce, are stupendous. The restaurant also offers a fixed-price four-course meal that ends with Biras Creek's signature offering of cheese and port. Most days, lunch is a barbecue on the beach. $ *Average main: $37* ✉ *Biras Creek Hotel* ☎ *284/494–3555* ⊕ *www.biras.com* ⌛ *Reservations essential.*

$$$
ECLECTIC

✕ **The Clubhouse.** The Bitter End Yacht Club's open-air waterfront restaurant is a favorite rendezvous for sailors and their guests, so it's busy day and night. You can find lavish buffets for breakfast, lunch, and dinner, as well as an à la carte menu. Dinner selections include grilled mahimahi or tuna, local lobster, and porterhouse steak, as well as vegetarian dishes. $ *Average main: $29* ✉ *Bitter End Yacht Club* ☎ *284/494–2745* ⊕ *www.beyc.com* ⌛ *Reservations essential.*

$$$
ECLECTIC
FAMILY

✕ **Fat Virgin's Café.** This casual beachfront eatery offers a straightforward menu of baby back ribs, chicken roti, vegetable pasta, grouper sandwiches, and fresh fish specials for lunch and dinner. You can also find a good selection of Caribbean beer. $ *Average main: $23* ✉ *Biras Creek Resort* ☎ *284/495–7052* ⊕ *www.fatvirgin.com.*

$$
AMERICAN

✕ **Hog Heaven.** Perched high above North Sound, with panoramic views and incredible BBQ ribs, this casual eatery earns its name. The atmosphere is friendly and down-home cooking includes buttery conch and BBQ with all the fixings, such as fried plantains, potato salad, and coleslaw. Hog Heaven is the perfect stopover during a day of island exploring. $ *Average main: $17* ✉ *The Valley* ☎ *284/547–5694.*

$$$
ECLECTIC

✕ **Restaurant at Leverick Bay.** The laid-back menu at this beach restaurant draws cruise-ship passengers on tour as well as hotel guests and locals.

The menu includes burgers, pizza, roti, chili, and fish-and-chips for lunch. Upstairs, there's an upscale restaurant that serves dinner with dishes that feature wild salmon and Anegada lobster. $ *Average main: $25* ⊠ *Leverick Bay Resort & Marina, Leverick Bay Rd., Leverick Bay* ☎ *284/340–3005* ⊕ *www.leverickrestaurant.com.*

$$$$ ✕ **Saba Rock.** Accommodating staff and congenial patrons make this
BRITISH   waterside restaurant, located on a miniscule 1½-acre island sitting in the middle of North Sound, a worthwhile trek by private boat or ferry. Fish tacos and burgers are among the lunch favorites, while seafood and steak lure dinner patrons. $ *Average main: $38* ⊠ *North Sound* ☎ *284/495–9966* ⊕ *www.sabarock.com.*

WHERE TO STAY

While villas are scattered all over Virgin Gorda, hotels are centered in and around The Valley, Nail Bay, and in the North Sound area. Except for Leverick Bay Resort, which is around the point from North Sound, all hotels in North Sound are reached only by ferry.

PRIVATE VILLAS

Visitors craving seclusion would do well at a villa. Most have full kitchens and maid service. Prices per week in winter run from around $2,000 for a one- or two-bedroom villa up to $10,000 for a five-room beachfront villa. Rates in summer are substantially less. On Virgin Gorda a villa in the North Sound area means you can pretty much stay put at night unless you want to make the drive on narrow roads. If you opt for a spot near The Baths, it's an easier drive to town.

BOOKING AGENCIES

McLaughlin-Anderson Luxury Villas. The St. Thomas–based McLaughlin-Anderson Luxury Villas represents about 15 properties all over Virgin Gorda. Villas range in size from one to five bedrooms, and come with full kitchens, pools, stellar views, and other amenities. The company can hire a chef and stock your kitchen with groceries. A seven-night minimum is required during the winter season. ☎ *340/776–0635, 800/537–6246* ⊕ *www.mclaughlinanderson.com.*

Villas Virgin Gorda. This management company's dozen properties stretch from The Baths to the Nail Bay area. Several budget properties are included among the pricier offerings. Most houses have private pools, and a few are right on the beach. A sister company at the same number, Tropical Nannies, provides babysitting services. ☎ *284/495–6493* ⊕ *www.villasvirgingorda.com.*

Virgin Gorda Villa Rentals. This company's 40 or so properties are all near Leverick Bay Resort and Mahoe Bay, so they are perfect for those who want to be close to activities. Many of the accommodations—from studios to six or more bedrooms—have private swimming pools and air-conditioning, at least in the bedrooms. All have full kitchens, are well maintained, and have spectacular views. ☎ *284/495–7421, 800/848–7081* ⊕ *www.virgingordabvi.com.*

THE VALLEY

$ RESORT **Fischer's Cove Beach Hotel.** The rooms are modest, the furniture is discount-store-style, and the walls are thin, but you can't beat the location right on the beach and within walking distance of Spanish Town's shops and restaurants. **Pros:** beachfront location; budget price; good restaurant. **Cons:** very basic units; thin walls; no air-conditioning in some rooms. *Rooms from: $145 Lee Rd. 284/495–5252 www.fischerscove.com 12 rooms, 8 cottages No meals.*

$ RENTAL **Guavaberry Spring Bay Vacation Homes.** Rambling back from the beach, these hexagonal one- and two-bedroom villas give you all the comforts of home—and that striking boulder-fringed beach is just minutes away. **Pros:** short walk to The Baths (and excellent snorkeling); easy drive to town; great beaches nearby. **Cons:** few amenities; older property; basic decor. *Rooms from: $255 Tower Rd. 284/495–5227 www.guavaberryspringbay.com 12 1-bedroom units, 6 2-bedroom units, 1 3-bedroom unit, 16 villas No credit cards No meals.*

$$$ RESORT FAMILY **Rosewood Little Dix Bay.** This laid-back luxury resort offers a gorgeous crescent of sand, plenty of activities, and good restaurants. **Pros:** convenient location; lovely grounds; near many restaurants. **Cons:** expensive; very spread out; insular though not isolated. *Rooms from: $405 Off Little Rd. 284/495–5555 www.littledixbay.com 78 rooms, 20 suites, 7 villas No meals.*

$ RENTAL **Virgin Gorda Village.** All the condos in this upscale complex a few minutes' drive from Spanish Town have at least partial ocean views. **Pros:** close to Spanish Town; lovely pool; recently built units. **Cons:** no beach; on a busy street; noisy roosters nearby. *Rooms from: $250 North Sound Rd. 284/495–5544 www.virgingordavillage.com 30 condos No meals.*

NORTHWEST SHORE

$ RENTAL **Mango Bay Resort.** Sitting seaside on Virgin Gorda's north coast, this collection of contemporary condos and villas will make you feel right at home. **Pros:** nice beach; lively location; easy drive to restaurants. **Cons:** drab decor; some units have lackluster views; need car to get around. *Rooms from: $195 Plum Tree Bay Rd., Pond Bay 284/495–5672 www.mangobayresort.com 17 condos, 5 villas No meals.*

$ RESORT **Nail Bay Resort.** On a hill above the coast, this beachfront resort offers a wide selection of rooms and suites. **Pros:** full kitchens; lovely beach; close to town. **Cons:** busy neighborhood; bit of a drive from main road; uphill walk from beach. *Rooms from: $240 Off Nail Bay Rd., Nail Bay 284/494–8000, 800/871–3551 www.nailbay.com 4 rooms, 4 suites, 2 apartments, 7 villas No meals.*

NORTH SOUND

$$$$ RESORT **Biras Creek Resort.** Tucked out of the way on the island's North Sound, Biras Creek has a get-away-from-it-all feel that's a major draw for its well-heeled clientele. **Pros:** luxurious rooms; professional staff; good dining options; private, white-sand beach. **Cons:** very expensive;

Bitter End Yacht Club, at Virgin Gorda's eastern end

isolated; difficult for people with mobility problems. $ *Rooms from: $790* ✉ *North Sound* ☎ *284/394–1000, 877/883–0756* ⊕ *www.biras. com* ⤳ *31 suites* ⃝ *Multiple meal plans.*

$$$$
ALL-INCLUSIVE
FAMILY
Fodor's Choice
★

⌕ **Bitter End Yacht Club.** Sailing's the thing at this busy hotel and marina in the nautically inclined North Sound, and the use of everything from small sailboats to kayaks to windsurfers is included in the price. **Pros:** lots of water sports; good diving opportunities; friendly guests. **Cons:** expensive rates; isolated; lots of stairs. $ *Rooms from: $646* ✉ *North Sound* ☎ *284/494–2746, 800/872–2392* ⊕ *www.beyc.com* ⤳ *85 rooms* ⃝ *All-inclusive.*

$
RESORT

⌕ **Leverick Bay Resort and Marina.** With its colorful buildings and bustling marina, Leverick Bay is a good choice for visitors who want easy access to water-sports activities. **Pros:** fun location; good restaurant; small grocery store. **Cons:** small beach; no laundry in units; 15-minute drive to town. $ *Rooms from: $149* ✉ *Off Leverick Bay Rd., Leverick Bay* ☎ *284/495–7421, 800/848–7081* ⊕ *www.leverickbay.com* ⤳ *13 rooms, 4 apartments* ⃝ *No meals.*

$
RESORT

⌕ **Saba Rock Resort.** Reachable only by a free ferry or by private yacht, this resort on its own tiny cay is perfect for folks who want to mix and mingle with the sailors who drop anchor for the night. **Pros:** party atmosphere; convenient transportation; good diving nearby. **Cons:** tiny beach; isolated location; on a very small island. $ *Rooms from: $150* ✉ *North Sound* ☎ *284/495–7711, 284/495–9966* ⊕ *www.sabarock. com* ⤳ *7 1-bedroom suites, 1 2-bedroom suite* ⃝ *Breakfast.*

Leverick Bay Resort and Marina

NIGHTLIFE

Pick up a free copy of the *Limin' Times*—available at most resorts and restaurants—for the most current local entertainment schedule.

THE VALLEY

Bath and Turtle. During high season, the Bath and Turtle is one of the liveliest spots on Virgin Gorda, hosting island bands Wednesday and Sunday from 8 pm until midnight. ⊠ *Virgin Gorda Yacht Harbour, Lee Rd., Spanish Town* ☎ *284/495–5239* ⊕ *www.bathandturtle.com.*

Chez Bamboo. This is the place for calypso and reggae on Tuesday and Friday nights. ⊠ *Lee Rd., Spanish Town* ☎ *284/495–5752* ⊕ *www.chez bamboo.com.*

Mine Shaft Café. The café has music on Tuesday and Friday. ⊠ *Near Copper Mine Point* ☎ *284/495–5260* ⊕ *www.mineshaftbvi.com.*

Rock Café. There's live piano music nearly every night during the Rock Café's winter season. ⊠ *Lee Rd.* ☎ *284/495–5482* ⊕ *www.bvidining.com.*

NORTH SOUND

Restaurant at Leverick Bay. This resort's main restaurant hosts music on Tuesday and Friday in season. ⊠ *Leverick Bay Resort & Marina, Leverick Bay Rd., Leverick Bay* ☎ *284/340–3005* ⊕ *www.leverick restaurant.com.*

Getting Your Goat

Roaming livestock is a fact of life in the tropics, particularly in less-developed places like Virgin Gorda. Indeed, residents who leave their car windows open occasionally return to find a freshly laid egg on the front seat. If you have time to sit a spell at places like Virgin Gorda Yacht Harbour, you might see a mother hen followed by a string of little ones.

While crowing roosters can rouse annoyingly early, grazing goats pose traffic hazards. Some have owners, but many of them wander off to forage for food. Be particularly careful when you're driving around bends or over the top of hills. You might find a herd of goats, or maybe a sheep or two, camped out in the middle of the road. Sound your horn and be patient. They'll move in their own time.

And should you happen to see a vendor selling local dishes, the relatives of those goats and chickens are probably bubbling in the pot.

SHOPPING

6

Most boutiques are within hotel complexes or at Virgin Gorda Yacht Harbour. Two of the best are at Biras Creek and Little Dix Bay. Other properties—the Bitter End and Leverick Bay—have small but equally select boutiques.

THE VALLEY

FOOD

Buck's Food Market. This market is the closest the island offers to a full-service supermarket, with an in-store bakery and deli as well as fresh fish and produce departments. ⊠ *Virgin Gorda Yacht Harbour, Lee Rd., Spanish Town* ☎ *284/495–5423* ⊕ *bucksfoodmarket.homestead.com.*

Rosy's Supermarket. This store carries the basics plus an interesting selection of ready-to-cook meals, such as a whole seasoned chicken. ⊠ *Rhymer Rd.* ☎ *284/495–5245* ⊕ *www.rosysenterprisesvg.com* ☾ *Closed Sun.*

Virgin Gorda Cash & Carry. The store isn't much to look at, inside or out, but it has the best wine prices on Virgin Gorda, along with the usual basic supermarket items. ⊠ *Lee Rd., Spanish Town* ☎ *284/347–1200.*

GIFTS

Allamanda Gallery. This shop showcases owner Amanda Baker's tropical photography, but it's also a good place to browse for cards, magnets, and other take-home gifts. ⊠ *The Baths, Tower Rd.* ☎ *284/495–5935* ⊕ *www.virginportraits.com.*

Caribbean Too. While this cozy store sells T-shirts and other vacation necessities, it's also a great place to shop for tropical wear in linen and other comfortable fabrics. ⊠ *The Baths, Tower Rd.* ☎ *284/495–6288.*

NORTH SOUND

FOOD

Bitter End Emporium. This store at the Bitter End is the place for local fruits, cheeses, baked goods, and gourmet prepared food. ⊠ *Bitter End Yacht Harbor* ☎ *284/494–2746* ⊕ *www.beyc.com.*

Buck's Food Market. Buck's is the closest to a full-service supermarket the island offers, and has everything from an in-store bakery and deli to fresh fish and produce departments. There are three branches. ⊠ *North Sound Rd.* ☎ *284/495–7368.*

Chef's Pantry. This store has the fixings for an impromptu party in your villa or on your boat—fresh seafood, specialty meats, imported cheeses, daily baked breads and pastries, and an impressive wine and spirit selection. ⊠ *Leverick Bay Marina, Leverick Bay Rd., Leverick Bay* ☎ *284/495–7677.*

GIFTS

Reeftique. This store carries island crafts and jewelry, clothing, and nautical odds and ends with the Bitter End logo. ⊠ *Bitter End Yacht Harbor* ☎ *284/494–2746* ⊕ *www.beyc.com.*

Thee Nautical Gallery. This boutique sells attractive handcrafted jewelry, paintings, and one-of-a-kind gift items, as well as books about the Caribbean. ⊠ *Leverick Bay Marina, Leverick Bay Rd., Leverick Bay* ☎ *284/495–7479.*

SPORTS AND THE OUTDOORS

DIVING AND SNORKELING

Where you go snorkeling and what company you pick depends on where you're staying. Many hotels have on-site dive outfitters, but if yours doesn't, one won't be far away. If your hotel does have a dive operation, just stroll down to the dock and hop aboard—no need to drive anywhere. The dive companies are all certified by PADI. Costs vary, but count on paying about $75 for a one-tank dive and $110 for a two-tank dive. All dive operators offer introductory courses as well as certification and advanced courses. Should you get an attack of the bends, which can happen when you ascend too rapidly, the nearest decompression chamber is at Schneider Regional Medical Center in St. Thomas.

There are some terrific snorkel and dive sites off Virgin Gorda, including areas around The Baths, the North Sound, and the Dogs. The Chimney at Great Dog Island has a coral archway and canyon covered with a wide variety of sponges. At Joe's Cave, an underwater cavern on West Dog Island, huge groupers, eagle rays, and other colorful fish accompany divers as they swim. At some sites you can see 100 feet down, but snorkelers and divers who don't want to go that deep will find plenty to look at just below the surface.

You can learn to sail at Bitter End Yacht Club.

FAMILY **Bitter End Yacht Club.** The BEYC schedules two snorkeling trips a day. ⊠ *North Sound* ☎ *284/494–2746* ⊕ *www.beyc.com* ⛵ *From $15.*

Dive BVI. In addition to day trips, Dive BVI also offers expert instruction and certification. ⊠ *Virgin Gorda Yacht Harbour, Lee Rd., Spanish Town* ☎ *284/495–5513, 800/848–7078* ⊕ *www.divebvi.com* ⊠ *Leverick Bay Marina, Leverick Bay Rd., Leverick Bay* ☎ *284/495–7328, 800/848–7078.*

Sunchaser Scuba. Resort, advanced, and rescue courses are all available here. ⊠ *Bitter End Yacht Club, North Sound* ☎ *284/495–9638, 800/932–4286* ⊕ *www.sunchaserscuba.com.*

SAILING AND BOATING

The BVI waters are calm and terrific places to learn to sail. You can also rent sea kayaks, waterskiing equipment, dinghies, and powerboats, or take a parasailing trip.

FAMILY **Bitter End Sailing and Kiteboarding School.** Bitter End Sailing and Kiteboarding School offers classroom, dockside, and on-the-water lessons for sailors of all levels. ⊠ *Bitter End Yacht Club, North Sound* ☎ *284/494–2746* ⊕ *www.beyc.com* ⛵ *Private lessons from $80 per hour for guests, $110 per hour for non-guests.*

Double "D" Charters. If you just want to sit back, relax, and let the captain take the helm, choose a sailing or power yacht from Double "D" Charters. Rates run from $89 for a day trip. Private full-day cruises or sails for up to eight people run from $950. ⊠ *Virgin Gorda Yacht Harbour, Lee Rd., Spanish Town* ☎ *284/499–2479* ⊕ *www.doubledbvi.com.*

OTHER BRITISH
VIRGIN ISLANDS

Jost Van Dyke, Anegada & the Smaller Islands

WELCOME TO OTHER BRITISH VIRGIN ISLANDS

TOP REASONS TO GO

★ **Snorkeling in Anegada:** The wrecks and reefs draw snorkelers from all over the world to this beautiful, beach-fringed island.

★ **Bar-hopping in Jost Van Dyke:** The BVI's nightlife capital is the place to go, especially for Foxy's Halloween and New Year's parties. The Soggy Dollar and Foxy's Tamarind are favorites.

★ **Lying on the beach in Peter Island:** Palm-fringed Dead Man's Bay is particularly conducive to a romantic picnic.

★ **Turning back the clock at Cooper Island:** Although it's been updated in recent years, a stay here is like visiting the old Caribbean, and that's exactly how guests want it.

★ **Sailing the BVI:** Pick up a charter yacht in Tortola and enjoy a variety of experiences throughout the 50-some islands that make up the BVI.

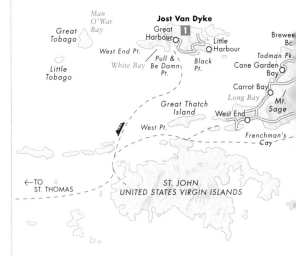

1 Jost Van Dyke. With only 300-some inhabitants, the number of day-trippers easily outnumbers the permanent islanders.

2 Guana Island. This private island hosts both a wildlife refuge and a luxe resort.

3 Marina Cay. A tiny island of only 8 acres, it's in Trellis Bay, just off Beef Island.

4 Scrub Island. A 250-acre island near Tortola's Beef Island Airport that's perfect for day trips.

5 Anegada. The only coral island in the BVI chain is surrounded by inviting (or dangerous) reefs, depending on whether you're a snorkeler or sailor.

6 Peter Island. A private island retreat, it is also popular with charter yachts.

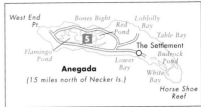

West End Pt.
Bones Bight
Red Pond
Loblolly Bay
Table Bay
The Settlement
Budrock Pond
Flamingo Pond
Lower Bay
White Bay
Anegada
(15 miles north of Necker Is.)
Horse Shoe Reef

Prickly Pear Island
Mosquito Island
Necker Island 8
Eustatia Island
Long Pt.
North Bay
Great Camanoe
Towing Pt.
Cockroach Island
George Dog
North
Sound
Berchers Bay
Guana Island 2
North Bay
West Dog
Long Bay
Virgin Gorda Peak
South Sound
Little Camanoe
Kitto Ghut
Scrub Island 4
Great Dog
Pond Bay
Handsome Bay
VIRGIN GORDA
Trunk Bay
Josiah's Bay
Monkey Pt.
Marina Cay 3
East End
Spanish Town
Virgin Gorda Airport
ROAD TOWN
Fort Shirley
Beef Island International Airport
Fat Hogs Bay
Beef Island
Copper Mine Pt.
Anegada Passage
Road Harbour
Buck Island
Sir Francis Drake Channel
Fallen Jerusalem
TORTOLA
Broken Jerusalem
Quart-a-Nancy Pt.
Round Rock
Manchioneel Bay
Great Harbour
Salt Island
South Bay
Ginger Island
Rock Hole
Dead Chest
Cooper Island 7
Big Reef Bay
Salt Island Bluff
Markoe Pt.
Pelican Island
White Bay
Peter Island 6
Privateer Bay
Peter Island Bluff
9
Money Bay
Norman Island

0 ——— 3 miles
0 ——— 5 km

7 Cooper Island. This hilly island is home to one of the more modest private-island resorts in the BVI, and it's also a popular anchorage for yachts.

8 Necker Island. Sir Richard Branson's private island is usually available to rent to large groups but is available for couples a few weeks out of the year—at an astounding price.

9 Norman Island. The caves here were the supposed inspiration for Robert Louis Stevenson's "Treasure Island", and are now one of the BVI's top snorkeling spots. The island's Pirate theme is also alive at "The Willy T", a floating bar and restaurant found here.

GETTING ORIENTED

More than 50 individual islands make up the British Virgin Islands. Jost Van Dyke, a sparsely populated island northwest of Tortola, has a disproportionate number of surprisingly lively bars and is a favorite for yachters. Flat Anegada, some 20 miles (32 km) northeast of Virgin Gorda, is the only coral island in the BVI chain, and its extensive reef systems attract snorkelers and divers. Several other islands have private resorts, though many are uninhabited.

Updated by
Susan Zaluski

Tortola and Virgin Gorda are the largest—and most visited—of the British Virgin Islands, but the chain is made up of 50-some islands and cays, many of them small and uninhabited. Of these outlying islands, Jost Van Dyke and Anegada get the lion's share of visitors, but several other smaller islands have notable resorts.

Anegada is most popular with snorkelers, sailors, and those looking to escape the modest crowds of the BVI, while Jost Van Dyke attracts partiers to its lively beach bars, along with a smaller contingent of visitors who spend a few days. Among the other islands, Guana, Necker, and Peter islands are luxe private-island resorts, while Cooper Island and Marina Cay are a bit more down-to-earth in terms of price. Norman Island is uninhabited, but it does have a floating restaurant on a ship moored off its coast. Billionaire entrepreneur Sir Richard Branson, owner of Necker Island, is building an ecoresort on Mosquito Island that is expected to open in 2016 with five three-bedroom villas.

Most of these islands are linked to Tortola by ferry. Some can be day-trip destinations (Peter Island, Jost Van Dyke, Marina Cay, Anegada, and Norman Island are all popular with day-trippers), and Cooper Island attracts many charter boats that moor for the night. Guana has no regular ferry service other than that offered to guests; Necker remains completely private.

GETTING HERE AND AROUND

You can fly to Anegada on a charter flight (affordable if you are traveling with a group), but all the other islands are reachable only by boat (or perhaps helicopter if you are visiting Necker Island). Anegada has ferry service from Tortola (via Virgin Gorda) three days a week, while Jost Van Dyke has regularly scheduled ferry service from Tortola, St. John, and St. Thomas, but not all these services run daily. You can rent a jeep on Anegada, and many people do, especially if they are staying for several days. It's possible to rent a car or jeep in Jost Van Dyke, but it's not really necessary.

CAR TRAVEL

You can rent a car or jeep on either Anegada or Jost Van Dyke. This may make sense in Anegada, where you might want to explore a variety of different beaches to maximize your snorkeling opportunities. However, in Jost Van Dyke, it's often just as easy to take a taxi or walk. On either island, both rentals and gas are expensive, so be sure to make room for those costs in your vacation budget.

ANEGADA

D.W. Jeep Rentals. Dean Wheatley can rent you a jeep for $65 per day. ⊠ *The Settlement* ☎ *284/495–9677*.

Lil' Bit Rentals. A small vehicle rents for $50, jeeps are $65, and a pickup truck with seating in the back for up to 10 people is $90. ⊠ *Setting Point* ☎ *284/495–9932*.

JOST VAN DYKE

Abe and Eunicy Rentals. This company's two-door Suzukis ($65 a day), four-door Suzukis ($75 a day), and four-door Monteros ($80 a day) will help you explore by land. There's pick-up and drop-off service from anywhere on the island. ⊠ *Little Harbour* ☎ *284/495–9329*.

Paradise Jeep Rentals. Paradise Jeep Rentals offers the ideal vehicles to tackle Jost Van Dyke's steep, winding roads. Even though Jost is a relatively small island, you really need to be in shape to walk from one bay to the next. This outfit rents two-door Suzukis for $60 per day and four-door Grand Vitaras and Sportages for $70. Discounts are availble for rentals of six or more days. It's next to the Fire Station in Great Harbour. ■TIP➔ Reservations are a must. ⊠ *Great Harbour* ☎ *284/495–9477*.

7

ESSENTIALS

ABOUT THE HOTELS AND RESTAURANTS

Both Anegada and Jost Van Dyke offer a choice of resorts and independent restaurants and bars; however, true luxury is in short supply. Most of the other smaller islands in the BVI are private and have a single resort, including the luxe choices Necker, Peter, and Guana islands, as well as the more modest Cooper Island and Marina Cay.

Hotel reviews have been shortened. For full information, visit Fodors. com

BANKS AND ATMS

Be sure to take cash if you travel to the smaller islands in the BVI. None has an ATM or a bank, though most resorts take credit cards.

Other British Virgin Islands

KEY
- **1** *Restaurants*
- ① *Hotels*
- 🛳 *Ferry*

A T L A N T I C

Man O'War Bay

JOST VAN DYKE

4 - 8 ① ②

14 **7**

Great Tobago

Great Harbour

Little Harbour

Great Harbour
Little Tobago

West End Pt.
White Bay

Pull & Be Damn Pt.

Black Pt.

1 - 3

9 - 13

3 - 6

Brewers Bay

Trunk Bay

Josiah's Bay

Cane Garden Bay

Todman Pk.

Fort Shirley

Road Town

Carrot Bay

Mt. Sage

Road Harbour

Long Bay

West End

Great Thatch Island

West Pt.

Frenchman's Cay

TORTOLA

Great Harbour

Rock Hole

← TO ST. THOMAS

Pelican Island

White Bay

Privateer Bay

ST. JOHN
UNITED STATES VIRGIN ISLANDS

Norman Island

15

16

Money Bay

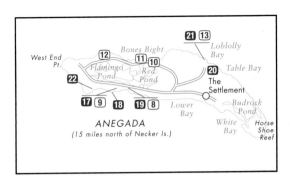

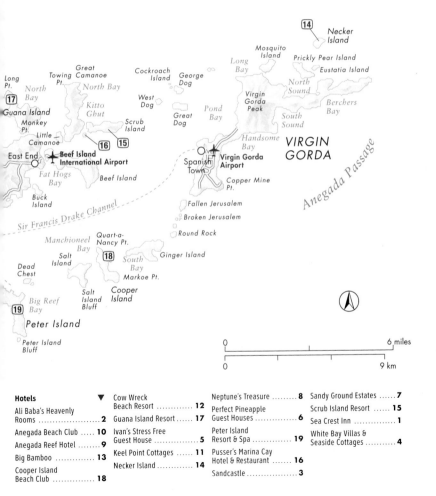

Hotels ▼

Ali Baba's Heavenly Rooms **2**

Anegada Beach Club **10**

Anegada Reef Hotel **9**

Big Bamboo **13**

Cooper Island Beach Club **18**

Cow Wreck Beach Resort **12**

Guana Island Resort **17**

Ivan's Stress Free Guest House **5**

Keel Point Cottages **11**

Necker Island **14**

Neptune's Treasure **8**

Perfect Pineapple Guest Houses **6**

Peter Island Resort & Spa **19**

Pusser's Marina Cay Hotel & Restaurant **16**

Sandcastle **3**

Sandy Ground Estates **7**

Scrub Island Resort **15**

Sea Crest Inn **1**

White Bay Villas & Seaside Cottages **4**

WHAT IT COSTS IN U.S. DOLLARS			
	$	$$	$$$	$$$$
Restaurants	under $13	$13–$20	$21–$30	over $30
Hotels	under $276	$276–$375	$376–$475	over $475

Restaurant prices are the average cost of a main course at dinner or, if dinner is not served, at lunch. Hotel prices are the lowest cost of a standard double room in high season.

JOST VAN DYKE

Named after an early Dutch settler, Jost Van Dyke is a small island northwest of Tortola and is *truly* a place to get away from it all. Mountainous and lush, the 4-mile-long (6½-km-long) island—with fewer than 300 full-time residents—has one tiny resort, some rental cottages and villas, a campground, a couple dozen cars, and a single road. There are no banks or ATMs on the island, and many restaurants and shops accept only cash. Life definitely rolls along on "island time," especially during the off-season from August to November, when finding a restaurant open for dinner can be a challenge. Electricity came to Jost in the 1990s, and water conservation is encouraged, as the primary sources are rainwater collected in basement-like cisterns and desalinized seawater. Jost is one of the Caribbean's most popular anchorages, and there is a disproportionately large number of informal bars and restaurants, which have helped earn Jost its reputation as the "party island" of the BVI.

GETTING HERE AND AROUND

The only way to get to Jost Van Dyke is by ferry or private boat. Daysail operators, both in the USVI and the BVI, take guests here daily, and there are regularly scheduled ferries from West End, Tortola (25 minutes), St. John (30 minutes), and St. Thomas (60 minutes, via St. John). Ferries from Tortola run several times daily from West End; the St. Thomas/St. John ferry runs generally just once a day, six days per week. Always check the schedules, as they change. Once on the ground, you can walk most everywhere you might need to go, but you can also hire a taxi driver.

BEACHES

The Bubbly Pool. A small opening in Jost Van Dyke's rocky cliffs channels the wild Atlantic's waters into a naturally formed Jacuzzi that bubbles with wave action during northerly winter swells. There is a tiny sand beach reached by a pleasant 15-minute hike along a trail that winds past small stands of mangroves and a salt pond filled with ducks and wading birds.■TIP➜ Ask locals for tips on finding the trail and about safety precautions. While the pool requires some swell to get things bubbling (and can be disappointing on a flat day), never climb rocks around the pool or attempt to exit the small opening. Use caution during stormy weather. ⊠ *Jost Van Dyke.*

Boaters docking at Jost Van Dyke

FAMILY **Great Harbour Beach.** Great Harbour has an authentic Caribbean feel that's not just for tourists. Small bars and restaurants line the sandy strip of beach that serves as the community's main street. While the island's main settlement may not have the unspoiled natural beauty of some popular beaches, it holds a quaint charm. Activity picks up after dark, but many of the restaurants also serve excellent lunches without huge crowds. There are a few areas suited to swimming, with calm, shallow water perfect for children; however, the attraction here is more about the facilities than the actual beach. Ali Baba and SeaCrest Inn have rooms on the bay. ⚠ **Bring your bug spray for sandflies in the early evenings. Amenities:** food and drink; toilets. **Best for:** walking; swimming. ⊠ *Great Harbour.*

Sandy Cay Beach. Just offshore, the little islet known as Sandy Cay is a gleaming sliver of white sand with marvelous snorkeling and an inland nature trail. Previously part of the private estate of the late philanthropist and conservationist Laurance Rockefeller, the Cay recently became a protected area. You can hire any boatman on Jost Van Dyke to take you out; just be sure to agree on a price and a time to be picked up again. As this is a national park, visitors are asked to "take only photos and leave only footprints." Nevertheless, it's become an increasingly popular location for weddings, which require approval from the BVI National Parks Trust. ⚠ **Experienced boaters can rent a boat or dinghy to go here, but be aware that winter swells can make beach landings treacherous. Amenities:** none. **Best for:** walking; snorkeling; swimming. ⊠ *Jost Van Dyke.*

FAMILY Fodor's Choice ★ **White Bay Beach.** On the south shore, this long stretch of picturesque white sand is especially popular with boaters who come ashore for a libation at one of the many beach bars that offer refuge from the sun. Despite the sometimes rowdy bar scene, the beach is large enough to find a quiet spot, particularly late in the day when most of the day-trippers disappear and the beach becomes serene. Accommodations directly on or just steps from the sand include the Sandcastle Hotel, White Bay Villas, Perfect Pineapple, and the Pink House Villas. ⚠ **Swimmers and snorkelers should be cautious of boat traffic in the anchorage.** **Amenities:** food and drink; toilets. **Best for:** partiers; swimming; walking. ✉ *White Bay.*

WHERE TO EAT

Restaurants on Jost Van Dyke are informal (some serve meals family-style at long tables), but charming. The island's a favorite charter-boat stop, and you're bound to hear people exchanging stories about the previous night's anchoring adventures. Reservations are not mandatory, but it's a good idea to call ahead in season for dinner. In all cases dress is casual. Most of the restaurants are also known for their nightlife, particularly during the weekends. Meal prices are fairly consistent across the island, with dinner entrées usually varying by a few dollars.

$$$ ECLECTIC 🍴 **Abe's by the Sea.** Many sailors who cruise into this quiet bay come so they can dock right at this open-air eatery to enjoy the seafood, conch, lobster, and other fresh catches. Chicken and ribs round out the menu, and affable owners Abe Coakley and his wife, Eunicy, add a pinch and dash of hospitality that makes a meal into a memorable evening. Casual lunches are also served, and an adjoining market sells ice, canned goods, and other necessities. Dinner reservations are required by 5 pm. [$] *Average main: $29* ✉ *Little Harbour* ☎ *284/495–9329* ✍ *Reservations essential.*

$$$ SEAFOOD 🍴 **Ali Baba's.** Lobster is the main attraction at this beach bar with a sandy floor, which is just some 20 feet from the sea. Grilled local fish, including swordfish, kingfish, and wahoo, are specialties and caught fresh daily. There's also a pig roast on Monday nights in season. Beware: Ali Baba's special rum punch is as potent as it is delicious. Reservations aren't mandatory for dinner, but you'll probably find yourself waiting a long time without them. [$] *Average main: $29* ✉ *Great Harbour* ☎ *284/495–9280* 💳 *No credit cards.*

$$ ECLECTIC 🍴 **B-Line Beach Bar.** The simple, open-air B-Line Beach Bar brings "getting away from it all" to a new level. If you're on mainland Jost Van Dyke you'll have to charter a dinghy or boat, or try to hitch a ride across the few hundred meters of water between Little Jost Van Dyke and Jost Van Dyke. Here you can have an ice-cold beer, assortment of rums, and great grilled items on a beautiful, remote beach. [$] *Average main: $13* ✉ *Little Jost Van Dyke* ☎ *284/342–4959* 🌐 *www.blinebeachbar.com.*

$$$ BARBECUE 🍴 **Cool's Breeze Bar & Restaurant.** This brightly colored eatery is often frequented by island locals. The establishment offers full dinner options, serving fresh grilled lobster, barbecue, and baby back ribs. [$] *Average main: $29* ✉ *Great Harbour* ☎ *284/496–0855* 💳 *No credit cards.*

$$$$ ECLECTIC 🍴 **Corsairs Beach Bar and Restaurant.** On an island known for seafood, it's the pizza that draws raves at this friendly beach bar considered by some to be Jost's version of *Cheers*. If pizza doesn't appeal, the lunch and dinner menus have a wide variety of selections with an eclectic, Continental flare, and the owners brought a new chef on board in late 2013. Bring an appetite to breakfast, when the choices include hearty omelets and breakfast burritos. The bar is easily recognized by its signature pirate paraphernalia and a restored U.S. military M37 Dodge truck parked next to the steps-from-the-sea dining room. [$] *Average main: $32* ✉ *Great Harbour* ☎ *284/495–9294* 🌐 *www.corsairsbvi.com.*

$$$$ ECLECTIC FAMILY 🍴 **Foxy's Taboo.** It's well worth the winding hilly drive or sometimes-rough sail to get to Taboo, where there's a sophisticated menu and friendly staff with a welcoming attitude. Located on Jost's mostly undeveloped East End, Taboo is less of a party bar than Foxy's in Great Harbour but usually has a great breeze and scenic views. You'll find specialties with a Mediterranean twist like eggplant cheesecake, kebabs, and hot-from-the-oven pizza. The lunch menu differs from the standard island fare. Even the burgers are a step up from average, and the salads are the best on the island. Coupled with a walk to the nearby Bubbly Pool (ask for a map at the bar), a visit to Taboo is a good way to while away a few hours. Dinner reservations are required by 4 pm. [$] *Average main: $33* ✉ *East End* ☎ *284/340–9258.*

$$$ ECLECTIC FAMILY 🍴 **Foxy's Tamarind Bar and Restaurant.** The big draw here is the owner, Foxy Callwood, a famed calypso singer who will serenade you with lewd and laugh-worthy songs as you fork into burgers, grilled chicken, barbecue ribs, and lobster. Check out the pennants, postcards, and weathered T-shirts that adorn every inch of the walls and ceiling of this large, two-story beach shack; they've been left by previous visitors. On Friday and Saturday nights in season, Foxy hosts a Caribbean-style barbecue with grilled fresh fish, chicken and ribs, peas and rice, salad, and more, followed by live music. Other nights choose from steak, fresh lobster, pork, or pasta; at lunch Foxy serves sandwiches and salads. Whether because of the sheer volume of diners or the experience of the management, Foxy's is one of the most reliable eating establishments on Jost. And it's also home to the only locally brewed beer in the BVI. You're unlikely to find Foxy performing at night, but he takes the mike many afternoons and makes time to mingle with guests—this is a popular happy-hour pit stop. [$] *Average main: $29* ✉ *Great Harbour* ☎ *284/495–9258* 🌐 *www.foxysbar.com.*

$$$ BURGER 🍴 **Gertrude's Beach Bar.** A casual bar right on White Bay Beach, Gertrude's will make you feel at home with burgers, conch fritters, and rotis. It's open for lunch and dinner, but it's a good idea to call ahead for dinner reservations. Sometimes Gertrude, and helpful staffer Olga, will let you pour your own drinks. [$] *Average main: $21* ✉ *White Bay* ☎ *284/495–9104.*

$$$$ ECLECTIC FAMILY 🍴 **Harris' Place.** Owner Cynthia Harris is as famous for her friendliness as she is for her food. Lobster in a garlic-butter sauce, and other freshly caught seafood, as well as pork, chicken, and ribs, are on the menu. Homemade key lime pie and expertly blended Bushwackers are "to live for," as Cynthia would say, but diners also praise the fresh fish and

7

The Famous Foxy Callwood

It's the laid-back attitude of Jost Van Dyke, which boasts a beach as its main street and has had electricity only since the 1990s, that makes the famous feel comfortable and everyday folk feel glorious. At no locale is this more true than at Foxy's Tamarind. Foxy Callwood, a seventh-generation Jost Van Dyker and calypsonian extraordinaire, is the star here, strumming and singing rib-tickling ditties full of lewd and laughable lyrics that attract a bevy of boaters, and even celebrities like Tom Cruise, Kelsey Grammer, and Steven Spielberg.

What began in 1968 as a lemonade-stand-size bar, albeit with "modern" fixtures like a galvanized roof and plywood walls, has evolved into a bona fide beach bar with sandy floors, wattle walls, and a thatched roof that defines the eastern end of the beach at Great Harbour. Since Jost lacks the bustle of St. Thomas, cachet of St. John, or grace of Tortola, islanders like Foxy knew they needed to carve out their own unique niche—and have done so by appearing to have done nothing at all. Unhurried friendliness and a slice of quintessential Caribbean culture flow freely here.

Foxy, who fished for a living before he started singing for his supper, has traveled the world and has the world come to him for endless parties for Halloween, Labor Day weekend, and the New Year. *The New York Times* named Foxy's one of its three top picks for ringing in the millennium, and even Queen Elizabeth chose to honor Foxy, making him a Member of the Order of the British Empire (MBE) in 2009. A local newspaper headline from the occasion read: "Is Foxy Wearing Shoes?"

So what makes Foxy and his bar so popular, some 40 years on? He sums it up himself: "It's the quantity of people and the quality of the party. You can dance on the tables and sleep on the beach. No one is going to bother you."

lobster. Call for the schedule of live music, which varies from season to season. Breakfast and lunch are served, too. Call ahead for reservations. $ *Average main: $34* ✉ *Little Harbour* ☎ *284/495–9302.*

$ **✕ Jewel's Snack Shack.** This little wooden shack sells the best—and

AMERICAN only—hot dogs on the island. You will also find burgers, fries, and ice-cream novelties on the simple menu. $ *Average main: $12* ✉ *White Bay* ☎ *284/495–9286* ▬ *No credit cards* ⊘ *No dinner.*

$$$ **✕ One Love Bar and Grill.** The Food Network's Alton Brown sought out

ECLECTIC this beachfront eatery and featured its stewed conch on a 2008 flavor-finding trip. Menu items include freshly caught seafood, quesadillas, sandwiches, and salads. Try their specialty drink, a Bushwacker. Seddy built the bar himself and decorated it with the flotsam and jetsam he collected during his years as a fisherman. $ *Average main: $28* ✉ *White Bay* ⊕ *www.onelovebar.com.*

$$$ **✕ Rudy's Mariner's Rendezvous.** Hamburgers, cheeseburgers, and barbe-

ECLECTIC cue ribs are the specialties at this roadside spot at the extreme western end of Great Harbour and next to the quaint JVD Methodist Church. You'll also find a supermarket where you can buy basic groceries or

CAMPING ON JOST VAN DYKE

Ivan's White Bay Campground. This bar, restaurant, and campground is a popular destination on Jost Van Dyke for those who don't mind roughing it. You can pitch your tent 6 feet from the sea or farther back under the sea-grape trees where there's an electric hookup and lamp. Or opt for a primitive cabin, where you can find just a bed, fan, light, and bucket of water to wash the sand off your feet. There's an outhouse, a sun shower (basically a plastic sack hung from a tree branch), and a communal kitchen stocked with pots and pans. Expect to pay $20 for a bare site, $40 for an equipped site, or $65–$75 for a cabin. Camping reservations are essential. ⊠ *White Bay* ☎ *284/495–9358* ⊕ *www.ivanscampground.com.*

enjoy a cup of coffee and Wi-Fi at outdoor picnic tables. Ⓢ *Average main: $28* ⊠ *Great Harbour* ☎ *284/495–9282.*

$$$$
ECLECTIC
Fodor'sChoice
★

✕ **Soggy Dollar Bar.** Candles illuminate this tiny, beachfront, palm-lined dining room during the evening meal, making it one of the most romantic dinner settings on the island. Native-born Jost Van Dyke chef Dwayne Donovan keeps things interesting with five to seven entrée and appetizer choices that change weekly and feature local flourishes like a passion-fruit demi-glaze. Don't miss the Painkiller ice cream, inspired by the Painkiller cocktail created here. For lunch, if you can find your way through the throngs ordering Painkillers at the bar, choices include mahimahi sandwiches, hamburgers, chicken roti, and conch fritters. ■ TIP→ Management has recently relaxed its reservations-only dinner policy, but it's still wise to call ahead. Ⓢ *Average main: $33* ⊠ *Sandcastle, White Bay* ☎ *284/495–9888* ⊕ *www.soggydollar.com.*

$$
AMERICAN

✕ **Sugar and Spice Snack Bar.** Those waiting on arriving and departing ferries will find this casual and convenient snack bar a handy choice for breakfast or simple sandwiches. It's open seven days a week. Ⓢ *Average main: $15* ⊠ *Great Harbour* ☎ *284/543–9016.*

$$$$
ECLECTIC

✕ **Sydney's Peace and Love.** Here you can find great local lobster and fish, as well as barbecue chicken and ribs with all the fixings, including peas and rice, corn, coleslaw, and potato salad. Book early for all-you-can-eat lobster on Monday and Thursday nights. Meals are served on an open-air terrace or in an air-conditioned dining room at the water's edge. The find here is a sensational (by BVI standards) jukebox. The cognoscenti sail here for dinner, since there's no beach—and therefore no annoying sand fleas. Breakfast and lunch are served, too, and guests help themselves at the honor bar. Ⓢ *Average main: $33* ⊠ *Little Harbour* ☎ *284/495–9271.*

WHERE TO STAY

$
B&B/INN

▦ **Ali Baba's Heavenly Rooms.** Just above Ali Baba's restaurant, owner Wayson "Baba" Hatchett has added three simple but attractive rooms, each equipped with air-conditioning and a private bath. **Pros:** convenient location. **Cons:** noisy area of Great Harbour. [$] *Rooms from: $140* ✉ *Great Harbour* ☎ *284/495–9280* *3 rooms* 🍴 *No meals.*

$ RENTAL **Ivan's Stress Free Guest House.** Ivan's will give you a quintessential Caribbean experience and allow you to have some comfort doing it. **Pros:** steps away from the best beach on the island; you can meet new friends at Ivan's convivial bar. **Cons:** basic furnishings; not within walking distance to other restaurants and nightlife (except Ivan's). [$] *Rooms from: $150* ✉ *White Bay* ☎ *284/495–9358* 🌐 *www.ivanscampground.com* *2 units* 💳 *No credit cards* 🍴 *No meals.*

$ B&B/INN **Perfect Pineapple Guest Houses.** One-bedroom suites, as well as one- and two-bedroom guesthouses, all come equipped with private bath, air-conditioning, stove, satellite TV, and refrigerator. **Pros:** located just steps from the popular White Bay beach. **Cons:** rooms have only basic furnishings; in need of updating. [$] *Rooms from: $160* ✉ *White Bay* ☎ *284/495–9401* 🌐 *www.perfectpineapple.com* *6 rooms* 🍴 *No meals.*

$$ HOTEL **Sandcastle.** Sleep steps from beautiful White Bay beach at this tiny beachfront hideaway, an island favorite for more than 40 years. **Pros:** beachfront rooms; near restaurants and bars; comfy hammocks. **Cons:** some rooms lack air-conditioning; beach sometimes clogged with day-trippers; no children allowed. [$] *Rooms from: $310* ✉ *White Bay* ☎ *284/495–9888* 🌐 *www.soggydollar.com* *2 rooms, 4 1-bedroom cottages* 🍴 *Multiple meal plans.*

$$ RENTAL **Sandy Ground Estates.** Each of these seven privately owned one- and two-bedroom villas is distinct in decor, with interiors ranging from spartan to stylish. **Pros:** a place to get away from it all; secluded feel; each villa is unique. **Cons:** only reachable by boat; not accessible for people with disabilities, and best for people in good physical shape. [$] *Rooms from: $278* ✉ *Sandy Ground Estates, Sandy Ground* ☎ *284/494–3391* 🌐 *www.sandygroundbvi.com* *7 houses* 🍴 *No meals.*

$ RENTAL **Sea Crest Inn.** Sea Crest offers the cheapest lodging on Jost Van Dyke, save for camping, and the location is smack-dab in the hub of Great Harbour. **Pros:** hospitable host; affordable rates; walking distance to restaurants and ferry. **Cons:** noise from nearby bar. [$] *Rooms from: $145* ✉ *Great Harbour* ☎ *284/495–9024* 🌐 *www.seacrestinn.net* *4 1-bedroom apartments* 🍴 *No meals.*

$ RENTAL FAMILY **White Bay Villas and Seaside Cottages.** Beautiful views and friendly staff keep guests coming back to these hilltop one- to three-bedroom villas and cottages. **Pros:** incredible views; full kitchens; friendly staff. **Cons:** 10- to 15-minute walk to White Bay and Great Harbour's restaurants and beaches; rental car recommended. [$] *Rooms from: $220* ✉ *White Bay* ☎ *410/571–6692, 800/778–8066* 🌐 *www.jostvandyke.com* *7 villas, 3 cottages* 🍴 *No meals.*

SHOPPING

The FoxHole Boutique. Foxy Callwood's Australian-born wife, Tessa, first arrived here back in the 1970s, and her shop offers a surprisingly large selection for such an out-of-the-way island. As a complement to Foxy's Tamarind Bar Restaurant, the boutique offers a wide selection of "Foxy's specific" merchandise. The large store also offers Cuban cigars, gift items, Foxy's own Firewater rum, and women's and men's clothing (including hats, board shorts, and sandals). Tessa has a unique style that's evident in the interesting handbags, accessories, and jewelry that she's found around the Caribbean and the world. ⊠ *Great Harbour* ⊕ *www.foxysbar.com.*

NIGHTLIFE

Fodor'sChoice ★

Jost Van Dyke is the most happening place to go bar-hopping in the BVI, so much so that it is an all-day enterprise for some. In fact, yachties will sail over just to have a few drinks. All the spots are easy to find, clustered in three general locations: Great Harbour, White Bay, and Little Harbour (⇨ *see Where to Eat, above*). On the Great Harbour side you can find Foxy's, Corsairs, and Ali Baba's; on the White Bay side are the One Love Bar and Grill and the Soggy Dollar Bar, where legend has it the famous Painkiller was first concocted; and in Little Harbour are Harris' Place, Sydney's Peace and Love, and Abe's By The Sea. If you can't make it to Jost Van Dyke, you can have a Painkiller at almost any bar in the BVI.

SPORTS AND THE OUTDOORS

Abe and Eunicy Rentals. This company's two-door Suzukis ($65 a day), four-door Suzukis ($75 a day), and four-door Monteros ($80 a day) will help you explore by land. There's pick-up and drop-off service from anywhere on the island. ⊠ *Little Harbour* ☎ 284/495–9329.

Endeavour II **Sailing.** Built entirely from scratch on the island with local high school students, this 32-foot traditional sailing vessel was part of a maritime heritage project initiated by the Jost Van Dyke's Preservation Society. Day sails aboard help fund dive and sail training for young Jost Van Dyke islanders. ⊠ *Great Harbour* ☎ 284/540–0861 ⊕ *www. jvdps.org.*

JVD Scuba and BVI Eco-Tours. Check out the undersea world around the island with dive master Colin Aldridge. One of the most impressive dives in the area is off the north coast of Little Jost Van Dyke. Here you can find the Twin Towers: a pair of rock formations rising an impressive 90 feet. A one-tank dive costs $95, a two-tank dive $115, and a four-hour beginner course is $120 plus the cost of equipment. Colin also offers day-trips to Sandy Cay and Sandy Spit, Norman Island, Virgin Gorda (The Baths), and custom outings. You can also rent snorkel equipment or dive gear. ⊠ *Great Harbour* ☎ 284/495–0271 ⊕ *www. bvi-ecotours.com* ⊗ *Closed Sat.*

Paradise Jeep Rentals. Paradise Jeep Rentals offers the ideal vehicles to tackle Jost Van Dyke's steep, winding roads. Even though Jost is a relatively small island, you really need to be in shape to walk from one bay to the next. This outfit rents two-door Suzukis for $60 per day and four-door Grand Vitaras and Sportages for $70. Discounts are availble for rentals of six or more days. It's next to the Fire Station in Great Harbour. ■TIP➔ Reservations are a must. ⊠ *Great Harbour* ☎ 284/495–9477.

Paradise Powerboat Rental. Franky Chinnery, who was born and raised on Jost Van Dyke, owns Paradise Powerboat Rental. The company offers day-trip boat tours to Sandy Cay, Sandy Spit, Normal Island, The Baths, and custom trips, along with dinghy rentals, sportfishing, and other services on board the *Betram* and *Renegade* powerboats. It also provides water-taxi service between Jost Van Dyke and Tortola or USVI (call for prices). ⊠ *Great Harbour* ☎ *284/442–4651.*

ANEGADA

WORD OF MOUTH

"If you explore the unknown spots of Anegada, you will be rewarded with unexpected gifts—such as a little altar of bleached conch, coral, and driftwood posed by the sea at the end of a spur off the road."—seasweetie

Fodor's Choice ★ Anegada lies low on the horizon about 14 miles (22½ km) north of Virgin Gorda. Unlike the hilly volcanic islands in the chain, this is a flat coral-and-limestone atoll. Nine miles (14 km) long and 2 miles (3 km) wide, the island rises no more than 28 feet above sea level. In fact, by the time you're able to see it, you may have run your boat onto a reef. (More than 300 captains unfamiliar with the waters have done so since exploration days; note that bareboat charters don't allow their vessels to head here without a trained skipper.) Although the reefs are a sailor's nightmare, they are a primary attraction for many visitors. Snorkeling, especially in the waters around Loblolly Bay on the north shore, is a transcendent experience. You can float in shallow, calm water just a few feet from shore and see one coral formation after another, each shimmering with a rainbow of colorful fish. Many local captains are happy to take visitors out bonefishing or sportfishing. Such watery pleasures are complemented by ever-so-fine, ever-so-white sand (the northern and western shores have long stretches of the stuff) and the occasional beach bar (stop in for burgers, local lobster, or a frosty beer). Several years ago, flamingos were reintroduced to the island. Seeking out the large bright-pink birds in Anegada's salt ponds has become a popular diversion from the island's beaches when touring by vehicle.

The island's population of about 180 lives primarily in a small south-side village called the Settlement, which has a handful of grocery stores, a bakery, and a general store. In 2009, Anegada got its first bank, but it is only open one day a week (and there is no ATM). Many restaurants and shops take only cash. Mosquitoes and sand flies can be murderous around dusk and dawn on Anegada; never come here without bug repellent and long-sleeved clothing.

GETTING HERE AND AROUND

You can get to Anegada from Tortola by ferry, which was upgraded in 2012 to include a scheduled, six-day-a-week service (no Saturday). There are morning and afternoon departures, making it possible to visit the island for the day. It's also possible to fly on a charter from Beef Island or St. Thomas; the flight from Beef Island takes only 10 minutes, and can be reasonably priced per person if you are traveling with a small group.

Anegada has miles of beautiful white-sand beaches.

BEACHES

Cow Wreck Beach. Named for the cow bones that once washed ashore, this stretch of sand on the island's northwest coast has soft white sand and a casual beach bar and restaurant. Cow Wreck Beach Resort is located directly on the beach, and small crowds congregate near the bar, but there's also plenty of room for those looking for solitude. Look for the palm-thatched benches that provide some shade on the beach. **Amenities:** food and drink; toilets. **Best for:** snorkeling; walking; kiteboarding. ⊠ *Cow Wreck Beach.*

Loblolly Bay. A curve of shore on Anegada's northern coast, this bay is home to the best snorkeling on the island. The two beach bars at Loblolly East are often closed and this is the place for solitude. Loblolly West has a popular beachfront reastaurant, showers, a gift shop, and snorkel rentals. The cottages at Big Bamboo are steps from the beach. Some palm-thatched shelters on the beach offer shade. **Amenities:** food and drink; showers; toilets; water sports. **Best for:** swimming; snorkeling; walking. ⊠ *Loblolly Bay.*

Pomato Point. A powder white-sand beach on Anegada's western shore, Pomato Point has the best sunset views. There is no easily accessible reef, but the water is calm (making it a good choice for children) and the views of Tortola and Jost Van Dyke are beautiful. There's a restaurant on the beach, but nearby Setting Point offers several restaurant options, along with lodging. **Amenities:** food and drink. **Best for:** swimming; walking. ⊠ *Setting Point.*

WHERE TO EAT

There are between 6 and 10 restaurants open at any one time, depending on the season and on whim. Check when you're on the island. Fresh fish and lobster are the specialties of the island. The going rate for a lobster dinner is $50, and it's almost always the most expensive thing on any restaurant menu.

$$$$ SEAFOOD Fodor's Choice ★

🍴 **Anegada Reef Hotel Restaurant.** Seasoned yachters gather here nightly to share tales of the high seas; the open-air bar is the busiest on the island. Dinner is by candlelight under the stars and always includes famous Anegada lobster, steaks, and succulent baby back ribs—all prepared on the large grill by the little open-air bar. The ferry dock is right next door, so expect a crowd shortly after it arrives. Dinner reservations are required by 4 pm. Breakfast favorites include lobster omelets and rum-soaked French toast; at lunch the Reef serves salads and sandwiches. [$] *Average main: $37* ✉ *Setting Point* ☎ *284/495–8002* ✍ *Reservations essential.*

$$$ SEAFOOD FAMILY

🍴 **Big Bamboo.** This beachfront bar and restaurant tucked among sea-grape trees at famous Loblolly Bay is the island's most popular destination for lunch. After you've polished off a plate of succulent Anegada lobster, barbecue chicken, or fresh fish, you can spend the afternoon on the beach, where the snorkeling is excellent and the view close to perfection. Fruity drinks from the cabana bar and ice cream from the freezer will round out your day. Dinner is by request only. If your heart is set on lobster, it's a good idea to call in the morning or the day before to put in your request. [$] *Average main: $29* ✉ *Loblolly Bay West* ☎ *284/495–2019* 🌐 *www.bigbambooanegada.com.*

$$$$ SEAFOOD

🍴 **Cow Wreck Bar and Grill.** Named for the cow bones that once washed up on shore, this wiggle-your-toes-in-the-sand beachside eatery on the northern shore is a fun place to watch the antics of surfers and kite-boarders skidding across the bay. Tuck into conch ceviche, lobster fritters, or the popular hot wings for lunch. The homemade coconut pie is a winner. Pack your snorkel gear and explore the pristine reef just a few strokes from the shore before you eat, or browse the on-site gift shop. Dinner is served by request; reservations required by 4 pm. [$] *Average main: $36* ✉ *Cow Wreck Beach* ☎ *284/495–8047* 🌐 *www.cowwreckbeach.com* ✍ *Reservations essential.*

$$$$ SEAFOOD FAMILY Fodor's Choice ★

🍴 **Neptune's Treasure.** The owners, the Soares family, have lived on the island for more than half a century, and the Soares men catch, cook, and serve the seafood at this homey bar and restaurant a short distance from Setting Point. The fresh lobster, swordfish, tuna, and mahimahi are all delicious. In 2013, Pam's Kitchen, a small bakery to the exterior of the property, was incorporated into the restaurant and rounds out offerings with freshly baked breads, sweet treats including made-from-scratch desserts (such as key lime pie, chocolate brownies, and apple pie), and pizzas. Dinner is by candlelight at the water's edge, often with classic jazz playing softly in the background. If you've tired of seafood, Neptune's has a nice variety of alternatives, including vegetarian pasta, pork loin, and orange chicken. The view is spectacular at sunset. Breakfast and lunch are also served. Dinner reservations are essential by

4 pm. $ *Average main: $32* ✉ *Bender Bay* ☎ *284/495–9439* 🌐 *www.neptunestreasure.com* ✍ *Reservations essential.*

$$$$ SEAFOOD 🍴 **Pomato Point Restaurant.** This relaxed restaurant and bar sits on one of the best beaches on the island and enjoys Anegada's most dramatic sunset views. Entrées include lobster, stewed conch, and freshly caught seafood. It's open for lunch daily; call by 4 pm for dinner reservations. Be sure to take a look at owner Wilfred Creque's displays of island artifacts, including shards of Arawak pottery and 17th-century coins, cannonballs, and bottles. These are housed in a little one-room museum adjacent to the dining room. $ *Average main: $38* ✉ *Pomato Point* ☎ *284/495–9466* ✍ *Reservations essential* 🕓 *Closed Sept.*

$$$$ SEAFOOD 🍴 **Potter's By the Sea.** Owner Liston Potter, a great staff, and a lively atmosphere just a few steps from the dock complement freshly grilled lobster and other seafood selections such as snapper and grouper. Potter's also offers a beach shuttle, free Wi-Fi, pool tables, and live music (ask about the schedule when you call ahead for dinner reservations). $ *Average main: $37* ✉ *Setting Point* ☎ *284/495–9182* ✍ *Reservations essential.*

WHERE TO STAY

$$ RESORT 🏨 **Anegada Beach Club.** This is a laid-back beach-club setting where beach enthusiasts can enjoy beach volleyball and badminton. **Pros:** with the option of adjoining king and "junior" suites (with two twin beds) and plenty of outdoor activities, this is a great spot for families; there is a bar and restaurant on-site. **Cons:** some find Anegada too remote. $ *Rooms from: $276* ✉ *Keel Point* ☎ *800/871–3551, 284/852–4500* 🌐 *www.anegadabeachclub.com* 🛏 *16 rooms, 7 luxury tents* 🍽 *No meals.*

$ HOTEL 🏨 **Anegada Reef Hotel.** Head here if you want to bunk in comfortable lodgings near Anegada's most popular anchorage. **Pros:** everything you need is nearby; nice sunsets. **Cons:** basic rooms; no beach; often a party atmosphere at the bar. $ *Rooms from: $265* ✉ *Setting Point* ☎ *284/495–8002* 🌐 *www.anegadareef.com* 🛏 *16 rooms* 🍽 *Multiple meal plans.*

$$ RENTAL 🏨 **Big Bamboo.** Location is this property's finest attribute: the four circular villas are just steps from beautiful Loblolly Bay. **Pros:** beachfront location; near restaurant and snorkeling. **Cons:** some may feel isolated; beach popular during the day. $ *Rooms from: $350* ✉ *Loblolly Bay West* ☎ *284/495–2019* 🌐 *www.bigbambooanegada.com* 🛏 *4 villas* 🍽 *No meals.*

$$ RENTAL 🏨 **Cow Wreck Beach Resort.** The resort's best attribute is its location at Cow Wreck Beach. **Pros:** secluded location; great snorkeling. **Cons:** the island's infamous, free-roaming livestock sometimes leave "presents" behind; location too remote for some. $ *Rooms from: $276* ✉ *Cow Wreck Beach* ☎ *284/495–8047* 🌐 *www.cowwreckbeach.com* 🛏 *4 units* 🍽 *No meals.*

$ RENTAL FAMILY 🏨 **Keel Point Cottages.** Picture yourself nearly alone in a tropical paradise; if that's your dream, then this may be your place. **Pros:** right on the water; new, well-kept property; rental car included. **Cons:** no on-site dining options (except your kitchen) and far from restaurants. $ *Rooms*

7

from: $250 ⊠ *Keel Point* ☎ *284/441–0296* ⊕ *www.keelpointcottages. com* ↩ *4 cottages* ⦿ *No meals.*

$ ⛱ **Neptune's Treasure.** Basic waterfront rooms with simple furnishings
B&B/INN and lovely views of the ocean are the hallmark of this family-owned
FAMILY guesthouse. **Pros:** waterfront property; run by a family full of tales
of the island; nice sunset views. **Cons:** simple rooms; no kitchens; no
beach. **$** *Rooms from: $150* ⊠ *Bender's Bay* ☎ *284/495–9439* ⊕ *www.
neptunestreasure.com* ↩ *9 rooms, 2 cottages* ⦿ *No meals.*

SHOPPING

Dotsy's Bakery. You'll find a tempting array of fresh-baked breads, sandwiches, pizza, cookies, and desserts at this bakery. ⊠ *The Settlement*
☎ *284/495–9667.*

Faulkner's Country Store. Stop here for a taste of old-time Anegada or just
to buy groceries or other necessities. ⊠ *The Settlement.*

SPORTS AND THE OUTDOORS

Anegada Reef Hotel. Call the hotel to arrange bonefishing and sportfishing outings with seasoned local guides. ⊠ *Setting Point* ☎ *284/495–
8002* ⊕ *www.anegadareef.com.*

Danny Vanterpool. Danny offers half-, three-quarter-, and full-day bonefishing excursions around Anegada. The cost ranges from $400 for a
half day to $600 for a full day. ⊠ *Anegada* ☎ *284/441–6334* ⊕ *www.
dannysbonefishing.com.*

OTHER BRITISH VIRGIN ISLANDS

Of the 50-odd islands in the British Virgin Islands chain only 15 are
inhabited, and several of those are privately owned, having been turned
into private-island resorts. Some of these—most notably Necker Island,
which is owned by Sir Richard Branson, and Peter Island, an upscale
private-island retreat often visited by the rich and famous—are well
known among the jet-set crowd; others are not as well known but
equally beautiful.

COOPER ISLAND

This small, hilly island on the south side of the Sir Francis Drake Channel, about 8 miles (13 km) from Road Town, Tortola, is popular with
the charter-boat crowd. There are no paved roads (which doesn't really
matter, as there aren't any cars), but you can find a beach restaurant,
a casual hotel, a few houses (some are available for rent), and great
snorkeling at the south end of Manchioneel Bay.

GETTING HERE AND AROUND

Unless you have your own sailboat, the only way to reach Cooper Island
is on a private ferry from Road Harbour Marina. The 35-minute ride
is included in the cost of your vacation at Cooper Island Beach Club if
your schedule meshes with the hotel's boat service.

WHERE TO STAY

$ Cooper Island Beach Club. Diving is the focus at this small resort, but ALL-INCLUSIVE folks who want to simply swim, snorkel, or relax can also feel right at Fodor's Choice home. **Pros:** lots of quiet; the Caribbean as it used to be. **Cons:** small ★ rooms; island accessible only by ferry; there is no nightlife. $ *Rooms from: $225* ⊠ *Manchioneel Bay* ☎ *284/495–9084, 800/542–4624* ⊕ *www.cooperislandbeachclub.com* ⤴ *9 rooms* ❍ *All-inclusive.*

GUANA ISLAND

Guana Island sits off Tortola's northeast coast. Sailors often drop anchor at one of the island's bays for a day of snorkeling and sunning. The island is a designated wildlife sanctuary, and scientists often come here to study its flora and fauna. It's home to a back-to-nature resort that offers few activities other than relaxation. Unless you're a hotel guest or a sailor, there's no easy way to get here.

GETTING HERE AND AROUND

Unless you have your own sailboat, the only way to reach Guana Island is by the resort's private ferry, which will pick you up at Beef Island, Tortola. You can also take a water taxi from St. Thomas.

WHERE TO STAY

$$$$ Guana Island Resort. Here's a good resort if you want to stroll the RESORT hillsides, snorkel around the reefs, swim at its seven beaches, and still Fodor's Choice enjoy some degree of comfort. **Pros:** secluded feel; lovely grounds. ★ **Cons:** very expensive; need boat to get here. $ *Rooms from: $1250* ⊠ *Guana Island* ☎ *284/494–2354, 800/544–8262* ⊕ *www.guana.com* ⤴ *15 rooms, 1 1-bedroom villa, 1 2-bedroom villa, 1 3-bedroom villa* ❍ *All meals.*

MARINA CAY

FAMILY Beautiful little Marina Cay is in Trellis Bay, not far from Beef Island. Sometimes you can see it and its large J-shape coral reefs—a most dramatic sight—from the air soon after takeoff from the airport on Beef Island. Covering 8 acres, this islet is considered small even by BVI standards. On it there's a restaurant, a Pusser's Store, and a six-unit hotel. Ferry service is free from the dock on Beef Island.

GETTING HERE AND AROUND

There's a regularly scheduled ferry from Beef Island, Tortola, direct to Marina Cay. It's a short, 15-minute trip.

WHERE TO STAY

$ Pusser's Marina Cay Hotel and Restaurant. If getting away from it all HOTEL is your priority, this may be the place for you, because there's nothing to do on this beach-rimmed island other than swim, snorkel, and soak up the sun—there's not even a TV to distract you. **Pros:** lots of character; beautiful beaches; interesting guests. **Cons:** older property; ferry needed to get here. $ *Rooms from: $175* ⊠ *West side of Marina Cay* ☎ *284/494–2174* ⊕ *www.pussers.com* ⤴ *4 rooms, 2 2-bedroom villas* ❍ *Breakfast.*

Peter Island, a private-island resort and popular anchorage for yachters

SCRUB ISLAND

The island is close enough to Tortola to spend a day exploring. That said, there are enough activities that you might not want to leave.

GETTING HERE AND AROUND

Scrub Island is easily reachable from Beef Island by the resort's private ferry. The dock is just minutes from the airport.

WHERE TO STAY

$$$$ RESORT Fodor's Choice ★ **Scrub Island Resort, Spa and Marina.** Part of Marriott's Autograph Collection, this swanky resort is located on a 250-acre island near Tortola's Beef Island Airport. **Pros:** new property; lots of activities. **Cons:** need ferry to get there; expensive. [$] *Rooms from: $480* ✉ *Scrub Island* ☎ *877/890–7444, 284/394–3440* 🌐 *www.scrubisland.com* *52 rooms, 7 villas* 🍴 *No meals.*

NECKER ISLAND

Necker Island sits off Virgin Gorda's northeast coast, reachable only by private ferry or helicopter. A mere speck in the British Virgin Islands, it's home to Sir Richard Branson's private estate. When he's not in residence, you and your friends are welcome to enjoy its gorgeous beaches and myriad amenities.

GETTING HERE AND AROUND

Guests (and only guests) of Necker Island will be whisked away from Beef Island or Virgin Gorda on a private boat or helicopter.

WHERE TO STAY

$$$$ ALL-INCLUSIVE 🏨 **Necker Island.** You probably won't run into British magnate Sir Richard Branson, but you can live in his luxurious style when you rent his estate on Necker Island. **Pros:** gorgeous setting; an island for you and a few dozen friends. **Cons:** very expensive; need boat to get here. [$] *Rooms from: $60,000* ✉ *Necker Island* ☎ *212/994–3070, 877/577–8777* 🌐 *www.neckerisland.virgin.com* 🛏 *10 rooms, 4 houses* 🍴 *All-inclusive* ☞ *Rate is per night for up to 30 people.*

NORMAN ISLAND

This uninhabited island is the supposed setting for Robert Louis Stevenson's *Treasure Island.* The famed caves at Treasure Point are popular with day sailors and powerboaters. If you land ashore at the island's main anchorage in the Bight, you can find a small beach bar and behind it a trail that winds up the hillside and reaches a peak with a fantastic view of the Sir Francis Drake Channel to the north. The island boasts nearly 12 miles of hiking trails. Call Pirate's Bight for information on ferry service, which was being upgraded in late 2014 to accommodate day-trippers.

GETTING HERE AND AROUND

The only way to reach this island is by private boat or on a charter boat that puts you aboard the *Willy T.* for a meal and drinks.

WHERE TO EAT

$$$$ ECLECTIC ✕ **Pirate's Bight.** This breezy, open-air dining establishment boasts quirky beach-bar eccentricities (a cannon is fired at sunset and bar-goers play games like "Giant Jenga"), while maintaining a slightly refined feeling that came with 2013 renovations. Sail Caribbean operates a dive shop on the property and owners offer ferry service, giving the restaurant the feel of a casual day resort. Dinner offerings include a variety of seafood and poultry options, and appetizers and bar food include choices such as tuna tartar and coconut shrimp. The restaurant hosts live entertainment several nights a week. Call ahead for the music schedule and for dinner reservations. [$] *Average main: $32* ✉ *The Bight* ☎ *284/443–1405* 🌐 *www.piratesbight.com.*

$$ ECLECTIC ✕ ***Willy T.*** *Willy T* is a floating bar and restaurant that's anchored to the north of the Bight. Lunch and dinner are served in a party-hearty atmosphere. Try the conch fritters for starters. For lunch and dinner, British-style fish-and-chips, West Indian roti sandwiches, and the baby back ribs are winners. Call ahead for dinner reservations. [$] *Average main: $17* ✉ *The Bight* ☎ *284/496–8603* 🌐 *www.williamthornton.com* ✍ *Reservations essential.*

PETER ISLAND

Although Peter Island is home to the resort of the same name, it's also a popular destination for charter boaters and Tortola vacationers. The island is lush, with forested hillsides and white sandy beaches. There are no roads other than those at the resort. You're welcome to dine at the resort's restaurants.

7

GETTING HERE AND AROUND

The only way to reach Peter Island is by private boat, private ferry, or helicopter from St. Thomas. Service from Beef Island Airport via private boat runs $60 per person round-trip. The resort also has transportation Tuesday and Saturday from Cyril E. King Airport on St. Thomas via taxi and ferry. It runs $125 per person round-trip. The scheduled ferry trip from Peter Island's shoreside base outside Road Town runs $20 round-trip for nonguests.

WHERE TO STAY

$$$$

RESORT

Fodor's Choice

★

☂ **Peter Island Resort & Spa.** Total pampering and prices to match are the ticket at this luxury resort. **Pros:** lovely rooms; nice beach. **Cons:** need ferry to get here; pricey rates. $ *Rooms from: $800* ⊠ *Peter Island* ☎ *284/495–2000, 800/346–4451* ⊕ *www.peterisland.com* ⤳ *52 rooms, 3 villas* ⏐◎⏐ *Multiple meal plans.*

TRAVEL SMART
U.S. & BRITISH
VIRGIN ISLANDS

GETTING HERE AND AROUND

While St. Croix has a four-lane highway and St. Thomas has multiple lanes running along the Charlotte Amalie waterfront, the other islands in the region have only paved two-lane main roads that twist and turn up and down the hillsides. Potholes are common. Once you get into neighborhoods, most roads are paved, but particularly on St. John and in the British Virgin Islands you may find some that are still dirt or gravel. Planes connect the larger islands, but travel to St. John and the smaller BVI is only by ferry. Ferries also connect the larger islands with the smaller ones and with each other.

■ TIP→ Ask the local tourist board about hotel and local transportation packages that include tickets to special events.

■ AIR TRAVEL

The nonstop flight from New York to St. Thomas or San Juan, Puerto Rico, takes about four hours; from Miami to St. Thomas or San Juan it's about three hours.

Reconfirming your flights on interisland carriers is still a good idea, particularly when you're traveling to the smallest islands. You may be subjected to a carrier's whims: if no other passengers are booked on your flight, you may be asked to take another flight later in the day, or your plane may make unscheduled stops to pick up more passengers or cargo. It's all part of the excitement—and unpredictability—of travel in the Caribbean. In addition, regional carriers use small aircraft with limited baggage space, and they often impose weight restrictions; travel light, or you could be subject to outrageous surcharges or delays in getting very large or heavy luggage, which may have to follow on another flight.

AIRPORTS

The major airports are Terrance B. Lettsome International Airport on Beef Island, Tortola; Cyril E. King Airport on St. Thomas; and Henry Rohlsen Airport on St. Croix, which is on the southwestern side of the island, near Christiansted. There's a small airport (so small that it doesn't have a phone number) on Virgin Gorda.

Airport Information **Cyril E. King Airport** (STT) ⊠ *Rte. 30, Lindbergh Bay, St. Thomas* ☎ *340/774–5100.* **Henry Rohlsen Airport** (STX) ⊠ *Airport Rd., off Rte 66, Anguilla, St. Croix* ☎ *340/778–1012.* **Terrance B. Lettsome International Airport** ⊠ *Beef Island Rd., Beef Island, Tortola, British Virgin Islands* ☎ *284/852–900.*

Ground transportation options are covered in the Essentials sections in individual island chapters.

FLIGHTS

There are nonstop and connecting flights, usually through San Juan, Puerto Rico, from the U.S. mainland to St. Thomas and St. Croix, with connecting ferry service from St. Thomas to St. John. There are no nonstop flights to the BVI from the United States; you must connect in San Juan or St. Thomas for the short hop over to Tortola or Virgin Gorda.

American Airlines is the biggest air carrier to the Virgin Islands, with several nonstop flights a day from New York and Miami to St. Thomas and several connecting flights through San Juan. American also flies nonstop to St. Croix from Miami. The frequency of flights is seasonal.

US Airways has nonstop flights from Philadelphia and Charlotte, North Carolina. Spirit Airlines flies nonstop every day from Fort Lauderdale. Delta flies nonstop from Atlanta. United also flies nonstop from Chicago and Washington, D.C. JetBlue flies direct from Boston but connects to many points on the mainland through San Juan.

Although connecting through San Juan is your best bet for getting to Tortola or Virgin Gorda, you can also fly from St. Thomas and St. Croix to Tortola and Virgin Gorda on Air Sunshine. Seaborne flies direct from San Juan to St. Thomas, St. Croix, Tortola, and Virgin Gorda and between St. Thomas and St. Croix.

Some islands in the British Virgin Islands are accessible only by small planes operated by local or regional carriers. International carriers will sometimes book those flights for you as part of your overall travel arrangements, or you can book directly with the local carrier.

Airline Contacts American Airlines ☎ 800/433-7300, 340/776-2560 in St. Thomas, 340/778-2000 in St. Croix, 284/495-2559 in Tortola ⊕ www.aa.com. **Delta Airlines** ☎ 800/221-1212, 340/777-4177 in St. Thomas ⊕ www.delta.com. **JetBlue** ☎ 800/538-2583 ⊕ www.jetblue.com. **Spirit Airlines** ☎ 800/772-7117 ⊕ www.spirit.com. **United Airlines** ☎ 800/864-8331 ⊕ www.united.com. **US Airways** ☎ 800/622-1015 ⊕ www.usairways.com.

Interisland Carriers Air Sunshine ☎ 800/327-8900, 800/435-8900 in Florida, 888/879-8900 in USVI, 284/495-8900 in BVI ⊕ www.airsunshine.com. **Antilles Helicopter Services** ☎ 284/499-0545, 284/441-7335 ⊕ www.antilleshelicopterservices.com. **Cape Air** ☎ 866/227-3247, 508/771-6944 outside the US/USVI ⊕ www.capeair.com. **Fly BVI** ☎ 284/495-1747 in BVI, 866/819-3146 in US ⊕ www.bviaircharters.com. **LIAT**

☎ 888/844-5428, 866/549-5428 in USVI, 284/495-1693 in Tortola ⊕ www.liatairline.com. **Seaborne Airlines** ☎ 787/949-7800 ⊕ www.seaborneairlines.com.

▌BOAT AND FERRY TRAVEL

Ferries travel between St. Thomas and St. John. You can also travel by ferry from both St. Thomas and St. John to the British Virgin Islands, and between the British Virgin Islands themselves. The companies run regularly scheduled trips, departing from Charlotte Amalie or Red Hook on St. Thomas; Cruz Bay, St. John; West End, Road Town, or Beef Island on Tortola; Spanish Town or North Sound on Virgin Gorda; and Jost Van Dyke. There's also regularly scheduled service between Tortola, Virgin Gorda, and Anegada a few times a week. Schedules change, so check with your hotel or villa manager to find out the latest. The ferry companies are all regulated by the U.S. Coast Guard, and prices are about the same, so there's no point in trying to organize your schedule to take one company's ferries rather than another's. Just show up at the dock to buy your ticket on the next ferry departing for your destination. If it all seems confusing—and it can be very confusing for travel to or around the BVI—just ask a local who's also buying a ticket. They know the ropes.

Although you might save a few dollars flying into St. Thomas if you're headed to the BVI, it's much easier to connect through San Juan for a flight to Tortola or Virgin Gorda. If you're headed to St. John or to points like North Sound, Virgin Gorda, or Jost Van Dyke, you'll have to hop a ferry regardless. If you're splitting your vacation between the U.S. and British Virgin Islands, ferries are the perfect way to get from one to another. You'll also get a bonus—views of the many small islands that dot the ferry route.

Dohm's Water Taxi runs from St. Thomas to St. John and any point in the BVI. You'll avoid the often crowded ferries, the crew will handle your luggage and navigate customs in the BVI, and you'll arrive at your destination feeling relaxed; however, you'll pay significantly more for the convenience.

There's frequent daily service from both Red Hook (15 to 20 minutes, $6 each way plus $2.50 for each piece of luggage) and Charlotte Amalie (45 minutes, $12 each way plus $2.50 for each piece of luggage) to Cruz Bay. The more frequent ferry from Red Hook to St. John leaves at 6:30 am and hourly starting at 8 am, the last at midnight; from St. John back to Red Hook, the first ferry leaves at 6 am, the last at 11 pm. About every hour there's a car ferry, which costs $42 to $50 (plus $3 port charges) round-trip; you should arrive at least 25 minutes before departure. From Charlotte Amalie the first ferry to St. John leaves at 10 am, the last at 5:30 pm; from St. John to Charlotte Amalie, the first ferry leaves at 8:45 am, the last at 3:45. The ferry between Charlotte Amalie and St. John is prone to cancellations, particularly in the slower fall months.

Reefer is the name given to both of the brightly colored 26-passenger skiffs that run between the Charlotte Amalie waterfront and Marriott Frenchman's Reef hotel every day on the half hour from 8 to 5. It's a good way to beat the traffic (and is about the same price as a taxi) to Morning Star Beach. The one-way fare is $6 per person, and the trip takes about 15 minutes.

There's daily service between Charlotte Amalie or Red Hook, on St. Thomas, and West End or Road Town, Tortola, BVI, by either Smith's Ferry or Native Son, and to Virgin Gorda, BVI, by Smith's Ferry. The round-trip fare is $55–$70 and the trip from Charlotte Amalie takes 45 minutes to an hour to West End and up to 90 minutes to Road Town; from Red Hook the trip is only a half hour.

There's also frequent service from Cruz Bay to Tortola aboard an Inter-Island Boat Service ferry. The half-hour trip costs $55 round-trip; bring your passport if you plan to go to BVI (it's now required for all travel there).

The 2¼-hour trip from Charlotte Amalie to Virgin Gorda costs $40 one way and $70 round-trip. From Red Hook and Cruz Bay, Inter-Island offers service on Thursday and Sunday; Speedy's offers service on Tuesday, Thursday, and Saturday.

On Friday, Saturday, and Sunday a ferry operates between Red Hook, Cruz Bay, and Jost Van Dyke; the trip takes 45 minutes and costs $80 per person round-trip.

Ferry Contacts Boyson Inc. General II and Mister B (*St. John Car Barge*) ☎ 340/776–6294 ⊕ www.boysoninc.com. **Dohm's Water Taxi** ☎ 340/775-6501 *in St. Thomas* ⊕ www.watertaxi-vi.com. **Global Marine's Tug Life aka Roanoke** (*St. John Car Barge*) ☎ 340/779–1739 ⊕ www.caribya.com. **Inter-Island Boat Service** ☎ 340/776–6597 *in St. John*, 284/495-4166 *in Tortola*, 340/473–8567 *St. John cell* ⊕ www.interislandboatservices.com. **Love City Car Ferry's Captain Vic** (*St. John Car Barge*) ☎ 340/779–4000 ⊕ www.lovecitycarferries.com. **Native Son** ☎ 340/774–8685 *in St. Thomas* (*Charlotte Amalie*), 340/775-3111 *in St. Thomas* (*Red Hook*), 284/495–4617 *in Tortola* (*West End*), 284/494-5674 *in Tortola* (*Road Town*) ⊕ www.nativesonferry.com. **New Horizon Ferry Service** ☎ 284/495–9278 *in Tortola* ⊕ www.newhorizonferry.com. **North Sound Express** ☎ 284/495-2138 *in Tortola*. **Peter Island Ferry** ☎ 284/495–2000 *in Tortola*, 800/346-4451 ⊕ www.peterisland.com. **Reefer** ☎ 340/776–8500 *in St. Thomas* ⊕ www.marriottfrenchmansreef.com. **Road Town Fast Ferry** ☎ 284/494–2323 *in Tortola*, 340/777-2800 *in St. Thomas* ⊕ www.tortolafastferry.com. **Smith's Ferry** ☎ 340/775–7292 *in St. Thomas*, 284/494–4454 *in Tortola* ⊕ www.bviferryservices.com. **Speedy's Ferries** ☎ 284/495-5235 *in Tortola* ⊕ www.speedysbvi.com. **Varlack Ventures** ☎ 340/776–6412 *in St. John* ⊕ www.varlack-ventures.com.

▌ CAR TRAVEL

A car gives you mobility. You'll be able to spend an hour browsing at that cozy out-of-the-way shop instead of the 10 minutes allotted by your tour guide. You can beach-hop without searching for a ride, and you can sample that restaurant you've heard so much about that's half an hour (and an expensive taxi ride) away. On parts of some of the islands, you may need to rent a four-wheel-drive vehicle to really get out and about. Paved roads are generally good, but you may encounter a pothole or two (or three). Except for one divided highway on St. Croix, roads are narrow, and in hilly locations twist and turn with the hill's contours. The roads on the north side of Tortola are particularly serpentine, with scary drop-offs that will send you plummeting down the hillside if you miss the turn. Drive slowly. Many villas in St. John and the BVI are on unpaved roads. Four-wheel drive could be a necessity if it rains. A higher-clearance vehicle will help you get safely over the rocks that may litter the road.

GASOLINE

Gas is up to $1 to $2 more per gallon than in the United States. USVI stations sell gas by the gallon; BVI stations sell it by the liter or the gallon, depending on the station. Most stations accept major credit cards, but don't count on that. Some stations have a pump-it-yourself policy, but it's still easy to find one with attendants, except on St. John. There's no need to tip unless they change a tire or do some other quick mechanical chore. You'll have to ask for a handwritten receipt if you're not paying by credit card. On smaller islands stations may be closed on Sunday.

PARKING

Parking can be tight in towns across the USBVI. Workers grab up the street parking, sometimes arriving several hours early to get prime spaces. It's particularly difficult to find parking in Cruz Bay, St. John. There are free public lots scattered around town, but they're usually filled by folks taking the ferry to St. Thomas. However, you can often find a spot in the public lot across from the tennis courts, but it's a 10-minute walk to the heart of Cruz Bay. Your rental-car company probably will allow you to park in its lot. Charlotte Amalie, St. Thomas, has a paid parking lot next to Fort Christian. A machine takes your money—$1 for the first hour and $5 for all day. In Christiansted, St. Croix, you'll find a public parking lot on Strand Street. Since the booth isn't staffed, there's no charge. There's also a public lot near Fort Christiansvaern, but that lot is locked at 4:30 pm. It costs $1 for the first hour, and $6 for all day. Tortola has several free parking lots near the waterfront, but daytime parking is a nightmare unless you get there early. On Virgin Gorda there's a free lot at Virgin Gorda Yacht Harbor. There are no parking meters anywhere in the USBVI. Even if you're desperate for a parking space in the USVI, don't park in a handicapped space without a sticker—unless you want to pay a $1,000 fine.

RENTAL CARS

Unless you plan to spend all your days at a resort or plan to take taxis everywhere, you'll need a rental car at least for a few days. While driving is on the left, you'll drive an American-style car with the steering wheel on the left. Traffic doesn't move all that fast in most USBVI locations, so driving on the left is not that difficult to master.

If you're staying on St. Thomas or St. Croix and don't plan to venture far off the main roads, you won't need a four-wheel-drive vehicle. On St. John and in the BVI, a four-wheel-drive vehicle is useful to get up steep roads when it rains. Many rental homes in St. John and the BVI are on unpaved roads, so a four-wheel-drive vehicle with high clearance may be a necessity if you rent a villa. While rental agencies don't usually prohibit access to certain roads, use common sense. If the road looks too bad, turn around.

Most car-rental agencies won't rent to anyone under age 25 or over age 75.

Some car-rental agencies offer infant car seats for about $5 a day, but check and check again right before you leave for your trip to make sure one will be available. If you don't use one, you may get a ticket since the law requires their use. You might consider bringing your own car seat from home.

Book your rental car well in advance during the winter season. Vehicles are particularly scarce around the busy Presidents' Day holiday. If you don't reserve, you might find yourself without wheels. Prices will be higher during the winter season.

You usually won't find any long lines when picking up your car or dropping it off. If your rental agency is away from the airport or ferry terminal, you'll have to allot extra time to get to there. Ask when you pick up your car how much time you should allot for returning it.

Rates range from $50 a day ($300 a week) for an economy car with air-conditioning, automatic transmission, and unlimited mileage to as much as $80 a day ($400 a week) for a four-wheel-drive vehicle. Both the USVI and the BVI have major companies (with airport locations) as well as numerous local companies (near the airports, in hotels, and in the main towns), which are sometimes cheaper. Most provide pick-up service; some ask that you take a taxi to their headquarters.

A driver's license from the United States or other countries is fine in the USVI and the BVI.

Major Agencies Alamo ☎ 800/462–5266 ⊕ www.alamo.com. **Avis** ☎ 800/331–1084 ⊕ www.avis.com. **Budget** ☎ 800/472–3325 ⊕ www.budget.com. **Hertz** ☎ 800/654–3001 ⊕ www.hertz.com. **National Car Rental** ☎ 800/227–7368 ⊕ www.nationalcar.com.

Local Agencies Dependable Car Rental ⊠ Estate Contant, 12 Lindbergh Bay, 1½ miles east of Cyril E. King Airport off Rte. 308, turning north at the Medical Arts Building, Lindbergh Bay, St. Thomas ☎ 340/774–2253, 800/522–3076 ⊕ www.dependablecar.com. **Itgo Car Rental** ⊠ Wickham's Cay I, Road Town, Tortola, British Virgin Islands ☎ 284/494–2639 ⊕ www.itgobvi.com. **Judi of Croix** ☎ 340/773–2123, 877/903–2123 ⊕ www.judiofcroix.com. **L&S Jeep Rental** ⊠ The Valley, Virgin Gorda, British Virgin Islands ☎ 284/495–5297 ⊕ www.landsjeeprental.com. **St. John Car Rental** ⊠ Bay St., near Wharfside Village, Cruz Bay, St. John ☎ 340/776–6103 ⊕ www.stjohncarrental.com.

RENTAL CAR INSURANCE

Everyone who rents a car wonders whether the insurance that the rental companies offer is worth the expense. No one—including us—has a simple answer. If you own a car, your personal auto insurance may cover a rental to some degree, though not all policies protect you abroad; always read your policy's fine print. If you don't have auto insurance, then seriously consider buying the collision- or loss-damage waiver (CDW or LDW) from the car-rental company, which eliminates your liability for damage to the car. Some credit cards offer CDW coverage, but it's usually supplemental to your own insurance and rarely covers SUVs, minivans, luxury models, and the like. If your coverage is secondary, you may still be liable for loss-of-use costs from the car-rental company. But no credit-card insurance is valid unless you use that card for *all* transactions, from reserving to paying the final bill. All companies exclude car rental in some countries, so be sure to find out about the destination to which you are traveling. It's sometimes cheaper to buy insurance as part of your general travel insurance policy.

ROADSIDE EMERGENCIES

To reach police, fire, or ambulance, dial 911 in the USVI and 999 or 911 in the BVI. There are no emergency-service companies such as AAA in the USBVI. Before driving off into the countryside, check your rental car for tire-changing equipment, including a spare tire in good condition.

ROAD CONDITIONS

Island roads are often narrow, winding, and hilly. Those in mountainous regions that experience heavy tropical rains are also potholed and poorly maintained. Streets in towns are narrow, a legacy of the days when islanders used horse-drawn carts. Drive with extreme caution, especially if you venture out at night. You won't see guardrails on every curve, although the drops can be frighteningly steep. And pedestrians and livestock often share the roadway with vehicles.

You'll face rush-hour traffic on St. Thomas (especially in Charlotte Amalie); on St. Croix (especially in Christiansted and on Centerline Road); and on Tortola (especially around Road Town). All the larger towns have one-way streets. Although they're marked, the signs may be obscured by overhanging branches and other obstacles.

Drivers are prone to stopping in the road to chat with a passerby, to let a passenger out, or to buy a newspaper from a vendor. Pay attention when entering curves, because you might find a stopped car on the other side.

RULES OF THE ROAD

Driving in the Virgin Islands can be tricky. Traffic moves on the left in *both* the USVI and BVI. Almost all cars are American, which means the driver sits on the side of the car next to the road's edge, a position that makes some people nervous.

Buckle up before you turn the key. Police in the USVI are notorious for giving $25 tickets to unbelted drivers and front-seat passengers. The police are a bit lax about driving under the influence, but why risk it? Take a taxi or appoint a designated driver when you're out on the town.

Traffic moves at about 10 mph in town; on major highways you can fly along at 50 mph. On other roads, the speed limit may be less. Main roads in the USVI carry route numbers, but they're not always marked, and locals may not know them. (Be prepared for such directions as, "Turn left at the big tree.") Few USVI secondary roads have signs; BVI roads aren't very well marked either.

▌ TAXI TRAVEL

Taxis run the gamut from sedans to huge, open, multipassenger safari-vans. Rates are set by the government, but that doesn't mean that the occasional taxi driver won't try to gouge you. In the USBVI you'll also pay extra for your bags. Fares vary by destination and the number of people in the taxi, but count on paying $15 per person from Cyril E. King Airport on St. Thomas to Charlotte Amalie; $9 per person from Henry Rohlsen Airport on St. Croix to Christiansted; and $27 per person from Terrance E. Lettsome Airport on Beef Island, Tortola, to Road Town. Tip taxi drivers 15%. It's pointless to argue if you think the taxi driver has overcharged you. You won't win, and you might be delayed further should the driver call the police. Instead, forego the tip. Taxis are found at airports and ferry docks, at most hotels, and in tourist locations such as popular beaches and main towns. If you're staying at a smaller hotel, ask the front desk to call one for you. Villa vacationers should line up a taxi in advance, but be aware that many taxi drivers are reluctant to drive on unpaved roads.

Taxi options are covered in the Essentials sections in individual island chapters.

ESSENTIALS

▮ ACCOMMODATIONS

Decide whether you want to pay the extra price for a room overlooking the ocean or the pool. At less expensive properties location may mean a difference in price of only $10 to $20 per night; at luxury resorts, however, it could amount to as much as $100 per night. Also find out how close the property is to a beach. At some hotels you can walk barefoot from your room onto the sand; others are across a road or a 10-minute drive away.

Nighttime entertainment is often alfresco in the USBVI, so if you go to bed early or are a light sleeper, ask for a room away from the dance floor. Air-conditioning isn't a necessity on all islands, many of which are cooled by trade winds, but it can be a plus if you enjoy an afternoon snooze or are bothered by humidity. Breezes are best on upper floors, particularly corner rooms. If you like to sleep without air-conditioning, make sure that windows can be opened and have screens; also make sure there are no security issues with leaving your windows open. If you're staying away from the water, make sure the room has a ceiling fan and that it works. Even in the most luxurious resorts, there are times when things simply *don't* work; it's a fact of Caribbean life. No matter how diligent the upkeep, humidity and salt air quickly take their toll, and cracked tiles, rusty screens, and chipped paint are common everywhere.

The lodgings we list are the cream of the crop in each price category. When pricing accommodations, always ask what's included and what costs extra. Properties are assigned price categories based on the range between their least and most expensive standard double rooms at high season (excluding holidays).

APARTMENT AND VILLA RENTALS

Villas—whether luxurious or modest— are popular lodging options on all the Virgin Islands.

Renting a villa lets you settle in. You can have room to spread out, you can cook any or all of your meals, and you can have all the privacy you desire. Since most villas are in residential neighborhoods, your neighbors probably won't appreciate late-night parties or your children playing too loudly in the swimming pool. And you may be disturbed by your neighbor's weekend yard maintenance. That said, there's no better way to experience life in the USBVI.

Many villas are set up specifically for the rental market with bedrooms at opposite ends of the house. This makes them perfect for two couples who want to share an accommodation but still prefer some privacy. Others with more bedrooms are sized right for families. Ask about the villa layout to make sure young children won't have to sleep too far away from their parents. Villas with separate bedroom buildings are probably not a good idea unless your children are in their teens.

Most villas are owned by people who live somewhere else but hire a local management company to attend to the details. Depending on the island and the rental, the manager will either meet you at the ferry or airport or will give you directions to your villa. Most of the companies offer the same services with similar degrees of efficiency.

You can book your villa through the numerous agencies that show up on the Internet, but they're usually not based on the island you want to visit. Booking through an island-based manager means that you can talk to a person who knows the villa and can let you know whether it meets your specifications. Your villa manager can also arrange for a maid, a chef, and other staffers to take care of myriad other details to help make your vacation go smoothly. They're only a phone call away when something goes wrong or you have a question.

Catered To Vacation Homes focuses on St. John. Vacation St. Croix is based on St. Croix. McLaughlin-Anderson has rentals across the USBVI.

Villa Management Companies Catered to Vacation Homes. Specializing in luxury villas, this company has listings mainly in the middle of the island and on the western edge. ✉ *Marketplace Suite 206, 5206 Enighed, Cruz Bay, St. John* ☎ *340/776–6641, 800/424–6641* ⊕ *www.cateredto.com.* **McLaughlin-Anderson** ☎ *340/776–0635, 800/537–6246* ⊕ *www.mclaughlinanderson.com.* **Vacation St. Croix** ✉ *400 La Grande Princesse, Christiansted, St. Croix* ☎ *340/718–0361, 877/788–0361* ⊕ *www.vacationstcroix.com.*

HOTELS

Hotels range from luxury beachfront resorts, where the staff caters to your every whim and where you'll find plenty of activities to keep you busy, to small, locally owned hillside hotels with great views that cater to more independent-minded visitors. They're priced accordingly. At the smaller inland properties you'll probably want to rent a car to get out to the island's best beaches and interesting restaurants.

The USBVI are quite Americanized thanks to television and the influx of U.S. visitors, but some traditional Caribbean customs still apply. Common courtesy is particularly important in the islands, so always say hello when you enter a store and make some small talk before getting down to

business. Also, watch out for cars that stop suddenly in the middle of the road for chats with passersby and be aware that nothing, and we mean nothing, ever starts on time.

▌ COMMUNICATIONS

INTERNET

Many hotels now offer high-speed Internet service. In most cases, Internet service is complimentary, but some resorts do charge a fee. Some provide computers in their lobbies if you've left your computer at home. You'll also find a few restaurants, bars, and businesses that offer Internet service for a fee.

PHONES

Phone service to and from the Virgin Islands is up-to-date and efficient. While you can still find a pay phone here and there, they are becoming a rarity.

CALLING WITHIN THE USBVI

In the USVI and BVI you dial just as if you were anywhere else in the United States.

The area code for the USVI is 340; for the BVI, 284.

In the USVI, dial 913 to reach the operator. In the BVI, dial 119. In both locations, dial 0 for advice on how to place your call.

CALLING OUTSIDE THE USBVI

The country code for the United States is 1.

Calling the United States and Canada from the USBVI is just like making a long-distance call within those countries: dial 1, plus the area code. To reach Europe, Australia, and New Zealand, dial 011 followed by the country code and the number.

MOBILE PHONES

If you have a multiband phone (some countries use different frequencies than what's standard in the United States) and your service provider uses the world-standard GSM network (as do T-Mobile, AT&T, and Verizon), you can probably use your phone abroad. Roaming fees can be steep, however: 99¢ a minute is considered reasonable. And overseas you normally pay the toll charges for incoming calls. Internationally, it's almost always cheaper to send a text message than to make a call, since text messages have a very low set fee (often less than 5¢).

There are no cell-phone rental companies in the USBVI. There are a few places that sell cell phones, but the price is much higher than in the United States. Cell phones from most U.S. companies work in most parts of the USVI if you have a roaming feature. If you're on St. John's north coast you may have some difficulties; you may find yourself connected to BoatPhone, a Tortola service. If you're on the south side of Tortola and at hilltop locations or near the ferry dock in Spanish Town on Virgin Gorda, you may be able to connect to AT&T, but other locations in the BVI have sporadic service.

Contacts AT&T ☎ *340/777–7777 on St. Thomas and St. John, 340/690–1000 on St. Croix* ⊕ *www.att.com.* **Digicel Cellular** ✉ *Virgin Gorda, British Virgin Islands* ☎ *284/300–1000* ⊕ *www.digicelbvi.com.* **Lime Wireless** ☎ *284/494–4444 in the BVI* ⊕ *www.time4lime.com.* **Mobal.** Mobal rents mobiles and sells GSM phones (starting at $49) that will operate in 140 countries. Per-call rates vary throughout the world. ☎ *888/888–9162* ⊕ *www.mobal.com.* **Planet Fone.** Planet Fone rents cell phones, but the per-minute rates are expensive. ☎ *888/988–4777* ⊕ *www.*

planetfone.com. **Sprint** ☎ *340/776–0770 on St. Thomas and St. John, 340/713–0055 on St. Croix* ⊕ *www.sprint.com.*

▌ CUSTOMS AND DUTIES

You're always allowed to bring goods of a certain value back home without having to pay any duty or import tax. But there's a limit on the amount of tobacco and liquor you can bring back duty-free, and some countries have separate limits for perfumes; for exact figures, check with your customs department. The values of so-called "duty-free" goods are included in these amounts. When you shop abroad, save all your receipts, as customs inspectors may ask to see them as well as the items you purchased. If the total value of your goods is more than the duty-free limit, you'll have to pay a tax (most often a flat percentage) on the value of everything beyond that limit.

As long as you're not bringing in meat, passing through BVI customs is usually a breeze. If you want to bring that special cut of steak from home, you'll need a $25 agriculture permit, but it's not worth the effort since you can buy meat all over the BVI. You don't clear customs entering the USVI if you're coming from the United States. You can't take fruits and vegetables out of either the USVI or BVI, so eat up that apple on the way to the airport. You may travel with your pets to the USVI without any special shots or paperwork, but you need an import permit from the BVI Agriculture Department to bring in your pet.

U.S. Information U.S. Customs and Border Protection ⊕ *www.cbp.gov.*

▌ EATING OUT

Everything from fast food to fine cuisine in elegant settings is available in the USBVI, and prices run about the same as what you'd pay in New York or any other major city. You'll find kid favorites McDonald's, Pizza Hut, KFC, and more on St. Thomas and St. Croix, but families will also find plenty of nonchain restaurants with kid-friendly menus. Resorts that cater to families always have a casual restaurant, but there are delis and other restaurants across the USBVI that offer something for everyone on their menus. Most chefs at top-of-the-line restaurants and even some small spots went to a major culinary school, which means innovative and interesting cuisine. Don't be afraid to sample local dishes at the roadside restaurants on all the islands. More and more restaurants have vegetarian offerings on their menus, though true vegetarian restaurants are hard to find. The restaurants we list are the cream of the crop in each price category.

Unless otherwise noted, the restaurants listed are open daily for lunch and dinner.

PAYING

Most USBVI restaurants accept Master-Card and Visa, and some take American Express. A rare few accept Discover. Only large hotels and their restaurants take Diners Club. You will find the occasional restaurant that doesn't accept credit cards.

For guidelines on tipping see Tipping.

RESERVATIONS AND DRESS

Regardless of where you are, it's a good idea to make a reservation if you can. In many places in the Caribbean it's expected, particularly at nicer restaurants. We only mention them specifically when reservations are essential (there's no other way you'll ever get a table) or when they're not accepted. For popular restaurants, book as far ahead as you can (often a month or more), and reconfirm as soon as you arrive. Large parties should always call ahead to check the reservations policy. We mention dress only when men are required to wear a jacket or a jacket and tie. Beach attire is universally frowned upon in restaurants throughout the Caribbean.

WINES, BEER, AND SPIRITS

Top-notch restaurants offer good selections of fine wines. Beer and spirits are available on all islands at all kinds of restaurants and roadside stands, but you may not find the brand you prefer. Cruzan Rum, manufactured in St. Croix, is available across the USBVI. Alcoholic beverages are available from the smallest corner rum shop to the fanciest resort at all hours of the day and night. The only prohibition comes during the day on Good Friday, when no one can sell drinks.

▮ ELECTRICITY

The USBVI use the same current as the U.S. mainland—110 volts. European appliances will require adaptors. Since power fluctuations occasionally occur, bring a heavy-duty surge protector (available at hardware stores) if you plan to use your computer.

▮ EMERGENCIES

Emergency personnel across the USBVI are well equipped to handle basic medical issues, but you'll find a bigger selection of doctors and dentists on St. Croix, St. Thomas, and Tortola. If you need one, ask your hotel or villa manager for a recommendation. There are hospitals on St. Thomas, St. Croix, and Tortola, and doctors and emergency facilities on the other islands. If you need hospital care on one of the smaller islands you'll face a boat ride to the closest hospital. St. John has an ambulance boat that whisks patients to Red Hook, St. Thomas, for an ambulance ride to Schneider Regional Medical Center, but the emergency staff will accompany you on the public ferry to Peebles Hospital on Tortola from the BVI outer islands. Air ambulances to the mainland are available from St. Croix, St. Thomas, and Tortola.

The emergency number in the USVI is ☎ *911*. In the BVI, dial ☎ *999*.

▌HEALTH

Water in the USBVI is generally safe to drink. Mosquitoes can be a problem here, particularly after a spate of showers. Insect repellent is readily available, but you may want to bring something from home, because it's more expensive in the Virgin Islands. Dengue fever and the Chikungunya Virus are a particular concern.

Less dangerous, but certainly a nuisance, are the little pests from the sand-flea family known as no-see-ums. You don't realize you're being had for dinner until it's too late, and these bites itch, and itch, and itch. No-see-ums start getting hungry around 3 pm and are out in force by sunset. They're always more numerous in shady and wooded areas (such as the campgrounds on St. John). Take a towel along for sitting on the beach, and keep reapplying insect repellent.

Beware of the manchineel tree, which grows near the beach and has green apple-like fruit that is poisonous and bark and leaves that burn the skin.

Even if you've never been sunburned in your life, believe the warnings and use sunscreen in the USBVI. If you're dark-skinned, start with at least an SPF of 15 and keep it on. If you're fair-skinned, use a sunscreen with a higher SPF and stay out of the sun during midday. Rays are most intense between 11 and 2, so move under a sea-grape tree (although you can still burn here) or, better yet, take a shady lunch break. You can also burn in

this part of the world when it's cloudy, so putting sunscreen on every day no matter what the weather is the best strategy.

OVER-THE-COUNTER REMEDIES
Over-the-counter medications like aspirin, Tylenol, and Mylanta are readily available in the USBVI. Kmart on St. Thomas and St. Croix have cheaper prices, but you can find a big selection of these products at grocery and drug stores across the USBVI. You can find a smaller selection (and considerably higher prices) on the smaller islands.

SHOTS AND MEDICATIONS
No vaccinations are required to visit the USBVI. The most serious tropical disease prevalent here is dengue fever, which has no vaccine.

Health Warnings National Centers for Disease Control & Prevention *(CDC)* ☎ *800/232–4636 international travelers' health line* ⊕ *www.cdc.gov/travel.* **World Health Organization** *(WHO)* ⊕ *www.who.int.*

▌HOURS OF OPERATION

Bank hours are generally Monday through Thursday 9 to 3 and Friday 9 to 5; a handful open Saturday (9 to noon). Walk-up windows open at 8:30 on weekdays. Hours may vary slightly from branch to branch and island to island.

Shops, especially those in the heavily touristed areas, are open Monday to Saturday 9 to 5. Those near the cruise-ship piers may also be open on Sunday, but usually only if there is a ship in port.

HOLIDAYS
In addition to the U.S. federal holidays, locals in the USVI celebrate Three Kings Day (January 6); Transfer Day (commemorates Denmark's 1917 sale of the territory to the United States, March 31); Holy Thursday and Good Friday; Emancipation Day (when slavery was abolished in the Danish West Indies in 1848, July 3); Columbus Day and USVI–Puerto Rico Friendship Day (always on Columbus Day weekend); and Liberty Day

(honoring David Hamilton Jackson, who secured freedom of the press and assembly from King Christian X of Denmark, November 1).

Although the government closes down for nearly 20 days a year, most of these holidays have no effect on shopping hours. Unless there's a cruise-ship arrival, expect most stores to close for Christmas and a few other holidays in the slower summer months.

The following public holidays are celebrated in the BVI: New Year's Day, Commonwealth Day (March 14), Good Friday (Friday before Easter), Easter Sunday (usually March or April), Easter Monday (day after Easter), Whit Monday (first Monday in May), Sovereign's Birthday (June 16), Territory Day (July 1), BVI August Festival Days (usually first two weeks in August), St. Ursula's Day (October 21), Christmas, and Boxing Day (day after Christmas).

▍MONEY

Prices quoted are in U.S. dollars, which is the official currency in all the islands. Major credit cards and traveler's checks are accepted at many establishments.

Prices in this guide are given for adults. Reduced fees are almost always available for children.

ATMS AND BANKS

You can find ATMs at most banks in the USBVI. The ATMs at FirstBank and Scotia Bank, the only two in St. John, sometimes run out of cash on long holiday weekends.

CREDIT CARDS

It's a good idea to inform your credit-card company before you travel, even if you're going to the USBVI. Otherwise, the company might put a hold on your card owing to unusual activity—not a good thing halfway through your trip. Record all your credit-card numbers—as well as the phone numbers to call if your cards are lost or stolen—in a safe place, so you're prepared should something go wrong. Both MasterCard and Visa have general numbers you can call (collect if you're abroad) if your card is lost, but you're better off calling the number of your issuing bank, since MasterCard and Visa usually just transfer you to your bank; your bank's number is usually printed on your card.

If you plan to use your credit card for cash advances, you'll need to apply for a PIN at least two weeks before your trip. It's usually cheaper (and safer) to use a credit card in the USBVI for major purchases (so you can cancel payments or dispute the charge if there's a problem).

▍PACKING

A pocket LED flashlight to deal with the occasional power outage, bug repellent for mosquitoes, sunglasses, a hat, and sunscreen are essentials for any USBVI vacation. If you forget something, those items are available at stores across the USBVI, but are usually more expensive than what you would pay at home. Pharmacies can fill prescriptions with a call to your home drug store, but this may be the week the drug shipment didn't arrive. It's always safer to bring everything you need. Dress is casual even at the most expensive resorts, but men are usually required to wear a collared shirt in dining rooms. For dinner out women typically wear what the locals call "island fancy" (a flowy skirt and nice top will do). Bring your bathing suit, a cover-up, sandals, sturdy walking shoes if you're a hiker, beach shoes if you plan on strolling those luscious strands of sand, and a sweater or fleece if you're visiting in the winter when the nights are cool. In these days of packing light, rent snorkel gear on the island rather than bringing it unless you have a prescription mask. Shorts and T-shirts will do everywhere during the day. Don't forget a good book for whiling away those afternoons in the beach chair and your camera for bringing home those USBVI memories.

▌PASSPORTS AND VISAS

For U.S. citizens, a passport is *not* required to visit the U.S. Virgin Islands, though you must still provide proof of citizenship by showing an original birth certificate with a raised seal as well as a government-issued photo ID. There are no immigration procedures upon arriving in St. Thomas or St. Croix for anyone arriving on planes from the U.S. mainland or Puerto Rico, but on your return you will clear immigration and customs before boarding your flight.

If you visit the BVI by ferry from the USVI, you must go through customs and immigration procedures and prove your citizenship. U.S. citizens must have a passport to enter the BVI by ferry.

If you fly into the BVI, you must go through customs and immigration upon arrival and have a valid passport. Aside from paying the departure tax, there are no special departure procedures.

▌RESTROOMS

Restrooms across the USBVI are usually clean, neat, and free. You won't often find attendants, even at swanky resorts. Most gas stations do have restrooms, and they'll do in a pinch, but using the restroom in a restaurant, attraction, or shopping area is probably a better bet.

▌SAFETY

In the USVI ask hotel staff members about the wisdom of venturing off the beaten path. Although it may seem like a nice night for a stroll back to your hotel from that downtown restaurant, it's better to take a taxi than face an incident. Although local police go to great lengths to stop it, crime does occur. The BVI has seen less crime than its neighbors to the west, but again, better safe than sorry.

Follow the same precautions that you would anywhere. Look around before using the ATM. Keep tabs on your pocketbook; put it on your lap—not the back of your chair—in restaurants. Stow valuable jewelry or other items in the hotel safe when you leave your room; hotel and villa burglaries do occur infrequently. Deserted beaches on St. John and the BVI are usually safe, but think twice about stopping at that luscious strand of lonely sand on St. Croix and St. Thomas. Hotel or public beaches are your best bets. Never leave your belongings unattended at the beach or on the seats of your rental car. Be sure to lock the doors on your rental villa or hotel room. Break-ins can happen across the USBVI, so it's better to be safe than sorry.

▌TIP➜ If you're wondering what to do with your cash and credit cards at the beach, consider buying a waterproof container to wear on a cord around your neck while you're in the water.

▌TAXES

There's no sales tax in the USVI, but there's a 10% hotel-room tax; most hotels also add a 10% service charge to the bill. The St. John Accommodations Council members ask that hotel and villa guests voluntarily pay a $1 per day surcharge to help fund school and community projects and other good works. Many hotels add additional energy surcharges and the like, so ask about any additional charges, but these are not government-imposed taxes.

In the BVI the departure tax is $15 per person by boat and $20 per person by plane. There is also an $8 departure tax from the USVI when traveling to the BVI. There are separate booths at the airport and at ferry terminals to collect this tax, which must be paid in cash in U.S. currency. Most hotels in the BVI add a service charge ranging from 5% to 18% to the bill. A few restaurants and some shops tack on an additional 10% charge if you use a credit card. There's no sales tax in the BVI. However, there's a 7% government tax on hotel rooms.

TIME

The USBVI are in the Atlantic Standard Time zone, which is one hour later than Eastern Standard or four hours earlier than GMT. During daylight saving time, between March and November, Atlantic Standard is the same time as Eastern Daylight Time since Daylight Saving Time is not observed.

TIPPING

Many hotels in the USVI add a 10% to 15% service charge to cover the services of your maid and other staff. However, some hotels use part of that money to fund their operations, passing only a portion of it on to the staff. Check with your maid or bellhop to determine the hotel's policy. If you discover you need to tip, give bellhops and porters 50¢ to $1 per bag and maids $1 or $2 per day. Special errands or requests of hotel staff always require an additional tip. At restaurants bartenders and waiters expect a 10%–15% tip, but always check your tab to see whether service is included. Taxi drivers in the USVI get a 15% tip.

In the BVI tip porters and bellhops $1 per bag. Sometimes a service charge of 10% is included on restaurant bills; it's customary to leave another 5% if you liked the service. If no charge is added, 15% is the norm. Cabbies normally aren't tipped because most own their cabs; add 10% to 15% if they exceed their duties.

VISITOR INFORMATION

Stop by the tourism department's local offices for brochures on things to do and places to see. The offices are open only weekdays from 8 to 5, so if you need information on the weekend or on one of the territory's many holidays, you're out of luck. *(For locations, see ⇨ Visitor Information in the Essentials section of each chapter.)*

British Virgin Islands Tourist Board BVI **Tourist Board** ☎ 212/563–3117, 800/835– 8530 in the U.S. ⊕ www.bvitourism.com.

United States Virgin Islands Department of Tourism USVI Government Tourist Office ☎ 340/774–USVI, 800/372–USVI ⊕ www. visitusvi.com.

INDEX

PHOTO CREDITS

Front cover: M. Dillon/CORBIS [Description: Beach at Trunk Bay, St. John, U.S. Virgin islands]. 1, SuperStock/age fotostock. 2-3, Walter Bibikow/age fotostock. 5, Carlos Villoch - Magic- Sea.com/ Alamy. Chapter 1: Experience the U.S. & British Virgin Islands: 8-9, Ellen Rooney/ age fotostock. 10, Jo Ann Snover/iStockphoto. 11, BVI Tourist Board. 13, George Burba/iStockphoto. 15, Sarah Holmstrom/iStockphoto. 16 (left), Ellen Barone/Alamy. 16 (top center), Guido Alberto Rossi/Tips Italia/ photolibrary.com. 16 (bottom center), Carlos Villoch - MagicSea.com/Alamy. 16 (top right), Concordia Eco-Resort. 16 (bottom right), Juneisy Q. Hawkins/Shutterstock. 17 (top left), Honky275/Flickr. 17 (bottom left), Nik Wheeler/Alamy. 17 (top center), Sunpix Travel/Alamy. 17 (bottom center), Super-Stock/ age fotostock. 17 (right), Ilja Hulinsky/Alamy. 18, BVI Tourism. 19, Charles Krallman/Surfsong Villa Resort. 20, Gary Blakeley/iStockphoto. 21, U.S. Virgin Islands Department of Tourism. 24, BVI Tourist Board. 25, Renesis/wikipedia.org. 26, Kborer/wikipedia. Chapter 2: St. Thomas: 27, Oscar Williams/Alamy. 28, Coral World Ocean Park, St. Thomas. 29 (top), Erik Miles/iStockphoto. 29 (bottom), U.S.Virgin Islands Department of Tourism. 30, Jeff Greenberg/age fotostock. 31 (top), Olga Lyubkina / Shutterstock. 31 (bottom), Atlantide S.N.C./age fotostock. 32, Juneisy Q. Hawkins / Shutterstock. 36-37, Walter Bibikow/age fotostock. 42, SuperStock/age fotostock. 51, Shutterstock / Andrei Medvedev. 66, Michael DeFreitas/age fotostock. 70, World Pictures/Alamy. 76, Alvaro Leiva/ age fotostock. Chapter 3: St. John: 79, Walleyelj | Dreamstime.com. 80, Jo Ann Snover/iStockphoto. 81. C. Kurt Holter / Shutterstock. 82, U.S. Virgin Islands Department of Tourism. 88-89, Ken Brown/ iStockphoto. 90, Walter Bibikow/ age fotostock. 107, Gavin Hellier/age fotostock. 109, Carlos Villoch - MagicSea.com/Alamy. 111, Kendra Nielsam / Shutterstock. 113, divemasterking2000/Flickr. 114 (top), Shirley Vanderbilt/age fotostock. 114 (center), Julie de Leseleuc/iStockphoto. 114 (bottom), Marjorie McBride/Alamy. 115, divemasterking2000/Flickr. 116 (top), David Coleman/iStockphoto. 116 (bottom), Steve Simonsen. 119, Nik Wheeler/Alamy. Chapter 4: St. Croix: 121, Bill Bachmann/Alamy. 122, Kelvin Chiu/iStockphoto. 123 (top), U.S. Virgin Islands Dept of Tourism. 123 (bottom), Steve Simonsen. 124, U.S. Virgin Islands Department of Tourism. 130-31, Bill Ross/Flirt Collection/photolibrary. com. 133, Walter Bibikow/age fotostock. 134, Marc Muench/Alamy. 146, The Buccaneer. 153, Danita Delimont/Alamy. 155, Stephen Frink Collection/Alamy. 157, Julie Hewitt / Alamy. Chapter 5: Tortola: 159, Alvaro Leiva/age fotostock. 160 (top), BVI Tourist Board. 160 (bottom), lidian neeleman/iStockphoto. 161, Aliaksandr Nikitsin/iStockphoto. 162, Ramunas Bruzas / Shutterstock. 168-69, Christian Heeb/age fotostock. 171, Walter Bibikow/age fotostock. 175, World Pictures/age fotostock. 181, Walter Bibikow/age fotostock. 186, Alvaro Leiva/age fotostock. 189, Eric Sanford/age fotostock. 190 (top), Randy Lincks/Alamy. 190 (bottom), Steve Dangers/iStockphoto. 191 (top), Doug Scott/age fotostock. 191 (bottom), Slavoljub Pantelic/iStockphoto. 192, Doug Scott/age fotostock. 194, Giovanni Rinaldi/iStockphoto. 195, Walter Bibikow/age fotostock. 197, Fotograferen.net/Alamy. Chapter 6: Virgin Gorda: 199, BVI Tourist Board. 200 and 201 (top), Joel Blit/iStockphoto. 201 (bottom), BVI Tourist Board. 202, Stefan Radtke/iStockphoto. 206-07, FB-Fischer /imagebroker.net/photolibrary.com. 208, BVI Tourist Board. 210, Ellen Rooney/age fotostock. 217, Bitter End Yacht Club International, LLC. 218, parasola.net/Alamy. 221, Carlos Villoch - MagicSea.com/Alamy. 222, Bitter End Yacht Club International, LLC. Chapter 7: Other British Virgin Islands: 223, BVI Tourism. 224, Paul Zizka / Shutterstock. 225, BVI Tourism. 226, Joel Blit/iStockphoto. 228-29, Kreder Katja/age fotostock. 233, Andre Jenny/Alamy. 241, Paul Zizka/Shutterstock. 246, S. Murphy-Larronde/age fotostock. Back cover, from left to right: Gary Blakeley/iStockphoto; U.S. Virgin Islands Dept of Tourism; Ken Brown/iStockphoto. Spine: Sasha Buzko / Shutterstock.

About Our Writers: Carol M. Bareuther, courtesy of Dean Barnes; Carol Buchanan, courtesy of Megan Lee Buchanan; Lynda Lohr, courtesy of Robert Charleston.

ABOUT OUR WRITERS

 Carol M. Bareuther, who lives in St. Thomas, works part-time for the government of the U.S. Virgin Islands. In her other life as a writer, she contributes to local, regional, and international publications on the topics of food, travel, and water sports. She's the author of two books, *Sports Fishing in the Virgin Islands* and *Virgin Islands Cooking*. She is the mother of Nikki and Rian, as well as the longtime partner of photographer Dean Barnes. She covered St. Thomas for this edition, and she contributed the spotlight on island cuisine and the yacht charter feature.

 Carol Buchanan started sailing the Caribbean in 1984 on four-masted sail boats and fell in love with the islands and the sea. Twenty years later she decided to leave the snow capital of Ohio to live "the dream," and she moved to St. Croix with her husband, daughter, and dog. She is currently working as a freelance reporter and photographer for an online publication serving St. Croix. She had published a weekly newspaper in northeast Ohio for ten years with her husband in the Cleveland area. She is the proud mother of two and has one grandson. She is a yogi, avid reader, hiker, tennis player, snorkeler, and traveler. And she takes full advantage of all the experiences life in paradise offers.

 Long-time St. John resident **Lynda Lohr** lives above Coral Bay with her significant other and a chubby cat. She moved to St. John in 1984 for a bit of adventure; she's still there and still enjoying the adventure. She writes for numerous national, regional, and local publications as well as travel websites. On her rare days off, she swims at Great Maho Bay and hikes the island's numerous trails. For this edition, she covered St. John.

Susan Zaluski is a freelance writer who resides on Jost Van Dyke. She serves as Executive Director for a small nature and heritage non-profit organization, the Jost Van Dykes Preservation Society. She holds a B.A. in Latin American & Caribbean Area Studies and a M.S. in Sustainable Development (Tulane University, New Orleans).